C. IRVING 3rd Yr Acc

PERGAMON INTERNA
of Science, Technology, Engin

The 1000-volume original paperba
industrial training and the

Publisher: Robert M

CW01653300

Management, Information and Systems

THE PERGAMON TEXTBOOK
INSPECTION COPY SERVICE

An inspection copy of any book published in the Pergamon International Library will gladly be sent to academic staff without obligation for their consideration for course adoption or recommendation. Copies may be retained for a period of 60 days from receipt and returned if not suitable. When a particular title is adopted or recommended for adoption for class use and the recommendation results in a sale of 12 or more copies, the inspection copy may be retained with our compliments. If after examination the lecturer decides that the book is not suitable for adoption but would like to retain it for his personal library, then a discount of 10% is allowed on the invoiced price. The Publishers will be pleased to receive suggestions for revised editions and new titles to be published in this important International Library.

Other Titles of Interest

BERNSTEIN S. J.
Computers in Public Administration

DAVIS S. M.
Managing and Organizing Multinational Corporations

DUBRIN A. J.
Casebook of Organizational Behavior

EILON S.
Aspects of Management

GOLD B.
Technological Change: Economics Management and Environment

HUSSEY D. E.
Introducing Corporate Planning

IBRAHAM I. B.
Readings in Managerial Economics

Management, Information and Systems

by

ARCHIE DONALD

Head of the Department of
Business and Administrative Studies, South East London College

SECOND EDITION

PERGAMON PRESS

OXFORD · NEW YORK · TORONTO · SYDNEY · PARIS · FRANKFURT

U.K.	Pergamon Press Ltd., Headington Hill Hall, Oxford OX3 0BW, England
U.S.A.	Pergamon Press Inc., Maxwell House, Fairview Park, Elmsford, New York 10523, U.S.A.
CANADA	Pergamon of Canada, Suite 104, Consumers Road, Willowdale, Ontario M2J 1P9
AUSTRALIA	Pergamon Press (Aust.) Pty. Ltd., P.O. Box 544, Potts Point, N.S.W. 2011, Australia
FRANCE	Pergamon Press SARL, 24 rue des Ecoles, 75240 Paris, Cedex 05, France
FEDERAL REPUBLIC OF GERMANY	Pergamon Press GmbH, 6242 Kronberg/Taunus, Pferdstrasse 1, Federal Republic of Germany

Copyright © 1979 Archie Donald

All Rights Reserved. No part of this publication may be reproduced, stored in a retrieval system or transmitted in any form or by any means: electronic, electrostatic, magnetic tape, mechanical, photocopying, recording or otherwise, without permission in writing from the publishers.

First edition 1967

Reprinted 1969

Reprinted 1975

Second edition 1979

British Library Cataloguing in Publication Data

Donald, Archibald Gordon
Management, information and systems.—2nd ed.
(Pergamon international library).
1. Management 2. System analysis
I. Title
658.4'032 HD20.5 78-40631

ISBN 0-08-021271-9 (Hard cover)
ISBN 0-08-021270-0 (Flexi cover)

Reproduced, printed and bound in Great Britain by
Cox & Wyman Ltd, London, Fakenham and Reading

Contents

Introduction to the First Edition

When Frederick Winslow Taylor died in 1917 the first revolution in management techniques had taken place. Taylor had shown the need for data from which useful control information could be extracted and used as a basis for management decisions. His method and time studies yielded the data to organize and control a process, and also provided a system of payment not without its denigrators yet probably more equitable than the contracting system then current.

The revolution of our own age has consisted of the explosion in data available, the computer to process this data, newer techniques of extracting useful information from the data and a start in finding out how systems work. New approaches to managerial problems—variously termed "cybernetics", "information technology", "operational research", "systems analysis"—have arisen with new terminologies. Progressive concerns, whether business enterprises or non-profit-making units, that adopt these new methods of thinking find themselves at a distinct advantage whether in matters of control of the current situation or in adapting quickly to change arising in the technology of the process or in the environment.

"Control" basically is of two sorts: the maintenance of an existing situation, bringing it back to normal when it deviates, and the introduction of change into a situation, whether by making alterations to the existing situation or by creating a new situation. In both cases the prime need is for information to guide action.

With the increased ease of handling the data flow and more powerful techniques available for extracting useful information from it, the manager's task has been made both easier and more difficult. This seeming paradox arises from the fact that although additional information may aid his decision-taking, he must know what type of information he requires in a particular situation and select the appropriate technique for the decision he is about to take. He must know the good points and limitations of the method he is using, what reliance he may place on its answers, and he must know the effect on the system of collecting information. Above all, he must realize that he himself still has to decide on the valuation of any particular method used. Each method of processing data will only give results in terms of the value criteria built into that particular method.

The purpose of this book is to outline these concepts and newer modes of thought, and then to examine the business enterprise and non-profit-making concern in the light of these concepts. Much current writing on management subjects concentrates on one aspect: Line Management or Work Study or Human Relations or Decision Theory or Cybernetics or Computers or Systems Analysis. An attempt is made here to show how these different disciplines overlap, and how an integrated approach will assist the manager in understanding how the undertaking functions and hence in achieving more effective control.

We first examine the objectives of an undertaking, the formulation of its policy, whether explicit or implicit, in terms of value judgements, and consider how fully this policy is understood and accepted by those responsible for implementing it. Next some attention is given to traditional techniques of control whereby management sets out to achieve its objectives; budgetary control, the most useful overall control so far devised, is seen to be deficient in that it may lack the flexibility which is necessary for growth and the best results. In order to understand better the "mechanics" of operation, the undertaking or appropriate part of it is then studied as a system, and the difficulties of successful definition are touched on. The cybernetic approach is then introduced to explain the manner in which an undertaking functions, and the concepts of "control", "feedback", "information" are given a business connotation. "Constraints" on the operation of the business system, influences which help to shape the structure of the enterprise and determine its objectives are then described in considerable detail; these include governmental policy, social environment, financial regulations and legal requirements. The individual undertaking is seen as part of a much larger comprehensive system, with much of the "input" and "output" beyond its control. The second half of the book deals primarily with the subject of information. Firstly we consider how information flows within a system and how it may be subject to "noise" and delay; we examine in turn what use the manager makes of this information to exercise effective control, in the dual sense discussed earlier. The problems of communication and obtaining adequate but not excessive information are then discussed. Statistical and Operations Research techniques emerge among the useful tools for analysing and presenting the information in a significant form, for deriving the optimum benefit from data, and hence improving managerial skill. In the final chapter the computer is seen in its role of co-ordinating, analysing and presenting meaningful information not only about historical data but also about possible courses of action in the future. Managers are reminded at this stage that with the advent of electronic data processing, they do not abdicate their moral responsibility to the undertaking and society; in the absence of manual intervention and with a more dynamic organization possible, the formulation of the right policy objectives will prove more important than ever.

This book is intended for businessmen, industrialists and administrators of all age groups who require a framework into which to fit their reading of the many specialized works on "new management thought". It should prove of value to those attending short business courses, as well as to full-time students at universities and technical colleges.

No one writes in isolation and I would like to acknowledge my debt to the authors listed in the bibliography whose books I have studied. Articles in professional and other journals on this subject increase in numbers yearly and reference to certain of these has been made in footnotes. Others may well have influenced my thought, for information presses in on every side, and to these also would I tender my thanks.

Specific thanks are due to Professor Tom Lupton who gave me much encouragement in the early stages; to Arthur Henderson of the Welsh College of Advanced Technology who dissected in detail my first three drafts; to D. B. Candlin of Leicester Regional College of Technology who helped with the final draft and to John N. Gibson, my colleague at Constantine, with whom I had many stimulating discussions in the later stages. Responsibility for what is written rests with the author alone.

Introduction to the Second Edition

The systems approach of viewing the world has become increasingly useful to us at the present time. Firstly, as a way of explaining the *interaction* of phenomena, and so increasing our knowledge of and insight into their working. Secondly, as a *planning and/or control methodology*, particularly in the area of constructed systems.

Because of the type of model that has been developed both for technical use, for example control engineering, and for abstract conceptual use and because of the type of problem-oriented and multidisciplinary questions we now find it interesting to ask, a particular world view is developing. In reply to questions we now ask within the constraints of this worldview the systems approach can provide "sensible" answers.

Attitudes to organization have passed through several stages in the last thousand years. The early Church attitude tended to regard with distaste the amassing of money capital through business operation. A reversal took place once the Protestant ethic praised thrift and the economic use of resources exemplified by the businessman who was successful, amassed and invested capital. Now, in a rapidly changing world, the systems viewpoint appears to gain ascendancy. The world environment has changed:

(i) We have vastly increased ability to handle (mainly numerical) data and information.

(ii) There has been a technological breakthrough enabling us to produce goods in vast quantities with less effort.

(iii) There appears to be some appreciation of our limited basic resources and of the need to rethink our world model.

In this new world situation, we have an incoming systems ethic in organizational life that operates on the assumptions (overt or covert) that,

Advancement is obtained by stating goals and solving problems, with implications that:

(i) Goals can be stated.

(ii) Problems can be solved.

(iii) Data (information) is required as a basis for problem solution and that this data requires quantification for easy manipulation.

(iv) The attainment of goals and the solution of problems is advantageous.

This standpoint is *part* only of the overall theory of systems; but it is the part that at present is receiving the most attention in organizational life. Where the "Systems Ethic" has penetrated an organization the managerial aspects emphasized are:

(i) The seen need to state (in writing) the organization's goals and objectives from which strategic and tactical plans of action are developed.

(ii) The designation of decision areas within the organization (subsystems) and the allocation of decision-makers to those areas.

(iii) The creation of data- (information) collecting systems. Most such systems admit specific types of data only.

(iv) The creation of communication channels through which the collected data may flow.

(v) The regular checking of the organization's present system state with that state anticipated in the plan and the initiation of action to bring the two into coincidence.

Organizational management falls into the category of Human Activity Constructed Systems (Fig. 0.1) where some of the "rules" are different to those of natural systems, and it is useful to consider the organization as carried on within the context of earth natural systems. Natural systems, shown outside the shaded area on Fig. 0.1, tend towards a position of "balance" whereas human activity systems have a "purpose" or seek a "goal". Laszlo[1] asks "Are we yet ready for intellectual acceptance

[1] E. Laszlo, *Introduction to Systems Philosophy*, pp. 4, 5 and 288–90, Harper Torchback, 1972.

SCHEMA OF NATURAL AND CONSTRUCTED SYSTEMS

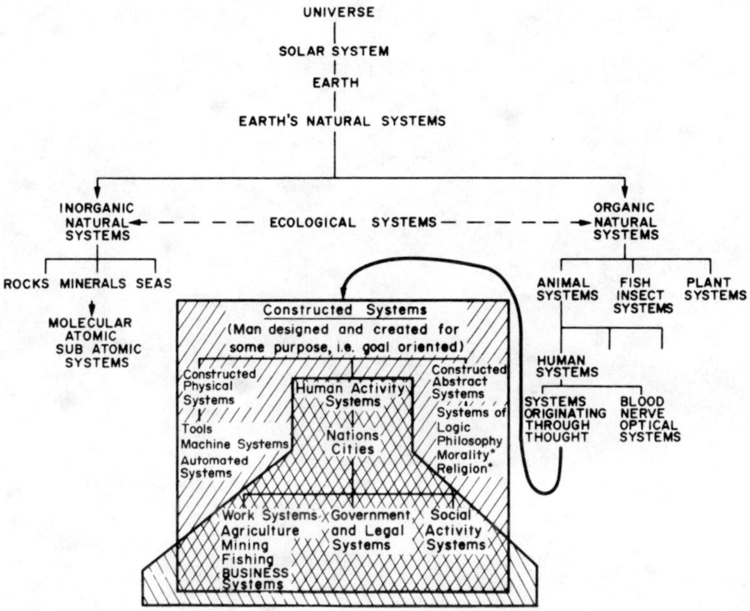

Constructed Systems exist within the context of Natural Systems

*Placed here in the schema for convenience only

Fig. 0.1.

of the overriding rules of world natural systems?" for ultimately there is no way for managers to avoid their constraints.

Since the first publication of *Management, Information and Systems* in 1967 there has been wider dissemination and acceptance of systems theory. The author has been encouraged by the translation of the first edition text into both Swedish and Japanese and in this enlarged second edition opportunity has been taken to rewrite and expand those parts dealing more particularly with systems.

Halstead, Kent 1978

CHAPTER 1

Management Objectives and Control

Within our society a business enterprise strives to produce an article or provide a service at a price that enables it to show a profit on its working. A non-profit-making concern will similarly attempt to reduce its costs and operate efficiently. All users of assets in our society are working within a financial context. In the long run these users will be measured by some financial standard, although it must be realized that many important aspects of life, for instance the benefit to be derived from an enlightened personnel policy, may not be fully susceptible to money measurement and thus may often be ignored, unless imposed by government legislation.

In most cases the financial context will deserve prime consideration when setting goals, as it is the universal unit of measurement. Businesses are expected to make a profit in the long run, and administrative departments which provide a service are similarly subject to control regarding the cost of that service. All aspects of business decisions, including those which may be termed the secondary aims (but which may in fact run a very close second to financial considerations), reflect the overall financial context: the size of the profit in relation to the scale of operations carried out.

Profit Motives

In businesses, the return on the total capital employed in the enterprise is the key figure and at least three attitudes towards the size of this profit can be distinguished.

(i) *Maximizing profit.* This is an amoral concept of obtaining as much profit as possible, more or less regardless of the consequences. It is a rather short-term view, most likely to be met with in areas of very rapid economic expansion.

As sections of an economy get older and settle down, the vested interest in the continuance of the enterprise as a unit becomes important to its members, and hence a longer-term view is more likely than the one of quick profits. The policy of maximizing profit at all costs may be acceptable legally, unless the position is monopolistic, but is seldom acceptable socially.

(ii) "*Satisficing*" *profit*. A word coined by economists to indicate a rate of profit on capital employed, considered "satisfactory" taking into account the risk involved and what could be earned elsewhere. The satisfactory rate tends to be kept down to such a level that it does not attract too many competitors into the same field and also does not attract legislation aimed at curbing the profits.

(iii) *Minimaxing*. In following this policy, the maximum profit obtainable is sought, but not at all costs as in (i): the necessity to guard against possible losses is taken into consideration when making decisions. So a description runs "maximizing the minimum expected gain whilst minimizing the maximum expected loss, taking into account competitors' actions".

In choosing its profit policy a business is usually concerned with "survival". Once created, there is a strong tendency for a system to adapt to internal changes and to changes in its environment in order to ensure continued survival. The system may even be seen to modify its goals, the better to survive and continue in existence. For this reason, there should be no expectation of finding rigid and unchanging goals when the business system is examined. At the same time a too frequent change in the goals is likely to cause confusion to managers and others carrying out the policy.

The administrative unit chooses its scale of operations in relation to the funds available to it. Efficiency in use of those funds will be a large factor in determining how effective its operations are. The allocation of funds may parallel that of the business:

(i) The lowest possible cost.

(ii) A satisfactory allocation in the light of public opinion.

(iii) As the administrative department is often in a monopolistic or semi-monopolistic position, there may be no real equivalent here. Perhaps the nearest parallel is the exposure of a department to have its services carried out by others on a "contract" basis.

Non-profit motives. Within the financial context, managers will also be motivated by other objectives which, although they may be evaluated financially, can be described as objectives of technical efficiency and of social standing. Often an enterprise will be found to pay particular attention to one of the objectives below and be proud of its reputation in this field, though each one of the objectives must have some consideration if the enterprise is to be well balanced.

(i) Customer satisfaction or user satisfaction of a service.

(ii) Position in the market, often linked with a desire for market leadership, which gives power.

(iii) Consideration for employee welfare and development of good personnel relations.

(iv) Public responsibility and corporate image.

(v) Technical efficiency; a high rate of productivity. Emphasis on research and development.

Evolving a Policy

When a "best" course of action is to be chosen out of, say, half a dozen possible courses open to the enterprise, a weighting system will be applied, perhaps unconsciously, to the profit and non-profit motives listed above. Having thus decided on the relative importance of the various criteria, the enterprise will be in a position to select which course of action appears to it to be most suitable at that time, i.e. "best". Another enterprise in a similar position might well choose differently. The objectives are all important and not necessarily exclusive, but it is seldom possible to follow all of them assiduously at the same time. It might well be that two business firms in the same trade emphasize different objectives and hence the whole character of the two is different. Similarly the administration of Welfare Services in different countries can have very different emphasis. These are *value decisions* and often reflect the personal values of the founding members. These values may persist until in due course it is necessary to effect a reappraisal of the situation with a possible change of emphasis.

Within the overall need to make a sufficient profit to survive in a competitive situation, or to disburse funds under the criterion of efficiency in the case of an administrative department, there is considerable scope for decision on what objectives are to be considered important and what are not. The costs may be obtainable, but how are the benefits to be measured; to whom do they accrue? This confronts one with the difficulty of measurement in the social sciences in the absence of a control group against which to measure the effect of a particular course of action. But the enterprise can only choose or follow *one* particular course of action, and when it does so it is first forced to consider its objectives, and their relationship to its local environment and the overall total environment.

Stating a Policy

Often firms have felt no need for an explicit statement of priorities of their objectives. Consequently the goals of many enterprises are held solely in the minds of senior management and may not be properly known to the staff. When the policy changes, as a result of the Chief Executive reassessing priorities, his decisions may be misunderstood and inadequately supported. With the increasing use of mathematical techniques to determine the "best" course of action, however, such a fault in management is rapidly exposed. The manager will need to be able to state his problem objectively and give his goal priorities explicitly enough both for his staff to gather relevant data and for the mathematician to work on the problem.

Carrying Out the Policy

The operations being carried out within a business enterprise or administrative unit at any given time can be classified in two groups, those that are considered to be working satisfactorily and those that require review. Management is faced with a continuing problem of control within the laid-down policy framework: to maintain the *status quo* in those areas of the enterprise that are considered to be running efficiently, and to introduce changes in those areas that are felt to be running inefficiently in order to give better service or to provide new products and markets.

The problems of controlling stability and change are common to business enterprises and non-profit-making concerns alike, and from now on the word organization will be used to cover both these managerial fields.

Control

Within the overall policy most managers and executives find themselves working to a plan designed to reach certain determined objectives. This plan may be no more than a tentative one of their own devising, or it may be a plan devised by members of the organization and laid out in detailed budgets. The plan may be worked out for only a month or two ahead or, again, it may be budgeted in detail for up to 3 years or more ahead.

Wherever there is a plan related to long- or short-term objectives, it is desirable to have some means of measuring divergence from the plan so that control may be exercised and corrective action taken as required otherwise the objectives may never be achieved.

How is the executive manager to keep his organization running on the lines that have been laid down?

The Role of The Controller

The controller by whatever name he may be known is the chief intelligence officer to top management. He marshals the necessary information on which the decisions are made. Such a person is necessary in an organization to guide and collate the thinking of departmental managers who may see their own departmental objectives as at least as important as the overall objectives of the organization.

Unless departmental information is integrated each department may be trying to achieve its departmental budget when conditions have changed from those obtaining originally. In so doing they may be upsetting the system as a whole and throwing the organization out of balance.

But in spite of his name the controller of the organization has not only to measure deviations from a plan. He must see that information is available to top management to enable them to formulate the "best" plan. This means presenting information in such a way that the effects of alternative courses of possible future action can be seen and judged. The controller must also ensure that others do take corrective action once divergence from the agreed plan is known.

Thus there are planning, interpretive and controlling functions bound up in the task.

In the United Kingdom, the person carrying out these control functions in an organization may be variously styled: Company Secretary, Director, Accountant, Financial Adviser or perhaps Chairman of the Board. Often the function of control is divided between two or more persons, acting individually, but in close liaison.

Where control is divided, each separate controller exercises control over his particular function. This is the piecemeal approach, allowable under budgetary control which acts as the co-ordinating influence and in which the allowed limits of the variables have been strictly defined. Control may, however, be better co-ordinated if all operational results are channelled through a single officer, the controller, who can co-ordinate and integrate the results, submitting possible courses of action to the Chief Executive for his decision in the light of *all* information. The Chief Executive as decision-maker may exercise his control at intervals and perhaps on the "management by exception" principle. That is, he is only brought in to make a decision when divergence from the plan exceeds a stated limit. He will attempt to bring balance to the system when it tends to go out of balance, and this should be done long before there is any chance of a complete breakdown.

The Nature of Control

The control of an organization as a whole may, at present, be seen operating at three levels of sophistication.

(i) *What has been done.* The historical process of recording and auditing, e.g. a company's financial accounts and the costs of jobs done.

(ii) *Forecasts and budgets.* The projection of the present situation into the near future of 1 or 2 years ahead.

(iii) *What can be done.* Taking the assets and showing the alternative courses of future action between which choice can be made. Some of the choices may fundamentally alter the course of the organization as at present envisaged, yet be entirely possible and be worthy of consideration.

A list of controls likely to be used by a business enterprise using budgetary control and standard costing is given in Appendix I.

Control Information

The measurement of data for control purposes is usually a continuous process, but the reporting of results on which decisions can be based is often carried out periodically, for example at monthly intervals. In the near future it may be possible to carry out continuous appraisal of current activities in real-time systems, control then being concerned with overall *trends* rather than with budget limits as at present. In the computer we have a tool which can make this type of control feasible, though its use in this mode of operation may be costly.

Broadly speaking, three categories of measurement are in use. Firstly, it will be noticed that much of the information needed for control is available in a *monetary unit* (these are the items which are shown in the Balance Sheet and Trading Account). Next are the statistical returns where the unit used is *quantity or weight*, e.g. labour returns. Thirdly, will be that class of qualitative items for which no unit of measurement is available, such as organization structures, attitude surveys, plant lay-out. The information on these items will take the form of a *subjective evaluation*.

Information is usually presented to management at definite periodic intervals. Some figures are presented daily; those requiring collating and digesting are more likely to be presented monthly or weekly. Such figures will, to some extent, be out of date at the time of presentation; the "out-of-dateness" bearing a relationship to the interval of presentation, perhaps being from one to three weeks out of date in monthly presented figures. Naturally the more up to date the figures can be on which management is to make decisions, the more useful that information is likely to be.[1]

On receiving his report, each manager, independently, will check his output and note its variance from his budget. He will tighten up the working of his department where he considers necessary and he will also have some authority to alter his input. This corrective action will be taken independently of other departmental managers, and these changes, in which some departmental managers decide to act in one way to achieve the budget and others choose another way, will affect the systematic plan laid down in the budget, which is as a rule rigid except for its acceptance of a limited change in volume. If conditions change much from those prevailing at the time of making the budget, inflexibility in *interaction* of its parts may become apparent and the budget may have to be recast. Budgeting is of great use and can be an efficient method of planning and control, but, seen in the light of cybernetic analysis, it tends to be somewhat inflexible.

Flexible Budget

Too rigid a budget may fail in its aim of control, since it will concentrate on maintaining the *status quo*, rather than making allowance for what may prove essential modifications to the system. External influences on the organization may be largely beyond its control, though not beyond its powers of prediction. It is advisable therefore to adopt a flexible budget, so that adjustments to the plan may be made in the light, for example, of changing market conditions or changes in governmental policies.

Normal budgeting consists of controlling many of the parameters (input values) during the budget period and only allowing certain of them to vary. From an analysis in the natural sciences of the action of systems

[1] A full working description of such a system in step-by-step operation can be read in T. G. Rose, *Higher Control in Management*, Pitman.

adapting to change whilst, under particular internal or environmental constraints, it has been found that the presence of rigid restrictions leads to a less than optimal adaptation. A better solution is found if *all* input parameters are alterable. It is hardly to be expected that all constraints can be removed from the functioning of an organization, but at least we should remove those that are artificially imposed and serve no really useful purpose.

Some administrative organizations admit a degree of flexibility to their budgets by allowing "virement" used in the sense of an ability to move budgeted funds between different heads of expense.

The following chapters develop the thinking that has been carried out in "systems" and "information" areas and point up its relevance for management.

CHAPTER 2

Systems Management

How can a knowledge of systems concepts help the manager and administrator in his operational task?
The systems way of looking at events will not automatically make a manager more efficient or more effective, but it may well give him insights which if properly applied could make him so.
Firstly a distinction between being efficient and being effective. Efficiency is a concept looking towards inputs and answering such questions as "What is the best way in which I can use my available resources?" Effectiveness looks towards outputs and the goals that are achieved "What is the best way to achieve my objectives?" In practice both are inextricably interwoven. Both approaches are necessary, and it is unwise to concentrate entirely on a management technique that is related to one aspect only, e.g. cost reduction, without at the same time considering the other aspect, e.g. the goal of providing a service, making profit or producing a quality article. A fairly obvious statement but one that is frequently ignored in times of stress when inputs or resources may be drastically curtailed regardless of the long-term effect on markets and clients or when services will continue to be given regardless of the rising costs of the inputs necessary to provide the service.
The manager and the administrator have under their charge a socio-technical system. It is a constructed system, and it is a system that must be used continuously and maintained continuously or it will disintegrate. Physical systems, a car, or even a complete industrial plant can be "mothballed" for a time, then brought back into use a couple of years later and still work as well technically as they did previously. The physical system does not lose its form quickly. But where the system is predominantly social, the system is bound together by motivations,

beliefs, habits, attitudes and expectations that sometimes may change overnight.

Any management situation can be regarded as a mixture of technological, mechanical, administrative, legal, social and psychological processes. Because these processes overlie and inter-penetrate each other in complex ways, the situation is difficult both to understand and to control. But the situation can be analysed; understanding and hence control of it is made easier if each process within it is regarded as a system and these various systems are analysed separately. Then it can be asked how they work and in what manner and to what extent each can be understood and controlled.

Finally a synthesis can be made.

What is a System?

To examine dictionary and other definitions of the word "system" gives evidence of the expansion in meaning this word has undergone from its

TABLE 1

Some definitions of the word "system"

The meaning of the word "system" has undergone considerable development, as can be seen from the following definitions:

A SYSTEM	consists of *orderly arrangement*, *classification* (static).
A SYSTEM	consists of *arrangement according to a plan.*
A SYSTEM	consists of "*a set of things* connected, associated or interdependent so as to form a complex unity".
A SYSTEM	consists of *a functioning whole* (dynamic) *controlled or regulated by the plan.* (Regulation implies feedback and a standard through which a balance is imparted to the activity the whole.) Expressed in business terms a man-created system is "a collection of men, machines and procedures by which any industrial or commercial activity is carried on".
A SYSTEM	consists of *the flow of communicated information, its inputs into a particular area and the response it elicits.*

The related adjectives bring out clearly the distinction between two of these meanings:

SYSTEMATIC	(in use by 1680) arranged according to a system, a plan.
SYSTEMIC	(in use by 1803) affecting the system, pertaining to the functioning (human) system.

earlier emphasis on the static order of a classificatory system to more recent dynamic definitions of a cybernetic system in action.

> "A set of things connected, associated or interdependent so as to form a complex unity"

is the definition given by the Institute of Cost and Management Accountants[1] following the *Oxford Dictionary*,[2] which itself adds to this definition the words

> "a whole composed of parts in orderly arrangement according to some scheme or plan".

All dictionaries trace the meaning of the word and many aspects of meaning are developed. *Odhams' Dictionary* of the English language[3] includes

> "a body of related principles, a classificatory scheme, a plan of categories listed in possible working relationship, a method of procedure worked out in accordance with an accepted set of principles",

whereas Skeats' *Etymological Dictionary of the English Language*[4] considers, a system to be a construct,

> "a complex whole, put together".

Wyld's *Universal English Dictionary*[5] develops other aspects:

> "a collection of related facts, principles, ideas exhibited and arranged so as to show the relations and bearings of each in respect of others and the whole; regularity of action; the body as a whole considered in relation to efficient performance of all its functions"

Whilst Funk and Wagnall's *Standard Dictionary*[6] (New York) notes that a system can consist of

[1] *Management Information Systems*, Institute of Cost and Works Accountants, 1967.

[2] *The Shorter Oxford English Dictionary*, 1933.

[3] *Odhams' Dictionary of the English Language* (undated).

[4] Skeats' *Etymological Dictionary of the English Language*, Oxford, 1882.

[5] Wyld's *Universal Dictionary of the English Language*, Waverley Book Co. Ltd., London, 1961.

[6] Funk and Wagnall's *Standard Dictionary of the English Language*, International Edition, New York, 1964.

"principles, facts or objects" and considers aspects of "equilibrium".

Whereas most dictionaries emphasize "system" in relation to a system occurring in nature, e.g. the solar system, and mention the hierarchical aspects of one system existing within another greater system, a more usual explanation of the word system as used in business[7] emphasizes its man-created nature,

> "a collection of men, machines and procedures by which any industrial or commercial activity is carried on".

Foundos'[8] description of a system illustrates the cybernetic approach

> "a system springs into life where there is response to communicated information. The communicated information becomes input (to the system), while the response creates the output (from the system)".

In this latter case there is no attempt at a description of the system itself which could be regarded as a black box; emphasis is on behavioural functions, what types of response or output are elicited by a particular stimulus or input.
Earlier descriptions emphasize a *collection* of parts, a classificatory system. The parts themselves can be concrete or abstract. It is only in the later descriptions that the concept of system develops into purposeful activity (first of all the human body system, the plant as a system and later the complex cybernetic constructed system), parts working to a plan, implying "feedback" and "homeostasis" or balanced activity.

Levels of Use of the Word "System"

The word "system" has several connotations. Currently the word is being used in management at at least two distinct levels which can best be explained by examples:

[7] Definition in general industrial use *circa* 1965.
[8] S. Foundos, *Cybernetics and Tax Law*, Association of Certified Accountants, 1971.

(a) A product or service is provided as a *system*, for example a reprographic system, an invoicing system, a heating system. These are physical systems existing in reality. Whereas in the past a boiler might be sold as a reliable well-made piece of equipment which the purchaser would then use as he required, the problem is now tackled from a wider viewpoint. The purchaser lays down what final results he requires from the equipment, "x cubic feet of air heated to a certain temperature in specified environmental conditions with running costs kept within certain limits". The supplier fully investigates the purposes for which his machines are needed and aims to provide the exact output requirements of the purchaser rather than merely to supply a machine. The supplier provides instruction in the use of the equipment and after-sales service. The purchaser is not interested in the merits of the machine he buys but only the extent to which his stated needs are satisfied. He is not interested in the machine itself, but its output. He has purchased a heating *system*, not just a boiler.

(b) A *model* of a given situation is built incorporating all the aspects it is wished to study. This model can then be used for analysis of the situation it represents and, if it is a good model, for prediction as well. In business it may be used as a planning model.

The information that flows within a management information system can be regarded as a model of the processes it represents. Such information is extracted by accountants and others from the processes management is in charge of. In a limited way, depending on how many attributes are measured and how accurately the measured information represents the real-life situation, such a model will represent what is happening or has just happened. The information is manipulated within the model by accountants who use their available techniques to analyse, control and predict the working of the model and the real-life processes it represents. Where the information is accurate and the techniques used sufficiently powerful, decisions made on the basis of model of the situation (the management information system) will control and influence the operational system of which it is a model. Thus the way reality is represented (the model constructed) will have a positive (feedback) effect on reality, because of the type of decisions made through the use of the model.

A third use of the word "system" is somewhat outside the scope of day-to-day operations, but is mentioned here for completeness and because developments at this level do in time filter down to and become absorbed in generalized everyday thinking.

At the top level of abstraction an approach continues to be made to build up a general theory of systems applicable to all systems, or limited perhaps to a defined subset of systems. Traditionally, the various sciences isolate and examine the various elements or *parts* of the universe, whereas General Systems Theory is concerned with the *interconnectedness* of the parts into wholes. Papers working towards systems theory were published in the 1920s and in 1939/40 the concept of open systems "trading" with their environment was developed by Burton and by Von Bertalanffy. What is now the Society for General Systems Research was founded in 1954. The dates show that the interest in systems is of recent origin.

Systems in Reality and Models of Systems

Most decisions and appreciations of specific systems take place on a *model* we have constructed of a situation rather than the situation itself.

This may not be so in the case of simple systems. If we are examining a system of pulleys and levers or a steam engine it may be possible to go to the equipment and move it physically whilst discussing its system, but even here it may be preferable to stay at home and draw diagrams on backs of envelopes. In more complex situations it is just not possible to examine the real system. We cannot physically examine the economic system of a country or the electricity grid system or the working of a large company and are forced instead to examine a model made of it.

Once the use of a model becomes necessary, great importance is attached to the "fit" between the model and the situation it describes. For a long time in studies of organization, such organizations were examined as "closed" systems unrelated to their environment. Now we examine organizations as open systems dependent on the environment with their consequent need to carry out market research, to be concerned with their image in their locality and to engage employees as persons not as hired "hands".

Reality or model? Which is more important, the actual situation or the model we make of it? Sometimes the model "runs away" and becomes more important than the reality it represents.

For example, money has been devised as a store of value and a representative of goods in exchange. The monetary system is representative and it is "managed", yet it controls the flow and interchange of goods in the physical reality system. At times we become carried away with the supposed reality of the monetary system and work it to make more money hardly noticing perhaps that the output is becoming greatly eroded in terms of what it will exchange for in the physical reality system. The "seen needs of people" and their ability to work may no longer coincide with the "resources within the existing monetary system". The representative system is controlling the reality system. Much effort is expended in trying to make the monetary system run smoothly and to some extent it does. Yet this is a very good example to show the difficulty of getting a good "fit" between a representative system and the system it purports to represent.

Different Types of System Model

For the Manager, the parts that have been defined as comprising a system may be viewed in two main ways:

(i) As a model on which the effect of the interaction of parts on each other may be *analysed*, including in certain circumstances the interaction the system may have with its environment.
This type of analysis and subsequent synthesis tends to emphasize the *relationship* of parts (rather than the parts themselves) and the *balance* that exists between them.

(ii) As a model of a system (physical or abstract) that has been designed and created by man's thought to achieve some purpose. In this type of analysis there will be emphasis on *goal*, and objectives of the system; what control is apparent in the system to ensure that objectives are achieved; how effectively the objectives are in fact achieved.

Management then makes use of systemic thought;

1. In *operational use*; in the processes of budgeting and planning, and

in the control of the day-to-day situation to the previously agreed plan

using systems concepts of

Feedforward

Feedback { Negative / Positive

Lower-level goal statement

Decision-making, using information in multiple and extended feedback loops

Contact with environment requiring

(i) estimate of environmental impact,

(ii) consideration of boundary permeability

(these words will be explained in the following chapter).

2. *To achieve structural change*; the structural change processes may often be regarded as part of planning and therefore not clearly distinguished from (i) above. Such changes can best be seen as a distinct process when systems engineering is employed as a technique to effect structural change.

The rigorous mathematical definition of a system is considered outside the scope of this text.

The Vocabulary of Systems

As has been shown from the dictionary definitions, the concept of systems has developed through several stages. The terms used in describing systems tend, in consequence, to be interdisciplinary, some having been taken from each of the relevant disciplines:

Classification systems. The fitting of all available information within some schemata or framework.

Mechanistic systems. Theories of pulleys and levers and of the mechanical speed-regulating governor.

Electrical and Radio Systems. Theories of working, in particular of radio receivers, and of the concept of feedback.

Control Engineering. Theories of control engineering, particularly that of regulation to a predetermined position or temperature.

Automated Processes. Epitomized by the concept of self-inspection and, after comparison with a standard, self-regulation.

Computer systems. Used (i) as analogues of the systems they represent or (ii) as corporate or other representational models for planning or prediction.

Cybernetics. Developed as the science of the working of and control in exceedingly complex dynamic systems.

From each of these various stages through which the concept of "a system" has passed has been built up the overall vocabulary.

CHAPTER 3

System Properties

Systems may be classified by type of component and operational area Such classification is useful for defining boundaries.

Examples:

Physical Systems
Mechanical systems
Chemical systems
Electrical systems
Electronic systems
Biological systems
Process systems
Heating systems
Production systems, etc.

Informational Systems
Management information systems
Administrative systems
Accounting systems
Economic systems
Many control systems, etc.

Attitudinal and Motivational Systems
Psychological systems
Industrial relations systems
Systems of morale building etc.

Social Activity Systems comprising a mixture of social systems and technical systems (socio/technical systems)
Company systems
Organizations of all types
Transport systems
City viewed as a system, etc.

Once boundaries have been defined in general terms it is then useful to classify the system by its system properties as a first step towards understanding and control.

Viewpoint of the observer (col. 1). Having defined the limits (boundaries), the observer must then declare his approach to the system; the stance he intends to take up in relation to the system whose properties he intends to investigate:

TABLE 2

A classification of viewpoints and system variables

Viewpoint of observer and Style of observation (1)	System analysed in relation to some specific system properties (useful for analysis and comparison of differing types of system)							
	Mode of composition (2)	Contact with environment and boundary permeability (3)	Complexity (4)	System stimulus (5)	Control (6)	Predictability of change (7)	Reaction to change (8)	Final state tends to (9)
Within/outside system	Existing in nature (in balance)	Closed system	Simple systems	Reactive system	Open-loop system	Static framework	Stable	Equilibrium (run-down)
Aspect of interest		↕	↓	—	—		↕	
Depth of analysis		↕	↓	—	—	—	↕	
Attitude of observation	—	↕	Complex systems	Proactive system	Closed-loop system with feedback control	Deterministic system	↕	—
Mode of observation		↕	↓	—	—	Probabilistic system	↕	
Cultural context	Constructed (man-designed) and goal-seeking	Open systems	Exceedingly complex systems (cybernetic)	Impactive system	Feedforward of process of information	Adaptive system	Unstable	Homeostasis (tension)

Position: from within or from outside the system.

Aspect of interest: flows or point values.

Depth of analysis: in general terms or in great detail.

Attitude of observation: descriptive, classificatory analytic, synthetic.

Mode of observation: static or dynamic.

Cultural context: any specific components relative to the analysis.

The declared approach will determine to a considerable extent where a given system stands in relation to the scales of system properties outlined in cols. 2–9.

Some important system properties are shown in cols. 2–9. Every defined system can be analysed in relation to each of these eight properties. To carry out such an analysis enables us to see how the system is likely to change over time and hence in what manner it may best be controlled. The list is not exhaustive but covers most of the categories important in an analysis.

Mode of composition (col. 2). A system describing the movement of the planets, or an ecological system describing the interrelationship of, say a colony of seals existing in ecological balance with its food supply, the birth of pups and survival into full membership of the colony of those who escape predators, can be described as *natural* systems. *Constructed* or man-made systems are innumerable and have the distinction of having been "put together" in their parts by man. A management information system, or any construct such as a car or a factory are constructed systems. The main emphasis in man-made systems is this putting together from parts (any of which may fail) rather than the overall system being the result of long evolution, in which latter case the parts have been tested over long periods of time and are less likely to fail. Most man-made systems have a goal or purpose. Natural systems seldom have a goal, but may be said to possess "on-going" drive. The seals if threatened will take what action they can to survive, not so much in order to achieve some particular goal, but in order to continue to exist in whatever manner they can. In natural systems any discerned goals are often found to have been imposed on the system by the observer and from the standpoint of his cultural background rather than being found implicitly in the system observed.

Contact with environment (col. 3). Where a system is completely isolated from its environment and examined under artificial or laboratory conditions as a separate entity, it is near to becoming a *closed* system. *Open* systems are those whose working is studied in relation to the environment in which they exist; importance is attached to examining the input from and output to the environment. The double-headed arrow in col. 3 indicates that although many systems that are examined can be classed as open or closed, some also exist where the environmental contacts are only partially made and so the system can be said to occupy a midway position. The thick skin of Fig. 3.1a represents its isolation from the environment. It cannot be permeated as can the boundary of Fig. 3.1b where traffic with the environment takes place.

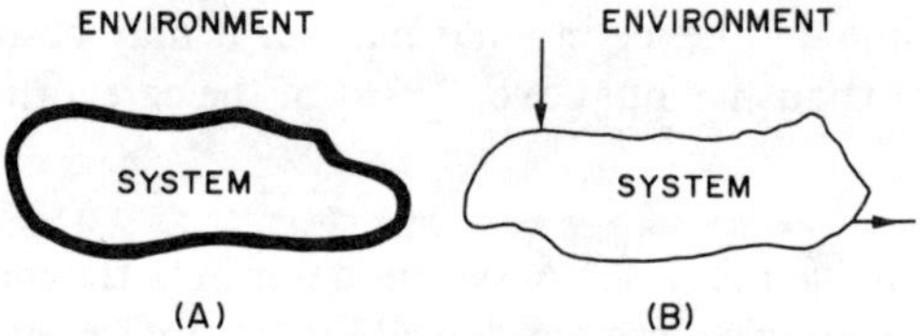

Fig. 3.1. (a) Closed system. (b) Open system.

Complexity (col. 4). The governor on an old-style gramophone, consisting of metal balls on a spring that are allowed to fly out a certain distance as the speed increases thus allowing the turntable to revolve at the set speed and no faster, is a good example of a *simple* system, in fact a simple system for regulating the gramophone mechanism. The same simple control system can be noticed at a steam rally on most traction engines where, as the speed increases, the governor balls fly out under centrifugal force until the moving ends are brought up against an adjustable stop which mechanically controls the speed. There are only a few parts in such systems. A company viewed as a system, or the economic system of the U.K. could be classed as exceedingly *complex* systems, systems in fact whose working we are just not able fully to describe in accurate detail because of the many parts that make them up and the complexity of the interrelationships between those parts. In such an analysis it is structure that is being examined and structure together with the amount of communication between each of the parts that determine the category.

A simple economic or psychological system would fall into the same category. The amount of complexity in a system is to some extent a function of the depth at which the observer has *chosen* to analyse its working. The more detail examined, the greater the complexity. In systems thinking, this approach is a very useful one, situations can be mastered as *simple* systems before moving on to more complex analyses of the same situation.

System stimulus (col. 5). A *reactive* system is one that reacts to a specific input stimulus. Its output is related in time and quality to the input. An *impactive* system is generally a large complex system that contains many resources within its own boundary. A course of action may be decided upon without there being any noticeable input stimulus. A Corporation or an individual may have many resources that can be rearranged and exported into the environment, often with great impact. Such systems are very difficult for outsiders, say a Government, to control.

The *Proactive* system comes midway. Planners within such a system are less inventive but nevertheless make plans, normally within the existing context of operations, to benefit the system by anticipating stimuli, adverse or favourable.

Control loops (col. 6). A bridge that breaks does not examine its condition and set about repairing itself, a watch that tells the wrong time does not automatically correct itself. A car that runs out of petrol does not fill itself up. But a car with driver should, however, act as a closed-loop system. On a long run the driver should regularly check the petrol gauge and as the tank is seen to be emptying, note this feedback of information and fill up again. There is nothing automatic here, the driver may be careless and not bother to look at the gauge, or he may not believe its reading and hence take no action. The feedback loop is there but it is somewhat tenuous.

Open-loop situations often exist in nature. A species of animal such as the goat that lives by browsing may find a lot of trees and shrubs at a suitable height, feed fully and so be in a fit state to multiply. As time goes on there is a larger herd but not so much food as the trees and shrubs take a longer time to replace themselves. Suddenly there is hardly any food left at all. The herd that was multiplying dies out through want of food input. Only a few of the hardiest survive. What to the herd (if they think in a dim way) must have seemed ideal conditions have suddenly evaporated. There was lack of information, and probably lack of means to process it even if it had been available. The same open-loop conditions can also exist in commerce and industry. Decisions are taken without basing them on available information or without seeking out information that is necessary.

Static systems (frameworks) may be able to exist satisfactorily without feedback, but for systems that are classed as open systems trading with their environment, and particularly if the system has mobility, some type of feedback is an absolute essential.

The closed-loop of feedback can be noticed in natural systems as an integral part of the system itself. A man is walking towards a door. He keeps his eye on the door and handle and judges his distance all the time

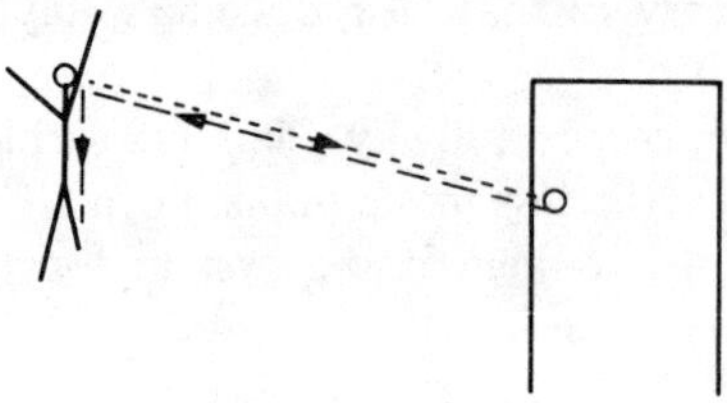

Fig. 3.2. Continuous negative feedback.

he is approaching it. If he does not bother to use his closed-loop integral feedback system when he is talking to a friend after lunch, he more often than not bangs into the door as he passes through. Where the door is fully of glass he may misjudge the hinge side and again bang into it. Watching the problems of a blind man trying to go through a door he does not know, soon brings home how effective in use are our own inbuilt closed-loop feedback systems that we use without even thinking about.

Inherent feedback systems are an integral part of many natural systems. Trouble arises when we are dealing with a constructed system, be it a

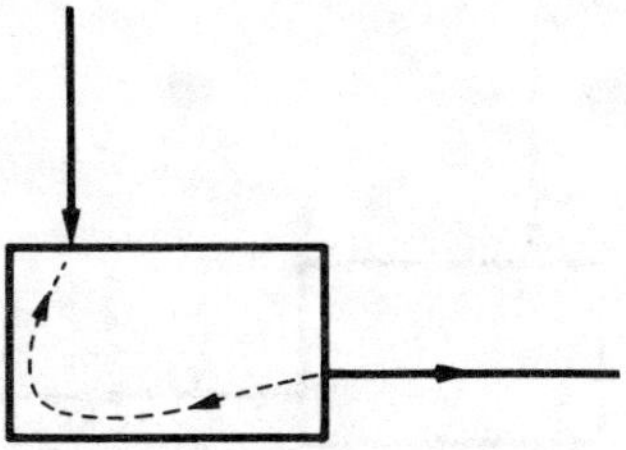

Fig. 3.3. Inherent feedback loop.

machine or a social organization, as the feedback loop has also to be constructed.

Problems of constructed feedback systems where the feedback loop is not an integral part of the system but a consciously constructed loop distinct from the main process system will be dealt with in detail in a later chapter.

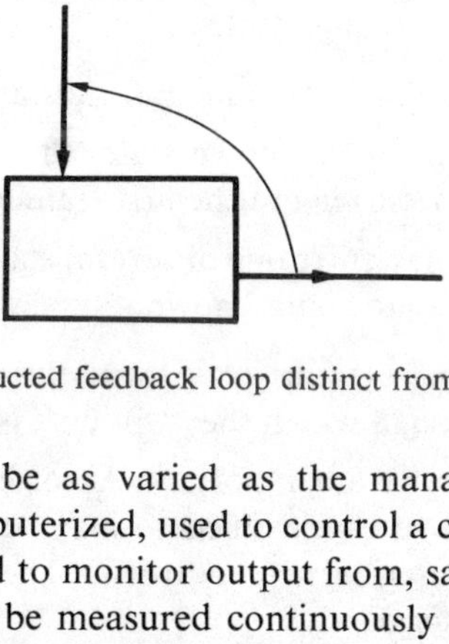

Fig. 3.4. Constructed feedback loop distinct from main process.

Feedback loops can be as varied as the management information system, probably computerized, used to control a company, to the more automatic devices used to monitor output from, say, a steel rolling mill where the output can be measured continuously by electronic devices and the pressure on the rollers adjusted without stopping as indication is given of thickness variance outside laid-down limits.

In radio work, feedforward has been experimented with but was found to be difficult to keep in balance. Feedforward as an alternative to feedback control may, however, have to be used in some chemical plants where the feedback loops take too long to function and so do not give effective control. Monitoring at one stage may indicate adjustments

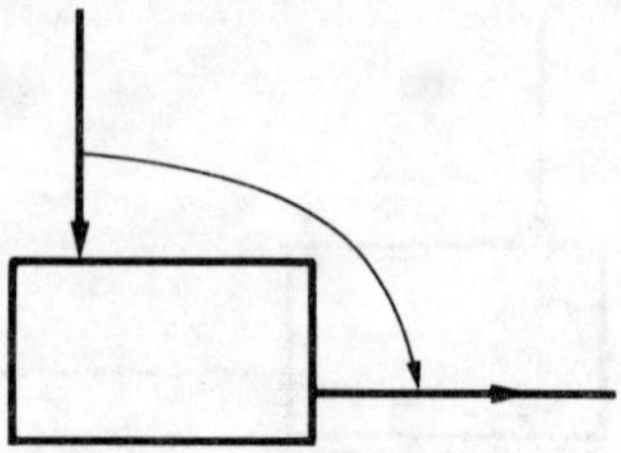

Fig. 3.5. Feedforward loop.

to be made to the process flow further downstream as a means of correcting "errors". Feedforward control can be considered "open-loop". When control does not function in the planned manner there will be none of the automatic self-regulation of the feedback loop. This is because the feedforward signal does not pass through the system again in the way that the feedback signal does.

Predictability of system change (col. 7)

Static systems have only one state and thus are "frameworks".

Deterministic systems have known states through which the systems must pass, often returning to the first state in a deterministic cycle.

Statistical systems may enter one of several states with the probability of entering each state being known.

Adaptive or learning systems may themselves alter their states and hence the pattern through which they will pass is difficult to determine. The four categories shown are important. According into which category a system may require to be classified so may be seen the related techniques available to describe and control it. These categories are dealt with further in Chapter 5.

Stable/Unstable (col. 8). Stability is a function of the structure of engineered systems and of the speed with which information passes through that structure. In Fig. 3(a) the system is stable as it operates outside the point of instability I; in Fig. 3(b) the point of instability is within the system mode of working and so the system will be inherently unstable. In Fig. 3(c) the system has been carefully engineered to avoid

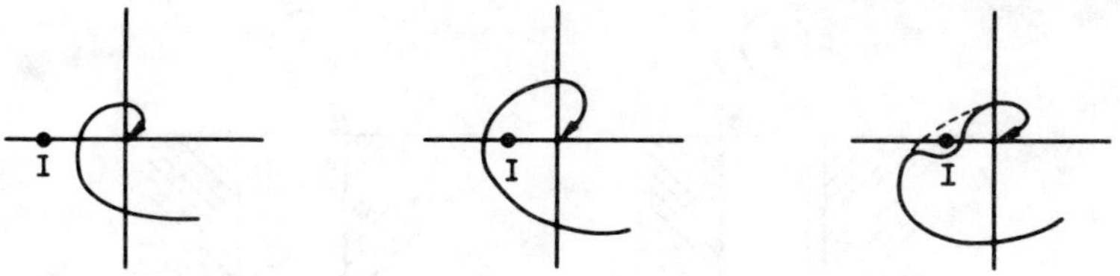

(a) (b) (c)

Fig. 3.6. (a) Stable. (b) Unstable. (c) Conditional stability

the point of instability and a condition of stability exists but any unexpected disturbance may make the system become unstable.

The speed with which a system responds to information, its response time, affects stability. If a system is so constructed as to have a very quick response time this may make it unstable if the changing inputs go outside certain limits. Stability of a system, that is its attribute not to go into a series of wild oscillations or to swing right out of control at the top or bottom of its limits, depends on keeping to a limited range of input values, dominance of particular feedback loops, response time to input changes, and the structure of system. To construct a system that has a quick response time yet is stable within the likely limits of input is not easy. Often stability is achieved by ensuring "checks and balances" and hence sluggish response to input.

In social systems stability again depends largely on the response time of the situation, how long it takes to react to changed conditions. Too quick a reaction means instability. Too long a response time causes an organization to become out of date. Most social systems can accommodate change within given limits, but environmental or internal changes outside these limits will cause perturbations to the system that cause it to become unstable.

Equilibrium and homeostasis (col. 9). Closed systems working under the second law of thermodynamics come to rest in a "run-down" state of *equilibrium*, where all their capacity for work has been expended, a state of entropy. All tension is released and the system attains a state of maximum entropy, a state of the most probable distribution of the elements comprising the system. Living systems, by contrast, exist as

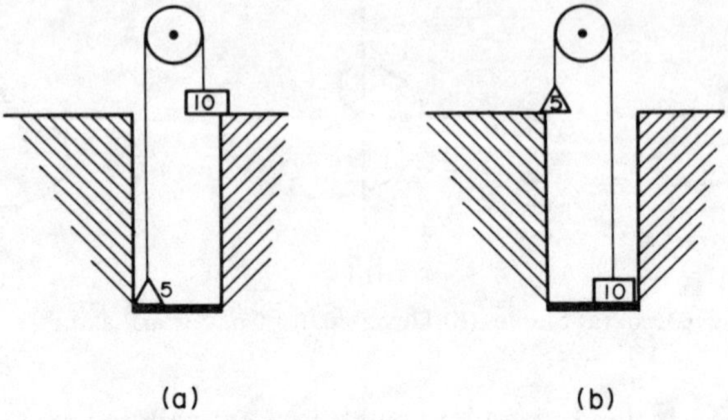

Fig. 3.7. (a) Tension in system: capacity for work. (b) Capacity for work expended. System has "run down".

"tension spots" within their environment. Most living systems behave as open systems. Open systems, depending on their input from and output to their environment, tend to become ever more complex, ever more differentiated and once established tend to grow, sometimes at the expense of other systems. Open systems are characterized by negative entropy.

The steady state that characterizes the input–output open system is not the motionless equilibrium of a closed system. Where conditions alter there is a drive to return to the steady state of the system. This action is best seen in the regulation of the human body system which is kept at a constant temperature regardless of external conditions. The principle of homeostasis, originally a biological term, implies a drive to return to the steady state of an open system. This steady state need not be absolutely fixed. The return after a disturbance can be to an exactly similar position, or developments of growth or decay can be accommodated, provided such growth or decay are within the programmed limits of the system. Normally these limits would allow only moderate growth within a specified time period. Growth outside these limits would probably lead to an unsecure (unstable) state of the system, the homeostatic principle is then not working, and the system enters a state of crisis, is vulnerable, and may cease to be viable and be destroyed. Some systems include within their programmed limits enormous capacity for change in size or quality; for example, grubs turn into butterflies without going outside the programmed limits of their systems.

Where the principle of homeostasis is applied to social organizations, it may be difficult to decide what are the programmed limits of such a system. Most social and psychological systems can react to change, but can only accommodate a given amount of change within a given time period.

System Boundaries and Environment

The closed system could be an actual system, say a system of pulleys and levers and weights, or it could be a model of a situation such as a closed system representing an economic situation. The closed aspect comes from the system's isolation from the environment in which it exists. Such closed systems are subject to the second law of thermodynamics, their final state is that of a stable equilibrium, a state of entropy, where points of tension have been evened out and a final "run down" state of equilibrium (liquidation in the case of a company) achieved. No further movement or action can take place without further input of energy and as this system is, by definition, isolated, this does not occur.

The *open* system has its boundary skin permeable and there is traffic across the boundary; for a business there is input of raw materials, energy and information about markets and output of finished goods. Isolated from its environment the open system would soon run down if, for instance, it was unable to purchase any more raw material or to sell its products. It would in effect become a closed system. The most important point about an open system is that, although the boundary is defined, there is traffic across it, both input and output. The open system exists within its environment.[1]

An open system cannot fully be described without in addition a description of its environment. Such open systems import energy from the environment and are viable as long as the importation of energy exceeds or at least balances the output. Open systems are viable as long as they remain points of tension and accumulations of energy. The viable open

[1] G. Sommerhoff, in *Systems Thinking*, Ed. F. Emery, pp. 147–204, Penguin, 1969.

system exists under conditions of negative entropy and the second law of thermodynamics does not apply. Human beings defy this law and remain points of tension but the price that has to be paid is the expenditure of time, a limited commodity that eventually runs out in death. Organizations appear to defy death for an indeterminate length of time as younger individuals arrive to take the place of the ageing ones. As long as the organization is able to balance the inflow against the outflow and remain a point of accumulated energy, it is viable. Once the outflow drains off the energy, the organization as an open system is no longer viable and liquidation or dissolution quickly ensues.

Sometimes an organization that could be regarded as an open system is considered as a closed system and plans and forecasts are made on the basis of a closed system without regard to the environment in which it exists and on which it depends. For example, plans are made to manufacture a product without examining the market. More than likely those plans and forecasts will be erroneous and more than likely they will lead to a run down in the organization.

Often it is useful to differentiate the environment[2] and to divide it into two parts: that which directly affects the system, the substantial environment, and the remainder, the general environment. It then becomes necessary to collect details relating to the substantial environment alone. In most cases when considering the open system, it is sufficient to consider that the output dissipates itself without trouble into the environment. A factory makes bread, its output is bought and paid for and a profit made to enable the business to continue in operation. The bread itself is eaten and assimilated satisfactorily into the environment. But on occasion products are not fully assimilated, the factory that makes soft drinks may produce unassimilable bottles, the wrappings of a product may become unassimilable. Often where only one factory is being examined the open-system model is satisfactory, but for some problems, particularly ecological ones, dealing with interaction of products and environment on a large scale, it may be necessary to take the concept a stage further and consider the boundary of the "environment that cannot be passed". The environmental boundary then becomes the aspect of the system that is closed.

[2] E. A. Lowe, *Journal of Systems Engineering*, Vol. 2, No. 1 (Summer 1971), University of Lancaster.

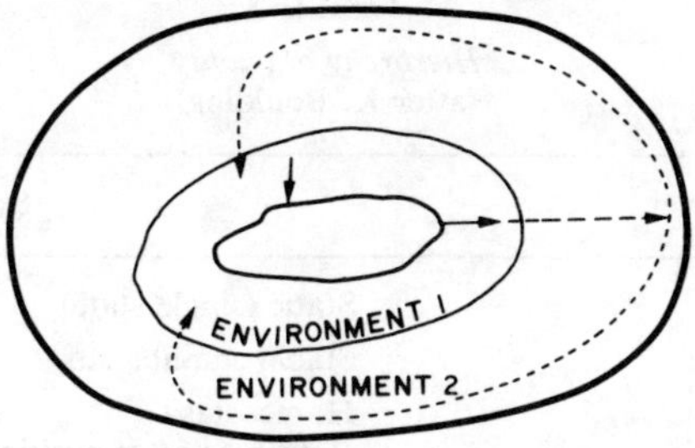

Fig. 3.8. Differentiated environment and closed environmental boundary.

The outer closed boundary may be taken as a national frontier, or for ecological systems "spaceship earth". The system is closed in that what it produces cannot escape and builds up. The output begins to affect other systems, often detrimentally, and finally begins to affect the environment (E_1) of the system that is itself producing the product that cannot be assimilated.

Hierarchy and System Properties

The concept of hierarchy previously introduced showed how smaller sub-systems exist within larger systems, but hierarchy in systems can also be related to a dimension other than size, that of the levels of complexity and hence the characteristics of systems.

These views have been widely accepted but are far from being fully assimilated into current thinking as a basis for action.

Table 3 is based on the nine levels distinguished by Boulding[3] with additional material added. The levels distinguished follow closely the changing dictionary definitions previously given, reflecting in a similar manner our growing interest in systems and the continued extension of our knowledge about systems.

For example, business companies which are a type of social organization were for many years viewed as static structures, frameworks epitomized by the formal organization chart. It is only recently that we are

[3] "General systems theory: the skeleton of science", *Management Science* (April 1956).

TABLE 3

Hierarchy of quality
(after K. Boulding)

System level	System
1. Frameworks	Static (single state)
2. Clockworks	Stable equilibrium
3. Cell	Homeostasis Return to a set position modified by growth/decay
4. Animal	Self-awareness
5. Human	Self-consciousness Self-reflectiveness End-seeking (teleological) behaviour
6. Abstract and symbolic systems	Formation of criteria, rules of the game, algorithms
7. Social activity organizations	Goal directedness. Value systems as criteria for determining goals
8. Eco-systems	Wider viewpoint of the totality of interaction
9. Transcendental systems	To be discovered

beginning to regard businesses as input–output open systems (Type 8) existing in and dependent on an environment, to be concerned with their goal-directedness and the interrelationships between the subsystems that are the parts of the business, and with the environment investigated by market research. This is not necessarily to say that the previous thinking was wrong at the time, but that further understanding has been gained so that it is possible now to give a much fuller description. The orderly classification of items required by the Static Type 1 system is a framework necessary of achievement before further work can be done. It is true that as more advanced types of system are described it may be necessary to question some aspects of the original classificatory work carried out under Type 1 but without a base on which to build it would be impossible to proceed to more advanced study.

CHAPTER 4

System Structure

The parts comprising a system can frequently be differentiated into sub-systems carrying out specific functions in relation to the main system. In any man-made system we would look for the

Perception sub-system	comprising the way in which the system finds out its place in relation to other systems and the environment and also the internal state which it is in;
Information sub-system	comprising the processing of the perceived data (internal and external) as in a management information system;
Advisory sub-system	bringing in further data and helping to interpret the information passing through the perception and information systems;
Goal-formulation sub-system	comprising positive feedback and the advisory sub-system, to determine what future system states are to be achieved;
Decision-making sub-system	comprising the way in which decisions are arrived at, which may be complex and include a power structure system;
Implementation sub-system	comprising the action elements. There are likely to be many implementation sub-systems;
Control sub-system	comprising negative feedback to control to the plan.

Some or all of which may be present. According to Katz and Kahn,[1] open systems move in the direction of differentiation and specialization. In an organizational system the amount of complexity will tend to depend on the authority system.
In every-day language the prefix "sub" is frequently dropped and the "control" sub-system may be discussed as a system in its own right. However, it is really a sub-system to the extent that it will disappear if the system it controls disappears.

Sub-system relationships

In examining the pattern of sub-system relationships in a system, important aspects are:

Number of sub-systems of each kind, and the number of parts of which each is comprised.
Coupling: the pattern of authority, responsibility and communication in which the sub-systems are joined.
Sub-system interfaces: opaqueness; gaps, overlap; the ease of communication.
Compatibility of the various sub-systems: can they work together in harmony?
Mutual dependency (or interrelatedness) of the parts. The degree to which change of state in one sub-system affects another sub-system.

Consideration of these relationships immediately brings into prominence the situation of variety and complexity.

Variety

Variety arises from the number of differentiated parts in a system and the number of ways in which they may be linked. Mechanical systems tend to be simple as the mechanical linkages are mostly on a 1 to 1 basis and they can be clearly seen. In social organizations, as example of

[1] *The Social Psychology of Organisations*, John Wiley & Sons, 1966.

exceedingly complex systems, the linkages are informational and these informational linkages assume great variety with startling rapidity.
Variety proliferates as the parts making up a system, such parts being similar or dissimilar, are regarded firstly as quite separate, then connected, then interacting dynamically.
There are, let us say, five simple parts within a system.
In the first case (Fig. 4.1) there are three parts of the identical type and a

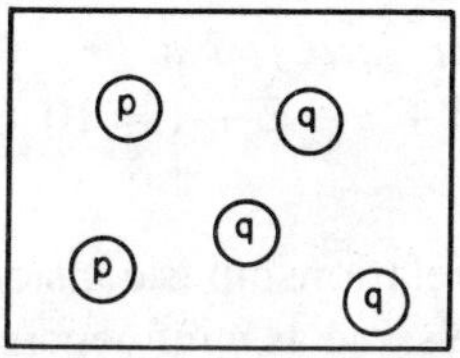

Fig. 4.1. Variety 2: system with five parts of two different kinds.

further two parts identical to each other but of a different type; the variety is two.
In Fig. 4.2 all parts are of a different type to each other; variety is five.

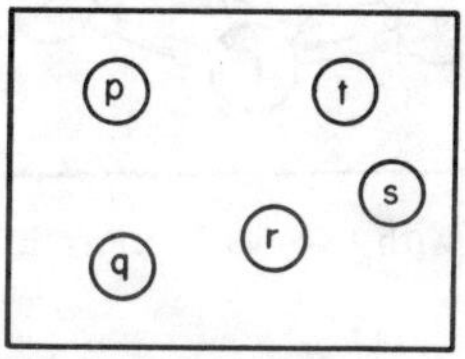

Fig. 4.2. Variety 5: system with five parts each of a different kind.

In Fig. 4.3 the dissimilar parts are connected. There is now variety not only in the different parts but also in their connectivity with the other

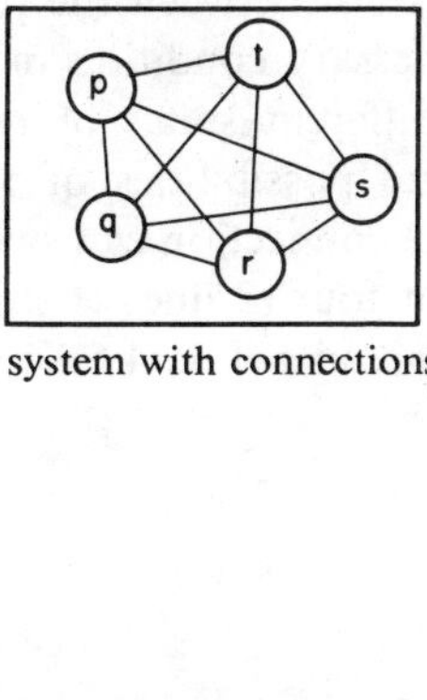

Fig. 4.3. Variety 10: system with connections between all five parts.

parts. Each item is fully connected to each of the other four items. We are now interested in the relationships, but no distinction is made in direction of relationship, *pq* is regarded as the same as *qp*.
The connections are

$$\begin{array}{llll} pq & & & \\ pr & qr & & \\ ps & qs & rs & \\ pt & qt & rt & st \end{array}$$

$$4 + 3 + 2 + 1 = 10$$

Variety is increased to ten.
In Fig. 4.4 direction of the relationship is considered; *p* influencing *q*(*pq*) is not regarded as being the same as *q* influencing *p*(*qp*).

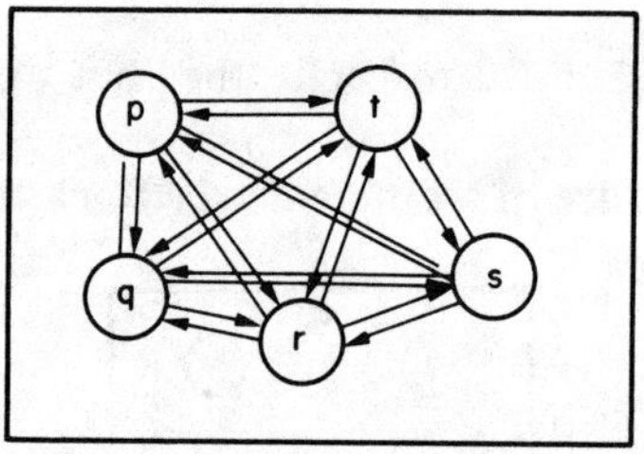

Fig. 4.4. Variety 20: system with two-way connections between all five parts.

Variety now becomes double that of the previous cases as there is a connection in each direction

$$8 + 6 + 4 + 2 = 20$$

But the influencing connections between the parts may not always be working. It is in fact a necessary condition of a dynamically working system that it can enter different states of relationship between the parts. Ignoring intermediate possibilities of the connection partially operating, let us say that the connection can switch on or off.
There are now not one, but four (2 lines × 2 position) possible states of the connection between *p* and *q* (Fig. 4.5).

p on *q* on, *p* on *q* off, *p* off *q* on, *p* off *q* off.

$(pq, \bar{p}q, p\bar{q}, \bar{p}\bar{q})$

As each further connection is brought into consideration, the possible states are multiplied ×2 for a single line or ×4 for a full connection.

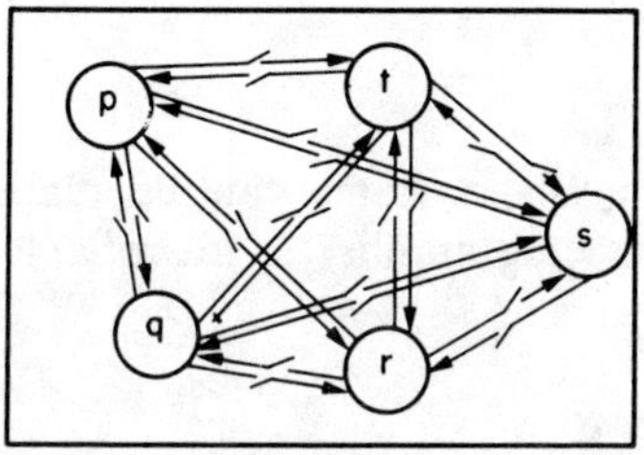

Fig. 4.5. Variety 1,048,576: system with on/off connections between all five parts.

The total variety of connections in this system of only five very simple parts now becomes

2^{20} (approx. 10^6) or 1,048,576.

The position so far is summarized in Table 4.

TABLE 4

Variety developed with five parts depends on the richness of the interconnections, "and"

Fig. 4.2	1 and 1 and 1 and 1 and 1.	Variety 5
4.3	1 and 1 and 1 and 1 and 1.	Variety 10
4.4	1 and 1 and 1 and 1 and 1.	Variety 20
4.5	1 and 1 and 1 and 1 and 1.	Variety 1,048,576

To add one further part, six parts, would raise the number of connections to 2^{30} (approx. 10^9) or 1,000,000,000, and for a dynamic system of 10 parts to 2^{90} (approx. 10^{27}) or 1,000,000,000,000,000,000,000,000,000. It may give some idea of the size of this number, to state that the number of atoms in the whole universe is calculated as 10^{73} or that our world was in a gaseous state less than 10^{18} seconds ago.

These calculations demonstrate the reason why it is impossible in any decision-making system to build a model taking in *all* the variables. Only those variables considered most important should be selected and put into the model (and, of course, there will always be argument as to which are the important variables).

Complexity

For the sake of analysis, systems can be placed into three broad categories according to the number of identifiable parts in their structure.

Simple systems,

Complex system,

Exceedingly complex (cybernetic) systems.

The *simple* system has few parts, perhaps ten or fifteen as in the case of the governor, and these parts can easily be described in their mechanical relationship either in reality or as a model.

At the other end of the scale, the *exceedingly complex system* is too wide to view in reality and the model created may be a highly complex one produced by a cybernetician comprised of many thousands of parts.

The problem here expressed links up with the comment made in Chapter 3 that the systems observer and investigator have to *choose* a particular depth of analysis at which to work. What depth of detail a systems man is able to work at in practice will depend on his own ability, the ability of those who have to "take over" the system he designs and the continuing development of techniques available to him, i.e. "the state of the art at any given moment".

Problems of variety and complexity have been taken up by cyberneticians. Cybernetics is described as the science of control in complex systems; systems that are highly complex and highly probabilistic.

The cybernetician's model of a situation is far more complex than the flow chart of a systems analyst. Although the cybernetician's system model will be a far more accurate model of the system it represents, yet there is often difficulty in bringing this cybernetic model from its depths of analysis to the operational day-to-day level at which it will have to be implemented. The barriers or interfaces that exist between different levels of analysis are by no means easy to cross. The day-to-day operational manager may not have the training to understand a complex analysis of the system he controls.

Certainly this training can be given. But even then the trained day-to-day operational manager may have great difficulty in translating the insights gained at deep level of analysis into the hurly-burly of operations in the market-place. Yet to an increasing degree this must be done.

A useful approach is the simplifying one of the economist's input–output analysis. Positing that the system itself is too complex to describe and model, examination is made only of input and its related output. What goes on within the system itself is considered too complex to trace through at all. This is termed *black-box* analysis. Where the inside of a complex system is partially traced through the technique is sometimes termed grey-box analysis.

Input–Output Analysis

The simplest method of examining a complex system is to examine the input and output to the system, and note how variations in input affect the output. For the time being the working of the system itself is ignored (Fig. 4.6).

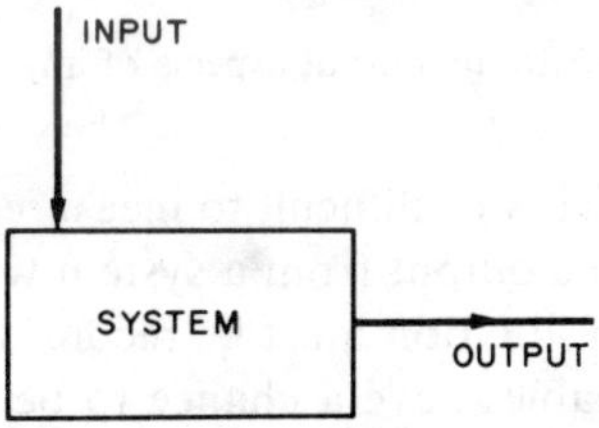

Fig. 4.6. Input–output system.

Input–output structure. The inputs to an open system, such as the socio-technical systems of business and industry, comprise information, materials and energy. These inputs are termed *parameters*, a word denoting that their values are determined; these inputs can be set to whatever level is desired or decided upon. The processes within the system convert these inputs in the established way. The subsequent outputs to the environment are termed *variables*. This word "variable" signifies that the outputs are dependent; dependent upon the inputs and conversion rates. The output variables are still dependents even though in a constructed system we may decide first what output we require and then work backwards through the known conversion rates of the system to calculate at what level to set the input parameters.

In the practical situation not all input is closely examined and not all output is susceptible to measurement, so that we arrive at the situation in Fig. 4.7. Only some of the input factors under our control are examined and controlled; only those output variables that we consider it profitable to examine, are measured.

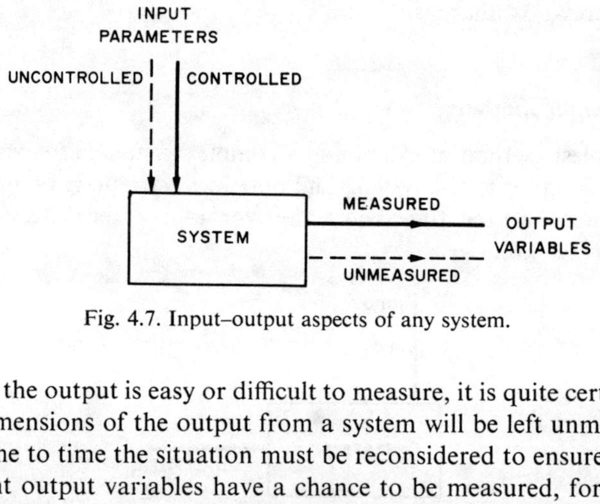

Fig. 4.7. Input–output aspects of any system.

Whether the output is easy or difficult to measure, it is quite certain that many dimensions of the output from a system will be left unmeasured. From time to time the situation must be reconsidered to ensure that all important output variables have a chance to be measured, for what is important may change, and input parameters may be controlled the more easily if they can be measured in some form. Output and input measurements are not concerned with flow of exactly the same items, for the purpose of the main system is to convert the input. Yet the general problem is the same. Input and output is differentiated into that which is controlled and that which is not controlled; output into that which is measured and that which is left unmeasured. Often in systems diagrams only one input and output line is shown, to represent the input that is controlled and the output that is measured in any given circumstance.

The sensor or measuring device is the most vital component of any control system. If the required dimensions of the output cannot be measured accurately and effectively, there is little likelihood of being able to control the system. The type of measuring device chosen depends to some extent on the type of output to be measured, as well as developments in the invention of measuring devices and measuring techniques.

Control of the System

In the business and administrative situation our first concern is *control* of the system which, in the first instance, we will take to be a satisfactory one.

Later the working of the system itself must be examined to see if a more efficient method or a more efficient process can be substituted for the existing one. This type of analysis, systems analysis, tends by its inherent nature to be intermittent. Once a satisfactory up-to-date process has been introduced it is often expected to remain for possibly up to 10 years or more without much revision, perhaps until it has been fully depreciated financially on some *ad hoc* basis whcih in fact may have no relationship to the obsolescence of the process.

The intervals at which systems analysis should take place will be discussed later. At present we must take it that we are confronted with an existing system that does not need to be, or cannot be (for financial reasons or lack of knowledge, etc.) revised. The problem is to keep this existing situation under control.

Whilst bearing in mind this temporary qualification regarding a system not in need of revision, it should be made clear at this stage that "control" signifies far more than maintaining the existing system in being. Elaborating on an earlier definition, control implies balance, and this balance is of two types:

(i) *Homeostasis*. This includes short-term control adjustments which are part of the programme of the system. These may cause the system to revert exactly to its original position, or may permit certain developments in the system, provided these changes remain within the programmed capacity.

(ii) *Innovation.* Controls may also permit developments which are outside the present capacity of the system, but within the information capacity of the persons responsible for directing the organization, and originating developments of this kind. Such changes may be termed controlled innovation.

Current situations need to be controlled as they occur. Uncontrolled systems may deviate from the agreed goals by increasing amounts until a crisis situation occurs. But control costs money and therefore the type of control used will depend on the likelihood of the system going out of control. This in turn depends on the type of system which is being controlled and the penalty involved in sorting out the crisis situation when this does occur. Where control is difficult or expensive, one solution is to exercise no control until breakdown occurs and then spend time sorting out the mess.

The simplest system to control is a closed mechanical process; this falls in our first category of determined systems. The description "closed" means that the system itself, including its control, will operate without outside attention. The control mechanism is *intrinsic*, built into the system and cannot fail to operate as long as the system itself is working. The engine governor is a good example. As the speed of the shaft increases, the weights fly out under centrifugal force and the sleeve to which they are attached moves up the shaft. This movement has the effect of turning off gradually the source of power until at last the shaft revolves at the required rate. It is the increase of speed of the shaft that causes the action which cuts off the power and so reduces its speed. The state at which the system settles down can be determined beforehand.

In other categories of systems, control tends to be mainly external to the system and not a part of it. The person in charge has to take action himself; it does not occur automatically. If he is not present, no action (or wrong action) may be taken, and the situation may consequently go out of control. *Extrinsically* controlled systems may require an operator in constant attendance to exercise control, correcting the system whenever

a divergence occurs; or it may be possible to exercise control at intervals, perhaps half-hourly in the case of a machine, daily or weekly in the case of information flow. It is possible to develop a management-control system which is intermittent and yet semi-automatic and hence tending towards intrinsic control. This is the basis of the "management by exception" principle.
We can then list the two basic categories of control:

Intrinsic Control

Those controls which are so bound up with and are part of the system that if the system is working the control must be operating.

Extrinsic Control

Those controls that are external to the system or only loosely linked to it and which may or may not be working when the system is in operation. Most control systems are neither completely *intrinsic* or *extrinsic*, but can be said to tend towards one or other of these types. The distinguishing types serve as the two poles of a continuum.

Definition of terms: process and control loops. Semantically, a problem now arises, just what elements does the word "system" apply to, now that the feedback loop has been distinguished as a separate element? In *descriptive* mode, business, industrial or administrative processes can be distinguished as production systems, the constructed management information process that controls it as a further system, both being classed as sub-systems of the main business system (Fig. 4.8).
In *analytic* mode, it becomes necessary to emphasize the systems aspects of the elements concerned, a process controlled by a feedback loop. The management information system loses its title and may be seen as a feedback loop controlling a main process, the *whole* being termed a system. Figure 4.9 shows the sub-systems in Fig. 4.8 redefined for analysis purposes.

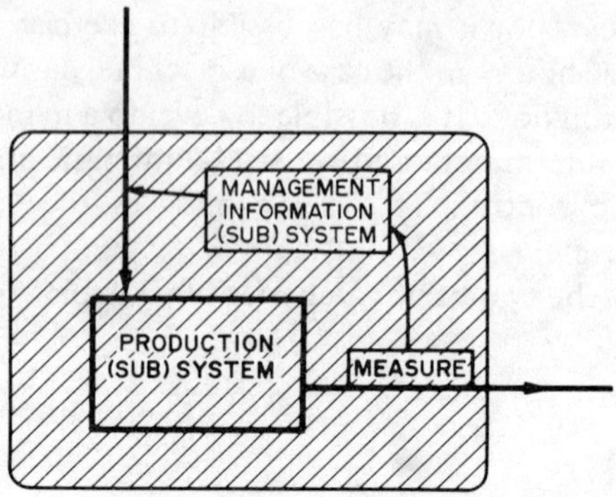

Fig. 4.8. A business system.

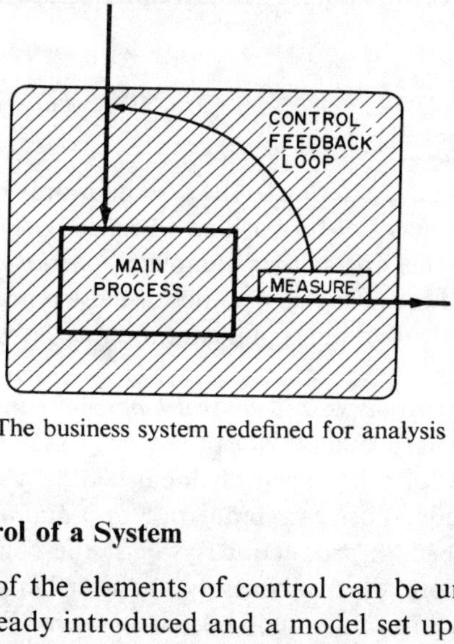

Fig. 4.9. The business system redefined for analysis purposes.

Elements of Control of a System

An examination of the elements of control can be undertaken on the basic diagram already introduced and a model set up capable of interpreting any control situation.

Measurement of output. For control, measurement of output and subsequent alteration of input parameters is required (Fig. 4.10). The measuring device, known as a sensor, will require a unit of measurement in which to work. This in itself may pose a problem; often a reason for

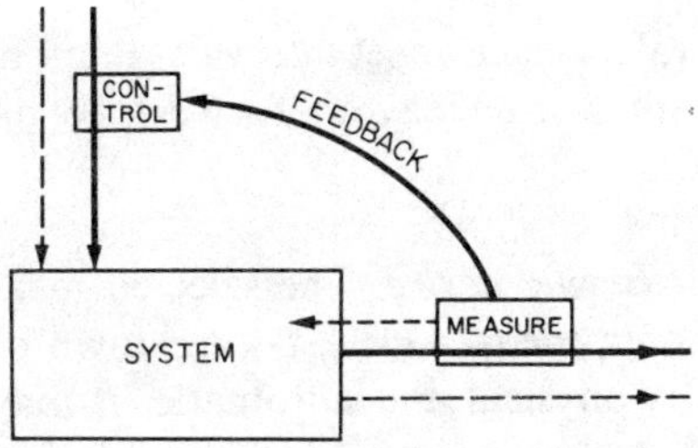

Fig. 4.10. Measurement, feedback and control.

leaving part of a system uncontrolled is that there is no suitable and accepted unit of measurement. Other parts of the system may not be measured because we do not consider it worthwhile, because it would be too costly or because we have no time to do so.

(i) *Aspects of the output*. The output to be measured may be continuous or discrete, A strip of steel being rolled may require continuous monitoring as to thickness. A device that is continually in operation whenever the process is in operation may be the ideal. Such a device is the electronic eye. Speed of measurement is vital as many feet of product per minute are being produced and any inaccuracies in thickness require to be checked and corrected within seconds. In other cases the output may arrive in discrete units, such as motor cars at the end of a production line which could be put to one side and it may not be important whether they have their final test drive within the next 2 minutes or next 2 days. Socio-technical systems may have feedback links that operate on greatly varying timescales, such as the daily or weekly balancing of books, the monthly management meeting, the annual general meeting of shareholders.

(ii) *Aspects of measurement*. Dependent on the type of output and the goals to be achieved by the system, so decisions will have to be taken in any constructed system as to whether the measurement of the output is to be continuous or intermittent. In the case of steel strip rolling or a radio set, output will be measured continuously. Statistical quality-control systems measurement may be of random items although the measurement itself takes place at set intervals. Bank inspectors visiting a branch to check cash will endeavour to work to both a random and intermittent pattern.

(iii) *The selected measuring device.* The selected measuring device may vary from an electronic eye to a clerk taking down pencil notes. Where the selected device is physical and automatic, it may be built into the process itself so that the process cannot work for long without its monitoring device also working; for example, the tachometer attached to a lorry. The lorry could complete a trip with the device out of action, but this would be checked at the end of the run. Often, particularly when the measuring device is human, the system may run for a considerable time with the measuring device out of action. A physical stores check on a sub-stores which should take place monthly may not be done at all throughout the year.

A sensor may be built to record output exactly as it arises, or specifically made to introduce lead or lag into a system. The fire-prevention sprinkler devices in a building are set to come into action at a temperature which arises long before a fire actually starts but after a critical temperature is passed. Even more important are the inaccuracies that a malfunctioning sensor is able to introduce into a system. The sensor may be biased and continually read too high or too low. Perhaps the most difficult malfunctioning to trace is intermittent incorrect readings, where a large proportion of the measurements are accurate, but where there are random inaccuracies that may be too high or too low. All sensors need calibration for accuracy at regular intervals, even human ones. The bad construction of a sensor may introduce "*noise*" into a system, and in most socio-technical systems, noise is not required, although it may be there in great quantities.

Noise can best be described as too much data or useless data that gets in the way relative to the job in hand. Occasionally it may be introduced on purpose by those working within the system who are interested in the system working at a low level of effectiveness.

(iv) *Redundancy.* How many sensors? Redundancy has a specific meaning in systems work. If one sensor is put out of action, will another record the information? And will there be sufficient channels for the information to pass. Redundancy is a term implying the existence of alternative ways of passing on the information if the accepted way is put out of action. The human brain has many circuits and sometimes, if some are damaged, other sections of the brain can pass the messages. In other parts of the brain there is not so much redundancy of circuits and if they are damaged we may irretrievably lose our sense of smell or control of particular muscles. In important circumstances an organization will pass a message over the loudspeaker system, by personal word of mouth possibly via supervisors and shop stewards, by printed notice on several noticeboards and by a personal letter, using a large number of alternative devices to make sure the recorded information is processed and passed on.

(v) *Measurement as information.* The measurement of output and the information gained in most cases enters the feedback loop as an information current. The section on Effectors will consider the problem of reconverting this information back into a physical action to alter the input parameters.

(vi) *Effect of measurement on the system being measured.* In most cases this effect is unwanted, and poses great problems of a wide range. In the physical sciences a physicist may be in difficulties because he can only measure the speed *or* the direction of a photon, whereas he would like to know both. On the shop floor an untactful cost clerk collecting information may upset a machine operator causing bad work or even a strike. The act of measuring creates a different situation to that which existed before measurement took place. A consciously measured socio-technical system does not operate in the same way once it is measured to the way it operated prior to measurement. The measurement unit is erected as a screen through which all action and work passes. A road-sweeper on a weekly rate may see his task as keeping certain pavements clean and may or may not take pride in the job. A roadsweeper working under a measured O & M bonus scheme may no longer see the pavement clearly but through a haze of figures as each action he takes clocks up his wages. The resultant attitude to work and the work done may or may not be considered better than the earlier unmeasured situation. Some argue that work is better done if clearly related to reward; some argue that the resultant measurement screen through which all of us now have to relate to our work instead of directly is the cause of present industrial attitudes. The point being made here is that feedback in constructed systems implies measurement and conscious measurement alters the system being examined. But it is the view of many that impersonal control is better than personal and hence there is a present-day tendency to erect measurement systems that work to a pre-set impersonal standard with either automatic recording or if the recording be personal by self-recording rather than through personal supervision by others.

(vii) *The purpose of measuring*, recording and transmitting output information is subsequently to alter input parameters so that agreed goals may be more effectively achieved. We endeavour to record the functioning of the system as it is, but our information about the system is only as good as the recordings that actually take place.
It is very important to realize that we alter the input to a system based on knowledge of what we *think* the system is doing rather than what it actually *is* doing. Efforts to control a system will only be effective if the variables that are of actual importance for that system are measured and not the variables we think are important; that the model system set up by selecting certain variables as important ones to be measured corresponds and is a reasonably good fit with the reality model, the situation as it really exists. Control will only be effective if measurement is reasonably accurate and the transmission of measurements is not unreasonably delayed.

Alteration of Input: the Controller and Effectors

When dealing with a radio or electrical circuit, i.e. an actual process system, it is often possible to feedback from the output takeoff direct to the input side. The character of the feedback and of the main process system are the same. The same statement can be made where the feedback is by mechanical linkage that itself regulates a mechanical process. When measuring the steel-strip output by electronic eye, however, the information is obtained as an impulse in a wire. Considerable physical effort will be needed to alter the pressure on the roller stands and so it is

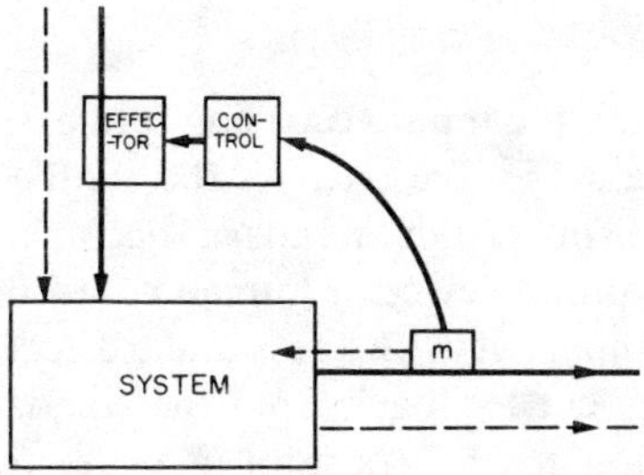

Fig. 4.11. Controller and effectors.

necessary to have a device to change information currents into processes that do actual physical work. Any device that effects such a change in a system is known as an *effector*. A specific example of such a device is a servomechanism. The output terminal of a measuring sensor is electrically connected to a servo-amplifier which in turn provides sufficient current to operate a servomotor. The servomoter is mechanically linked to the specific mechanical control of the input to the system and hence alters the parameters. In social systems an area sales manager may alter input to the sales system by writing weekly to his salesmen to inform them which lines to push and which to soft-pedal on.

He may like to reinforce (redundancy) his instructions by bringing all salesmen into a meeting once a month. Whereas in the servomotor case the alterations to input would take place automatically as long as the motor had not broken down, the sales manager must take additional precautions to see his instructions are obeyed. His orders may not be understood fully, or they may be wilfully ignored. "It is easy to give an order, more difficult to ensure it is carried out". The concept of the effector entails carrying out the action; in social systems this entails both giving the necessary final instructions and seeing they are carried out.

Information can be produced at several points, say by buying several terminals without significant loss of energy, though perhaps at considerable cost. Physical action consumes energy when being reproduced at more than one point. The conversion of information into physical action also consumes a considerable amount of energy.

The Standard

The concept of altering the input according to measured output implies a standard, if only a subjective one. As the feedback system becomes differentiated and distinct, this standard becomes objectivized. The function of the controlling device or human controller is then to collect information and compare it with the standard, calculate the "error", the divergence of present feedback from the standard, and to pass on correcting information to the effectors in order to bring the output more nearly in line with the standard.

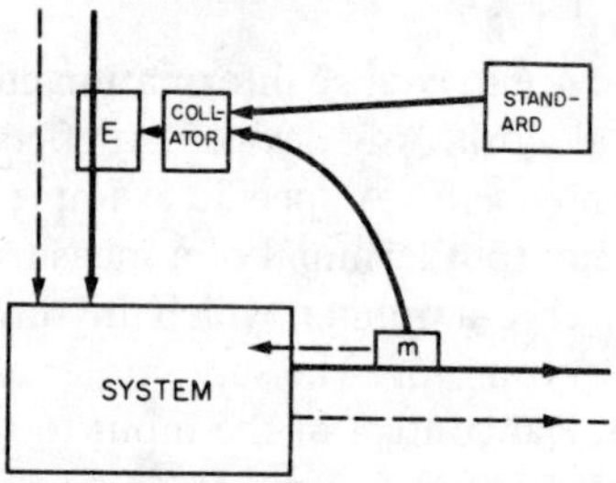

Fig. 4.12. Introduction of a standard for comparison.

Standards do not have to be definite fixed points or levels. A heating system might be considered as working satisfactorily within the limits of 32°C ± 2°C and correcting information would be passed to the effectors only if the temperature fell below 30°C or went above 34°C. Upper and lower limits to a standard are well known in statistical quality-control systems and in budgeting. In analysis it is important to consider how the standard was obtained and whether it is still a valid one to control the present situation. It may be that the standard requires to be revised periodically in which case pertinent questions are:

At what intervals is the standard being revised?

Are present data being fed in to keep it up to date, both internal and external data?

On whose authority is it revised?

Interaction of the Several Dimensions of Feedback

Where several aspects of the output are measured, it may make considerable difference to the manner in which the input parameters are altered, depending on whether each measurement is separately compared with standard and altered or whether all output measurements are centrally processed and interpreted in their overall aspects before passing on control information to alter the input parameter concerned. In the first case, the relationship between the variables remains static in the pattern decided upon when the standard was developed.

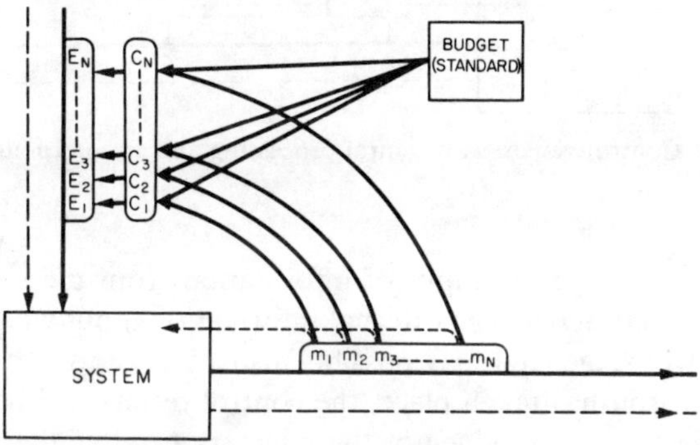

Fig. 4.13. Control system of an undertaking with several departmental controllers.

This may be satisfactory when making an artefact to exact laid-down dimensions. However, in many situations, it may be better not only to examine the "error" of each dimension but also to examine in an interpretive unit how these "errors" *interact*, for each variable measured is seldom completely independent, more often it is a function of some other measured variable. Also it is particularly necessary to achieve this examination of interaction where the system being controlled is a sociotechnical system in which the change in relationship between the various dimensions of the output measured may be dependent on changes in the environment. It will be no good, for instance, controlling to a budget to produce a particular "mix" of products as laid down 6 months ago, if the relative profits to be obtained on the several lines has altered. In this

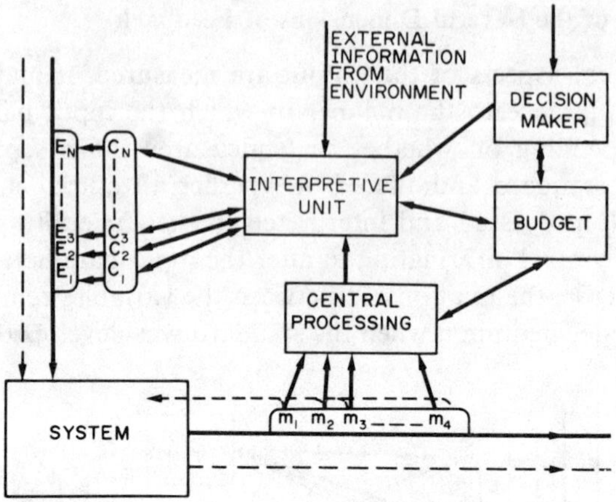

Fig. 4.14. Control system with central processing and an interpretive unit.

second case, effects of an input of information from the environment must also be considered. The external information input will come in at the interpretive stage, and may possibly also affect the standard.

Once comparison has taken place, the control results will be passed to the controllers and subsequently the effectors to alter the input. The whole purpose of adding an interpretive unit is firstly to take account of the interactions that may exist between dimensions, secondly to allow any input of new information from the environment to be fed into the system.

Interfaces

The length of the constructed feedback loop can be seen to be growing as also are the number of elements in it. Wherever there is a change or break in the loop there is an interface.

For instance, the physical output is recorded as pencil marks on paper or counted electronically. The pencil digits are punched onto cards. The cards after processing are printed out. A manager must read the print-out. He may consult with colleagues. Their deliberations are punched onto cards. Further sorting and tabulating takes place. Another printout is read by the controller who interprets it in a specific way. He summons effectors and gives instructions of action to be taken, the action is finally taken. At each stage there is a possible break in the even flow of information, its character changes in some respects. Like the synapses in the brain or body nerves that require a certain amount of charge before they "fire" and pass on a message, so it is with interfaces. It requires an appreciable amount of effort or energy to cross an interface. Not only is energy required to cross it, but the interface itself may be "opaque", not a good transmitter of information or action and so there is often a significant loss of information or action when an interface is crossed. The manager may receive a computer printout, but the information it contains may not stir him to action as it should do if he really understood its import; he may actually ignore it so that the loop is effectively cut. It is interesting to note that interfaces may have different "opacities" depending on the direction in which they are traversed. The computer printout/manager passage of information may be a much easier interface to cross than the manager/computer input interface. At least the two present very different problems. Interfaces should always be checked as possible weak links.

The Monitor or Control of Control

Is the control system working? Many mechanical linkage control systems such as the mechanical governor are built into the system so that while the system is working the control system is working. Few control systems are absolutely intrinsic; it is a relative term. The opposite situation is the extrinsic control that is outside the main system and may or may not be working. Exception reports sent to a supervisor may or may not be read. The supervisor may examine them very closely when he is there, but when ill or called away to an emergency the reports may simply pile up awaiting his return. Such a control is *extrinsic*. When the main system is working, we are not sure whether the control is working or not until we examine it. In complex feedback control systems it may be necessary to introduce redundancy, several channels of communication, to make sure the control information passes.

Where the feedback loop is not working effectively the control is ineffective and the main system is working "out of control". This may or may not be dangerous. Many control systems are so made that if they fail they will fail in such a way that the main system is safe. An electrical circuit that is overloaded blows the fuse, brings the system to a halt and so *fails-safe*. This is often the case in mechanical systems where a specially designed piece of metal is introduced, a mechanical fuse, that breaks if the system is overloaded thus bringing the system to a halt without damaging expensive parts. Most socio-technical systems *do not* fail-safe. Their control loop may or may not be working effectively; it is extrinsic and we cannot tell whether the system is under control unless we continually monitor the control system. Many legal enactments are of this type. H.M. Factory Inspectorate make spot checks on factories to ensure that safety systems are working. Auditors check accounts yearly and report to shareholders.

CHAPTER 5

System Processes

Having considered system structure, our interest now shifts to process; system history and change.

Modes of Working

The mode of working of a system, the manner in which it changes from one system state to the next, can usefully be analysed in the following categories:

Static system (no change of state),
Deterministic change of system state,
Probabilistic change of system state,
Adaptive, learning or self-organizing mode of system state change,
Reactive and impactive mode of system state change.

Available techniques to control such types of system state change include inspection, full system state description and input–output analysis.

The Static System

The static system, a construct such as a bridge or the set of rules for an algorithm or a method of logic, does not change its state. That single state is known. The static system can therefore be classified as a deterministic system that has only one state.
The only need for control is regular inspection to see that the framework is *not* changing state, i.e. through rust in the case of a bridge or through unauthorized change in the case of a set of rules or a classification.

The Deterministic Mode of Working

The deterministic mode of working most usefully describes a simple dynamic closed system. A matrix of the states through which the system can pass is set up. Everything about the system is known. If we examine the system and note that it is in state t_3, then we can tell exactly what state or position it will be in when, after a time lapse, it has moved to the next state, t_4. The states may be cyclical, after state t_{24} the system may revert to t_1, or the states may be moving towards a final state, t_{24} might represent the final state from which there is no further movement. Many car-maintenance books will show the position of the valves and pistons as the engine is moved. It takes two complete cycles to return to the original starting point in a four-stroke engine. If the engine is partially taken down and the actual positions noted, the matrix chart can be examined to see what the next position should be after a stated interval (expressed probably as half a cycle). The engine can be turned half a cycle and the positions noted. If the pistons do not correspond to the chart, the engine is either maladjusted or broken down. In correct running the engine passes through all the states exactly as laid down and finally comes to rest in one of them after running out of petrol. Deterministic systems, and this category includes a large proportion of the tools, artefacts and technology man has created, are relatively easy to control. Difficulties arise once the system being examined is expanded to include an operator. Unless he can be made to operate as a deterministic machine, we have a more complex system that may require analysing in one of the two following categories.

The Probabilistic Mode of Working

Whereas in the previous system we could draw up an exact matrix of all states, in this type of system probability enters in at some stage making us uncertain of what course the system will actually follow. A chemical reaction may or may not follow a certain path. Some systems are inherently probabilistic from the start, others gradually move from deterministic systems to probabilistic systems as they wear. At first a new lathe may work in a deterministic way. As parts wear its operation may become increasingly erratic and the system be best treated as a probabilistic one. Depth of analysis is another factor in determining how to treat a system. It might be regarded as an overall deterministic system that an employee has to work one day a week in Manchester, then two in London and two in Slough. But looked at in detail he may travel by train, plane, by using different routes, may arrive at different times, may sometimes attend in different order, may occasionally miss one town out. Examined in depth his itinerary assumes a probabilistic aspect. This change from deterministic to probabilistic viewpoint is frequently brought about by the observer deciding to change his viewpoint, rather than by change in the system. Thus it can be seen how important it is that the observer at the outset declares the position he intends to take up. On the other hand, some systems are obviously probabilistic and cannot be treated otherwise.

Charting a probabilistic system is not as easy as charting the deterministic one. At one stage the possible pattern the system can follow will start to branch. It will not be known which path will be taken by the system but perhaps it will be possible to allocate percentage probabilities to the various courses of action. A chemical plant might produce the correct mixture 85% of the time, the incorrect mixture (waste) 13% of the time and explode 2% of the time, i.e. once every 50 times the process is carried out.

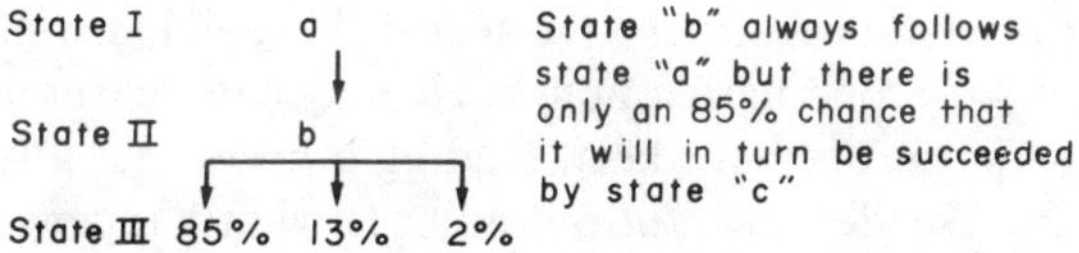

As what will happen on any particular occasion is not known, strategies must be developed for each situation. Firefighting and rescue equipment, safety procedures and insurances for when it explodes; methods of selling or disposing of the unwanted incorrect mixture. All the time efforts will be made to improve the process, to make it more deterministic, so that correct mixtures are always produced. But there is no inherent reason why a probabilistic system should necessarily yield to these efforts.

Techniques and tools have been developed to control probabilistic situations, most of these being statistical techniques, and to mitigate the unwanted effects by spreading the load using the actuarial techniques of the insurance companies.

The "Learning", Adaptive or Self-organizing Mode of Working

Any of the three words, learning, adaptive or self-organizing may be used to describe the same type of system. Some systems can learn from their mistakes, organize and adapt themselves so that their reaction to specific stimuli changes as time elapses. Typically such systems have a frame of reference through which the stimuli passes, or standard against which the stimuli is tested before any output is allowed to pass. The frame of reference or standard can be changed through experience and learning and hence the reaction is altered.

> "A man is punched on the nose, he retaliates and his aggressor gives him a harder punch back."

Next time he meets the same person, who as before punches him on the nose, he may not retaliate. He has learnt and adapted his course of action. But we cannot always tell *what* he has learnt or *how* his frame of references is altered (unless he chooses to tell us). To the outsider such systems tend to contain a larger element of probability than the previous category.

He may not retaliate because he has learnt through experience that this action leads to a second harder punch. He may have learnt nothing from his own experience but have been reading a book that advises against retaliation and decided to try it out and see what happens. As we may not know why his reaction has altered this second time, we will have no idea of how he will react when the situation is repeated a third time.

Compared with probabilistic systems there is a second stage of uncertainty in adaptive systems. It may be known (but not always) what courses of action are possible at a given stage, but it is not known with any certainty the probability of each course of action.

When examining adaptive systems we constantly look for a *pattern* of response. Luckily in human, social and now machine-adaptive systems there can nearly always be discerned a pattern of adaptive response rather than completely random change in response. Control of adaptive systems depends on coming to recognize and predict such changes in patterns of response. Such recognition would, for instance, be particularly important in examining industrial strikes and the action taken by unions viewed as adaptive systems, which may learn from experience and alter their response to given stimuli.

This category of self-organizing systems covers living systems, social systems, psychological systems and even certain types of machine systems. Machines that do not always follow a set pattern but can learn from their "mistakes", such as a computer programmed to play noughts and crosses, also fall into this category.

Reactive and Impactive Systems

Most systems are treated as reactive. Their output is a reaction to an input stimulus and this model is suitable in most cases where a small system is being examined.

Some organizations, however, are very large and contain many resources within their own boundaries. The interplay of these resources may produce local tension spots *within* the system and produce an output without any need for an input stimulus. Such systems have been called "inventive" systems and also impactive systems because of their frequent large impact on their environment and the difficulty of control by outside agencies.

The typical impactive system is the "think-tank", particularly in its applied aspect. No longer does such an organization necessarily respond to ascertained needs of the environment, but rather the output of such systems may be imposed upon the environment. In a sense the impactive system has grown out of the adaptive system, but it has attained the position of a distinct type of system in its own right. The effects of such a system's output are not related to the scale of inputs. The impactive effects come about from the inventive capacity of groups *within* the system and the availability to them of the required technology.

Whereas the reactive system would respond to regulation (e.g. by governments), the scale of effects on environment produced by *impactive* systems, is so many times greater that "after the event" control becomes a poorly operating method of control.

At present it is not known how to control such systems apart from legislation which arises *after* the offending event and which consequently is not always effective as a means of control.

The cultural constraint of civilization, that it is not necessary to do something just because we are technically able to do it, does not always operate very effectively. The emergence of the impactive system poses many problems.

Organizations Seen as Systems

The mechanical linkage system was given as an example of a deterministic system, thus implying that it is unlikely that an organization containing human elements will fall into this category. Despite this it is interesting to examine to what extent an organization contains deterministic elements. A prison or highly disciplined school will contain many such elements, and bureaucracy instituted for its own sake, the means mistaken for the ends, can grind life to a halt in a deterministic way. Other organizations change over time; for example, an army unit must be largely deterministic in response during training; once in operation it will show more of the self-organizing principle to ensure survival.

Categorizing a Particular System

In the practical situation having defined the limits of the system to be reviewed, it next becomes necessary for purposes of understanding and control to decide what type of system is being dealt with. Often a system may fall into two or even all three of the categories mentioned above, depending on the detail of phenomena by which it is being described. A general working description of a closed heating system with thermostats in each room may be treated as deterministic. If, however, more variables are considered, such as the weather, the opening and shutting of doors and windows and the worn state of the equipment, it may be necessary to treat the system as a probabilistic one. The expanding progress of a company may appear steady from year to year judged by money sales turnover, but highly erratic and unpredictable if judged by product mix. This same need for different models by which to deal with varying depths of analysis is apparent in the material world, where Euclidean geometry is ideal to describe everyday life, but special geometries are required for space travel and to explain the movement of atoms.

Control Models

Full system-state description: a technique for deterministic and probabilistic systems.

Where a system is reasonably simple, it may be possible to examine and note down the states through which it passes.

	P1	P2	P3	P4
T1	↓	↓	↓	↓
	P2	P3	P4	P1

The above transformation (T1) shows that the system being described passes through a set sequence of four changes. Starting at P1, the system then moves to P2. From P2 it moves on to P3 and so on until finally it returns to its original state P1. This example is a *closed* transformation, that is the system returns to state P1. A transformation could go on with an infinite number of different states. This transformation is also *single valued*; starting from any of the given states, there is only one following state that the system moves on to. A transformation is a specification of a system's changes. The sequence of changes the system passes through being termed the trajectory.

Figures 5.1 show in diagrammatic form two closed single-valued systems each of which moves through four states before returning to the original position. But they are very different types of system. The traffic light system is *discrete*, a light is either on or off. The car engine is moving continuously and the four states shown merely represents certain points in the system, they are, however, important points of change and also they are spaced at set intervals of time. A transformation does not necessarily represent time. The traffic light system which is discrete exposes the lights for varying lengths of time. Normally, the trajectory

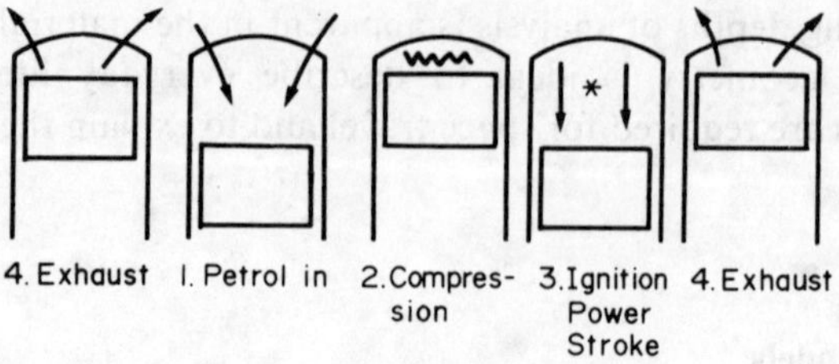

Fig. 5.1. (a) Four-stroke engine. (i) Petrol in. (ii) Compression. (iii) Ignition and power stroke. (iv) Exhaust.

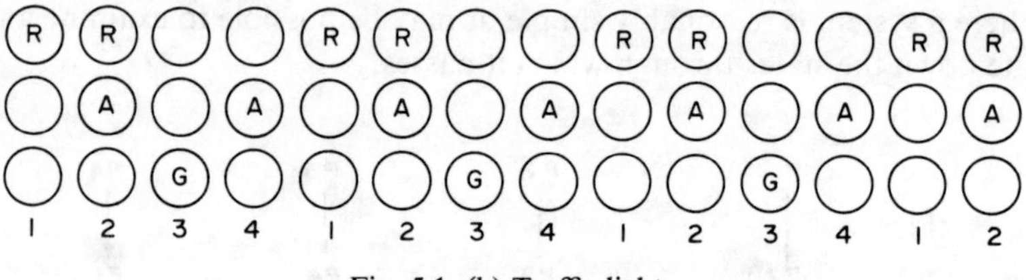

Fig. 5.1. (b) Traffic lights.

of a system will be based either on time or on events. The trajectory might show the state of the system as given intervals of time elapse, or it might refer to the important events in the system, the sequence of changes through which it passes, and such changes may occur at irregular intervals as in the case of the traffic lights.

Kinematic graph. Where the system states become numerous and the transformation complex it may be useful to draw a kinematic graph in order to have some insight into the nature of the system.

T	A	B	C	D	E	F	G	H	I	J	K	L	M	N	O	P
↓	C	C	B	A	D	G	H	M	O	P	L	C	C	B	Q	Q

can be shown graphically as:

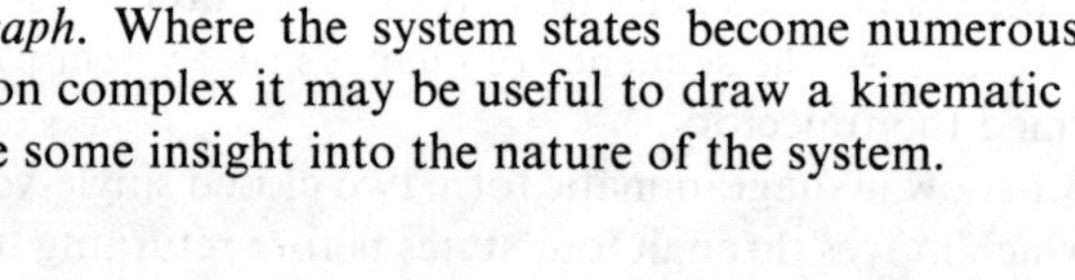

This particular system has two modes in which it may settle, depending on its initial state. Either it settles in state Q or it cycles between states B and C. This method of graphing applies to a transformation that is closed and would obviously be useless where the trajectory consisted of an infinite number of states. So far no digits have been used, yet as Ashby[1] states, "a theory of such unanalysed states can be rigorous".
Vector and matrix algebra can handle both algebraic notation or numerical digits and in a specific case it may often be possible to assign numerical values to a transformation.
To operate on a transformation often discloses its nature:

$$T \quad \downarrow \begin{matrix} 1 & 2 & 3 \\ 5 & 6 & 7 \end{matrix}$$

can be condensed to $n \longrightarrow n + 4$
the operand becomes itself plus 4

$$T \quad \downarrow \begin{matrix} 1 & 2 & 3 \\ 5 & 10 & 15 \end{matrix}$$

can be condensed to $n \longrightarrow 5n$
the operand becomes "itself multiplied by five"

$$T \quad \downarrow \begin{matrix} 1 & 2 & 3 \\ 2 & 1\tfrac{1}{2} & 1\tfrac{1}{3} \end{matrix}$$

Can be condensed to $n \longrightarrow 1 + \frac{1}{n}$

Markov chains. Where it is possible to observe a system over a long series of events, the system's pattern of states may show the stochastic properties of the Markov chain. It may then be possible to calculate the probability of the system entering one of the possible states. Suppose an investigation reveals the following system states:

P Q Q R P R P R Q R P P R Q R P P P R Q P R Q R P P R Q R
P R Q R R R P Q R R Q R P

By analysing the above sequence we could discover what the probabilities are of the system, being found in one of the states P, Q, R, next moving on to one of the other states or remaining as it is. The series of forty-three

[1] W. Ross Ashby, *An Introduction to Cybernetics*, p. 30, University Paperbacks, Methuen, 1964.

items must be analysed as between the existing states and the next following one for the forty-two changes it embodies.

Number of times next state is ↓	Existing state P	Q	R	
P	5	1	9	15
Q	2	2	6	10
R	6	8	3	17
	13	11	18	42

This table can be reduced to a total figure of 1 to give the transition probabilities,

↓	P	Q	R
P	5/13	1/11	1/2
Q	2/13	2/11	1/3
R	6/13	8/11	1/6
	1	1	1

EXISTING STATE

or

↓	P	Q	R
P	0.39	0.09	0.50
Q	0.15	0.18	0.33
R	0.46	0.73	0.17
	1.00	1.00	1.00

that is, if the system is found in state Q, it has an 18% chance of remaining as it is, a 9% chance of moving to state P and an overwhelming 73% chance of moving to state R. This is a first order analysis. We could further analyse what state a system is likely to move into depending on the combination of the previous two, or even three states.

Such a state analysis could have been the basis of the probabilities assigned to the chemical process previously mentioned.

Input–Output Analysis for More Complex Systems

Socio-technological systems of business and administration are often so complex and can enter so many different states that it may not be satisfactory to attempt to list those states. A successful technique in this situation is to regard the system as a "black box" and confine examination to input and output, altering the input parameters and checking what effect on output this action has. In a practical control situation the input alterations that are made will normally bear some relationship to the information carried in the feedback loop.

The Control Cycle

The basic control components are seen in Chapter 4. On whether or not these will in practice operate to keep the system stable, depends the effectiveness of the control cycle. Many questions may be asked about the structure of the control cycle. Is the control to be continuous, or intermittent? If intermittent, at what intervals? What is the delay in the feedback cycle? Is the system to be kept at a fixed level, or must it fluctuate, perhaps seasonally? In tracing the feedback of information in the control loop of the system it is quite usual to use radio terminology and these terms will be introduced here and briefly explained.

"Information"

The basis on which any control system works is information. In the simple determined system this information will be transmitted by a direct mechanical linkage but, in any more sophisticated system, control will be effected by the collection of information regarding the output of the system and the feedback of this information. The actual situation is being compared with the planned situation (the standard), and action initiated according to the size and nature of the divergence. The need for information on what is happening is of prime importance for the control of any system. In addition to controlling the current situation this collected information is used to build up sufficient data which, together with external information, will be used at some time in the future as the basis for a decision to modify or change completely the standard.

The information measured by the sensors can be of three types of increasing complexity:

(i) the size of the error (i.e. divergence from standard), where the output has to be held constant;

(ii) the rate of change, where the system is oscillating;

(iii) the rate of change of change (i.e. acceleration and deceleration), where the system is to be controlled at a fluctuating level.

Most business systems require controlling to a fixed limit (requiring feedback on amplitude and rate of change alone) or to fluctuating limits (requiring in addition feedback on rate of change of change) depending on the extent to which they are subject to seasonal fluctuations. They do therefore need a combination of all three types of information in a feedback system which is essentially dynamic to be effectively controlled. Feedback systems covering the third type are not yet fully developed for the business and administrative situation.

Attributes of feedback that are of interest to those attempting to control a process are:

(i) The positive or negative aspects of the feedback information in the loop at the time it is used for control purposes.

(ii) Response time of the system to the feedback input.

(iii) The amplitude and timing of the correcting information contained in the loop.

(iv) Noise in the feedback loop.

(v) Oscillation in the feedback loop.

Positive feedback is the type of feedback associated with growth or decline. Positive feedback moves a system away from a point of origin. This is in contrast to negative feedback which constantly seeks to bring a system back to a predetermined level or state.
Positive feedback is difficult to control and tends to be unstable. Positive feedback works in the same direction as the output "error" measured, thereby increasing the divergence. An example well known at the moment is the exponential growth of population. Each generation more individuals are born and these additional persons have the ability

themselves to add to the increase in population; and so the population develops not only in actual numbers but at an ever-increasing rate.
All positive feedback does not necessarily act in as fierce a manner as this, some growth curves may show a very gentle increase, yet situations of growth or controlled decline are difficult to maintain without the system moving into a crisis situation of uncontrolled growth or decay.

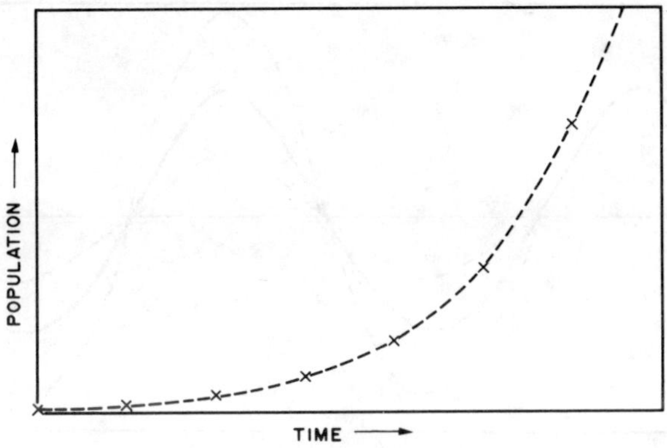

Fig. 5.2. Exponential growth curve.

The earlier rundown of operations in the British coal industry was by no means easy to achieve in a smooth manner. Similarly when organization is being operated in a growth situation it is very likely to run into a crisis, often because it can see many opportunities and hence starts to overtrade, a form of uncontrolled growth. Nearly always a crisis occurs, a crisis often solved by being "taken over".
Positive feedback was first brought to notice in medical cases. Certain patients have what in effect is a reversal of the visual/motor reaction. As they stretch out to pick up an object, their eye measures how far away their hand is, but instead of this action helping them to touch the object, the impaired feedback channel tells the muscles to work in the opposite direction, so that the harder they attempt to pick up an object, the more wildly their hand and arm is likely to swing away from it.

Negative feedback. Negative feedback implies control. The difference (error or variance) between the actual output and the desired standard output is measured. The controls of the input parameters are then operated in the opposite (negative) direction to the measured "error" so bringing the system back to the standard output.

In Fig. 5.3 a system output may be fluctuating seasonally (line A). The desired output may be a constant level (line B). Negative feedback will

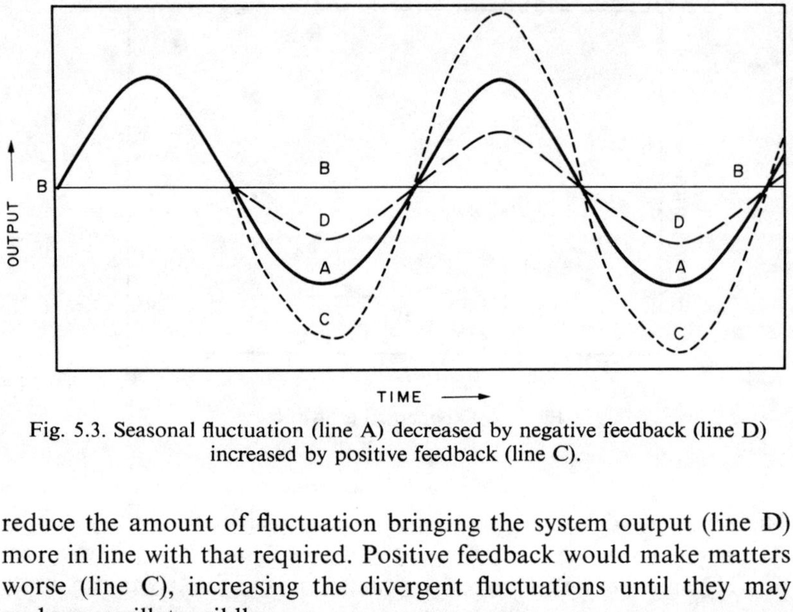

Fig. 5.3. Seasonal fluctuation (line A) decreased by negative feedback (line D) increased by positive feedback (line C).

reduce the amount of fluctuation bringing the system output (line D) more in line with that required. Positive feedback would make matters worse (line C), increasing the divergent fluctuations until they may perhaps oscillate wildly.

The negative feedback control approach is so well tried in administration that it is used to control a growth (positive feedback) situation. High-level planning may decide that the undertaking is to operate in a positive feedback (growth) situation.

Creative decisions are made at top level to expand the company with new capital, to bring in new methods and new products. The scene is set for an overall positive feedback growth situation. But once the expansion has been decided upon and planned, negative feedback controls will be used in the short-term day-to-day situation to control growth to

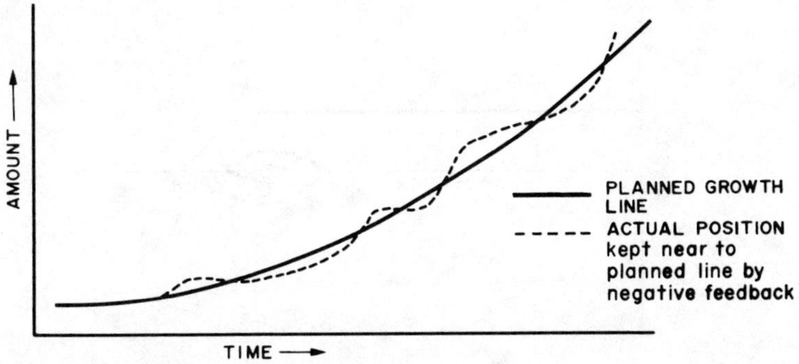

Fig. 5.4. Negative feedback used to control a positive feedback "growth" situation.

the set budget expansion. Thus negative feedback operating controls are being used to guide a system which in the longer term is following a growth, positive feedback, budget (Fig. 5.4).

Timing of the correcting process. The problem of when to apply the correcting process (effectors) and when to shut it off requires careful consideration.

As a mechanical example, take the case of a car which is moving and has to be halted at a fixed position, but where the speed is not controlled until it reaches the required point (Fig. 5.5). It will overshoot and have to be reversed. When reversing, if the driver does not brake until the car is again at the required position it will overshoot in the opposite direction. As this backwards and forwards process is repeated, the car will each time gather less initial speed and so be halted nearer the mark, and finally be halted more or less on it.

As an administrative example, take the case of information required by an executive at a particular deadline. Overtime has been initiated at a sufficiently early date, so that all requirements can be met by this deadline. But suppose the work has been completed in advance, the continuing arrangements for overtime may not be cancelled as promptly as they should be, or the number of staff concerned may not have been correctly assessed. The work load will suddenly appear to have reached

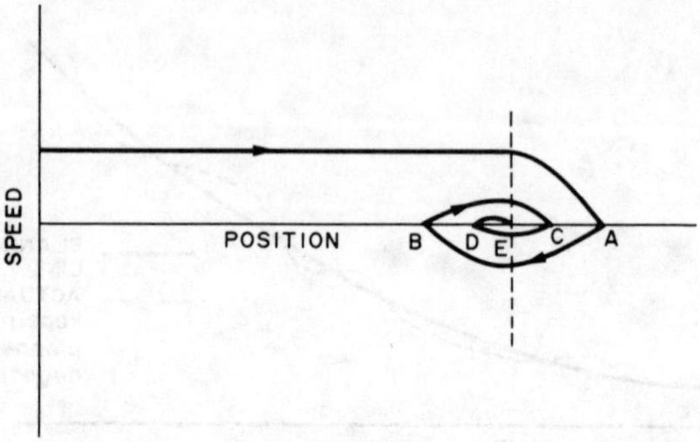

Fig. 5.5. Car approaching a fixed position, overshooting and reversing several times.

a record low level, and panic arrangements may be made to reduce working hours. This measure in turn is probably too drastic and will require corrective action in due course, so that in the return to the normal level of activity a dampened oscillation (Fig. 5.6) takes place. The diagram represents what would take place where staff worked at a specified pace and without any unofficial breaks. Often this effect is obscured by the fact that when there is a change of workload it is absorbed by a change in intensity cf work and a change in the continuity

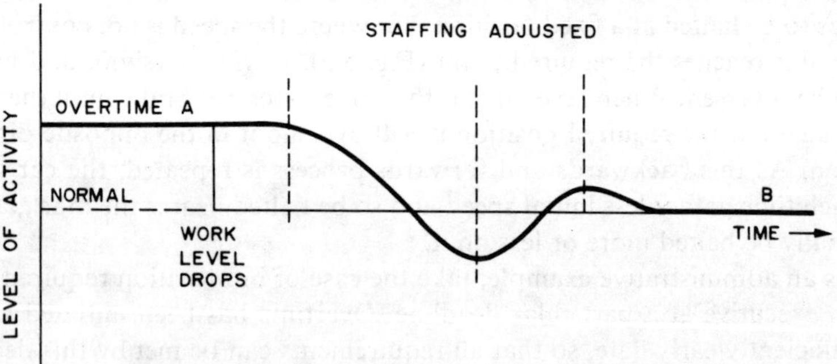

Fig. 5.6. Diagram showing that as the work level drops there is a dampened oscillation from (a) equilibrium at overtime level to (b) equilibrium at normal level.

of work. Figure 5.6 is in effect, Fig. 5.5 unwound. In the former case the horizontal axis is position, in the latter it is time, which only flows in one direction.

Response Time of the System to Input Changes

The information given by the feedback loop is the basis for changes that are subsequently made in the input parameters. How long does this changed input take to work its way through the system? In a simple system the time may be but a matter of seconds. A complex system such as the economic system may take from 4 to 6 months for input changes such as alterations in tax to work through. Any controller of a system has to be conversant with his system's response time if he is to work effectively. Once an alteration has been made, the output measurements will still show as incorrect until the change has had time to work itself through. To make a second change to input parameters to speed up changes in output before the results of the first change have been noted will not improve matters. If the first change was sufficient and would have been seen to be sufficient if enough time had been allowed to elapse to let it work through, a second change may only produce "errors" in the reverse direction to those first noted.

The Chancellor of the Exchequer is constantly under pressure to free the economy. His reply at all times is that he has already made the right decisions but that they must take time to work through. No one can be absolutely certain when given economic changes have worked through the system. The response time of a system is generally taken to be function of its structure. If we want to alter the response time, then alter the structure or at least find the "pressure points" in the system where changes to be made have maximum effect. Such delays in the effect of feedback information on output are often referred to as "lags" or "transport lags". One of the lags that will be examined subsequently in a numerical example is the exponential lag, exemplified by the time it takes to reach a given stock level if a constant ordering policy is used. It will be noticed (Fig. 5.7) how long such a system takes to achieve a desired level, dependent on its structure. In a numerical example, this time will be dependent on the equations we use to describe the structure. To try and hurry up the procedure in the same given structure produces

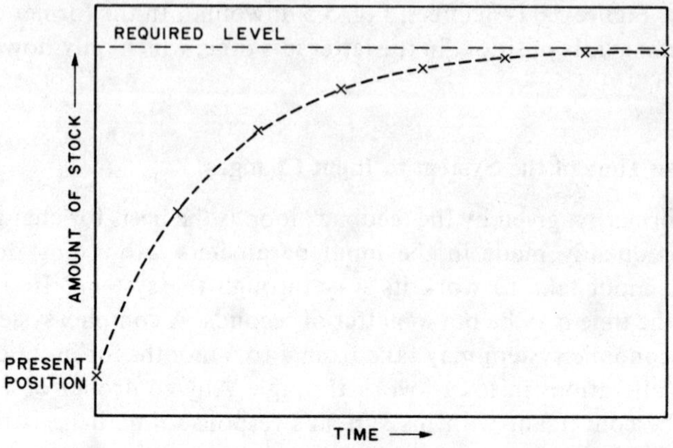

Fig. 5.7. Exponential lag.

the effect in Fig. 5.8, an overshoot which if then corrected in the same manner will overshoot in the opposite direction finally damping down to the level required but taking much longer to do so than the first case took. Electrical engineers and control engineers, being in charge of mainly physical systems and being in the happy position of knowing nearly everything about the system they are controlling, will accept the

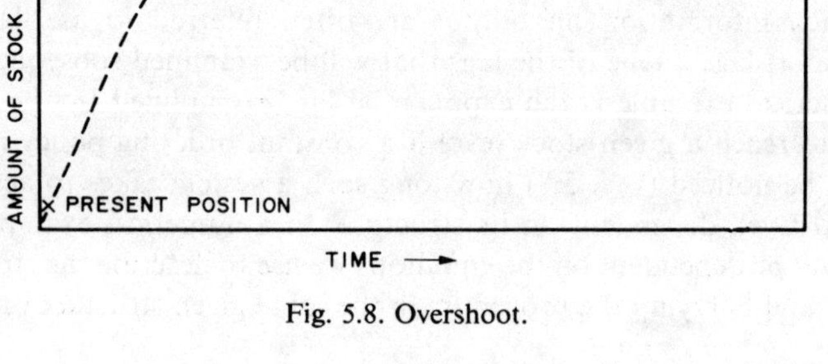

Fig. 5.8. Overshoot.

time lag shown in Fig. 5.7 and know it can be altered only by structural changes in the system which may themselves be too costly to undertake. Managers are controlling systems whose inner structure it is difficult to elucidate. Managers like to get things settled and so have a tendency to overcorrect in the hope that the overcorrection may "beat the system". It seldom does and overcorrection is generally an important source of unwanted oscillation so often met in business and industry and sometimes in administrative work. But managers seem to have lived so long with "ups and downs" (oscillation) that they become a way of life possibly because they link with human rhythms, and might be missed if they did not occur.

Amplitude of Correcting Information and Delays

To apply correcting negative feedback smoothly it has already been mentioned that we need to have information of three orders of complexity:

(i) the size of the "error",
(ii) the rate of change,
(iii) the rate of change of change (acceleration and deceleration).

The manager often behaves in the manner described in the previous paragraph simply because he has no information in categories (ii) and (iii), or very little of it. The control engineer would insist on having the necessary information. It is only fair to say that socio-technical systems can be classed as highly complex and tools of control difficult to develop. Such tools of control as are developed have a great tendency to be linear ones. There are tools of control that are dynamic and non-linear, but such control tools themselves are complex and expensive. For reasons of cost we excuse ourselves and say that static and linear tools of control will do us. But life and socio-technical systems are both dynamic and non-linear. The manager is probably trying to control not so much with inadequate information as with inadequate *types* of information. The tendency is to do something fairly drastic as soon as he is aware of the situation, which is often a little later than should be. In the negative feedback situation overcorrection and delay can both lead to oscillation. However, in the negative feedback-control situation amplitude of the correcting factor is not as critical as it is in the situation of positive feedback. In the negative feedback situation two or three or perhaps even more times the required correction can be applied without too much trouble arising, apart from increasing a little the oscillations that appear endemic in socio-technical systems. Real problems may arise where there is delay in a feedback loop that is controlling a fluctuating situation as this delay may convert the negative feedback wholly or partially to positive (growth and decay) feedback and so greatly increase the fluctuations rather then decrease them slightly.

Positive feedback applies a correcting factor in the same direction as the "error" and so increases the swing away from a point of origin, in either growth or decay. The extreme example is the population exponential curve previously mentioned. Positive feedback applied to a fluctuating output increases the fluctuation, very easily setting up a wildly swinging oscillation. The amplitude of the correcting factor is crucial. To keep a controlled situation the correcting amount is normally a small fraction of the error. Amplitudes of one-quarter or one-half might be experimented with to see the results in a particular system. A car driver wishing to leave his line of direction and turn a corner, moves his steering wheel over a little and then eases off the correcting factor, gradually returning his steering wheel to the normal position, as the car completes the turn. If he applied a large correcting factor straight away or if he went on increasing the correcting factor as the car went into the corner, the steering wheel would lock and the car probably overturn. A heavy hand can be used in the negative control situation, but it needs a lightness of touch and a sureness to control the positive feedback situation, without it "getting out of hand".

Where negative feedback is delayed in a fluctuating output situation, the effects in application gradually change from negative to positive feedback as one-half cycle elapses. So that instead of damping down the fluctuations, they may be increased (Fig. 5.9).

No business that operates seasonally is going to use control information that is 6 months out of date (the extreme case of moving completely from negative to a positive feedback position). But this extreme position can well illustrate that control information delayed 2 or 3 months could cause control problems of a lesser nature. An organization may well pride itself that its internal information is quickly available, but this by itself

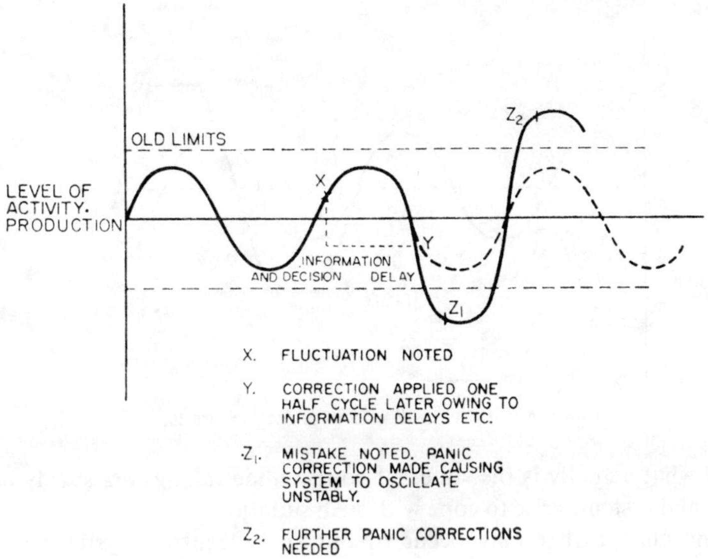

Fig. 5.9. Effect of introducing a correcting decision after a half-cycle delay.

is of little avail if its external information on markets, etc., is 4 months out of date. Forrester has pointed out that where wild oscillations occur in socio-technical systems, the swings do not operate without disturbing the timescale. A skeleton labour force is kept on even if orders are low and even with working overtime there is a maximum limit to what can be produced. This deformity of the swings at their peaks and nadirs leads to a second problem, the timing of the cycles may change (Fig. 5.10). So that not only do we have a problem of controlling a widely fluctuating system but the length of the fluctuations are disturbed from what previous experience with the system would lead us to expect.

Organizations are controlled by the information presented to managers. Considering the inaccuracies that may be present in the sensors that pick up the information, the information that is not considered, and the delay that can occur in presenting this picture of the state of the system to the controller, organizations need to be pretty sturdy, insensitive and adaptive in their structure to continue as viable entities when subject to such control; that is control by what we think is the state of the system rather

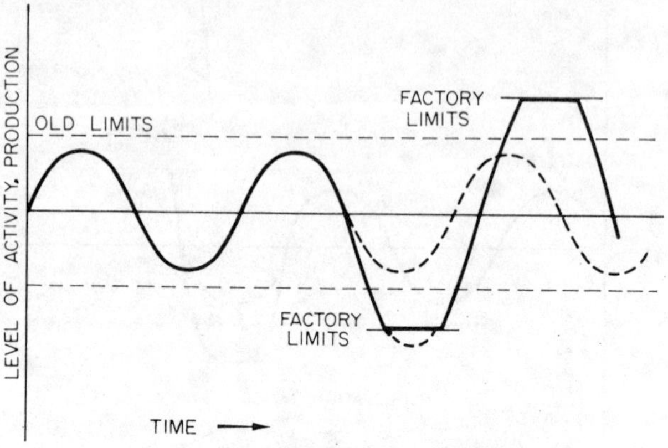

Fig. 5.10. Cut-off effects of factory limits.

than what actually is the state. Of course undertakings *are* sturdy, and informal systems arise to cope with such situations.

One change that may occur to our socio-technical systems is the gradual move towards real-time control, as seen developing, for example, in airline seat reservation. By tradition most administrative control feedback is batched before it is examined and control implemented. Batching intervals may be any time from 1 day to 6 months. If cost barriers can be broken through, a more sensitive form of control for an organization may turn out to be some form of cumulated information, accumulating on a real-time basis. Where such sensitive overall control develops, there could be a drop in the need for informal operator-originated controls. A detailed worked example of negative feedback of first and second order is shown in Appendix V.

Noise, as in a bad radio receiver, may be present in the system so that information may be distorted; important information may be lost and excess unimportant information may come through. What is important is the "signal-to-noise" ratio, ensuring that the important information, the signal, is sufficiently strong or goes on sufficiently long to overcome the interruption.

Oscillation. Information once collected may move backwards and forwards within the control loop itself and never finally emerge as a decision.

CHAPTER 6

The Organization as a System

Choice of Model

The purpose for which the analysis or investigation is taking place determines which system model it will be best to set up. It may be necessary to use any or all of four distinct types of model already mentioned:

1. The open system existing within an unlimited environment.
2. The open system interacting with a differentiated local environment which itself exists within an unlimited environment.
3. The open system existing within an environment that is itself bounded.
4. The closed system (a) completely closed, (b) information-tight.

Unless specific reasons dictate otherwise, an undertaking will probably use model 1 or model 2, but increasingly for large operations model 3 (the "spaceship earth" approach) may be necessary.

Operational Use by Organizations of the Systems Model

The routine *operational* control of an organization involves the collection of data (through the word and number filters) in order to monitor processes. This involves

Recording
Budgeting and Estimating
Planning
Controlling

Much of this collection of information falls to the accountant who is involved in recording and controlling to preset standards. Here the negative feedback-control processes are dominant and most of the accountant's work is of this nature. At intervals when planning and budgeting takes place the creative positive feedback process come into play. Planning (whether for an increase or a decline) will involve a divergence from a point of origin (except in the single unlikely case of no change from last period) and this is the description of positive feedback. Once the plan is agreed, the positive feedback process stops and control to the (divergent) plan is achieved by negative feedback, as was shown on Fig. 5.4.

In *Budgeting*, the participants are exhorted to look at:

1. Company strengths and weaknesses.
2. Sources of funds.
3. Environment including resources and markets.

This act requires goal statement (minor goals within the overall company objectives) and examination of the environment as the current organization model is the "open system" one.

Once agreed, the budget can be regarded as a feedforward of information, a description of the future system state it is hoped to achieve.

In socio-technical systems, all budgeting data, employee rulebooks and manuals and other attempts at future programming, even perhaps advertising, can be regarded as a feedforward loop. Army discipline training is an extreme example of this, future behaviour is drilled into a recruit.

In socio-technical systems *both* feedforward and feedback loops are in operation at the same time—there is a double loop that leaps forward and backward iteratively based on the time period chosen for control purposes.

Such control loops must be examined minutely and continuously to ensure that they continue to operate: the control loops are extrinsic, that

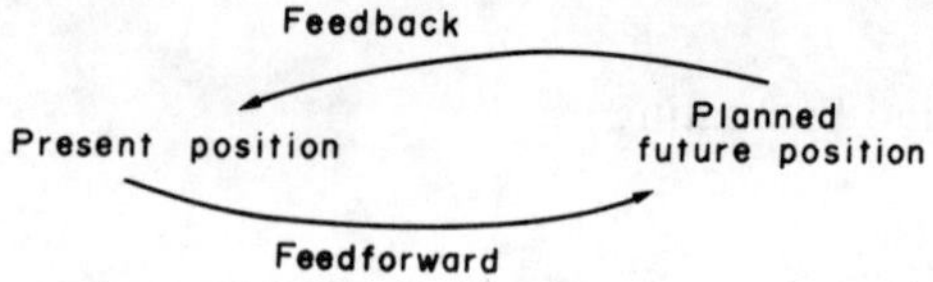

is they are separate from the main process and their failure to operate may not show up until a crisis occurs. Additionally the feedforward loop control is open-loop and does not feed back through the process as does the information in the feedback loop.

Feedforward

The controller may wish to distinguish between

1. a feedforward system,
2. a system with feedforward command loop,
3. a planning feedforward loop.

The true feedforward loop (1) operates where the time lag in a feedback system would make it useless as a control method.

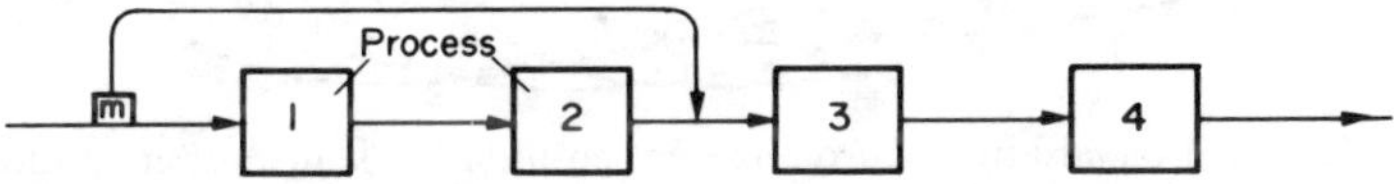

Fig. 6.1. Feedforward of information to correct the process at the third stage.

Such a loop is not far removed from the "crisis manual" loop (2) that gives laid-down procedures to be followed in certain predetermined circumstances, as when no reference can be made to higher management for a decision or in an emergency "command" situation.

To be successful feedforward control requires that:

(i) All or at least most of the possible disturbances to the system are known in advance.

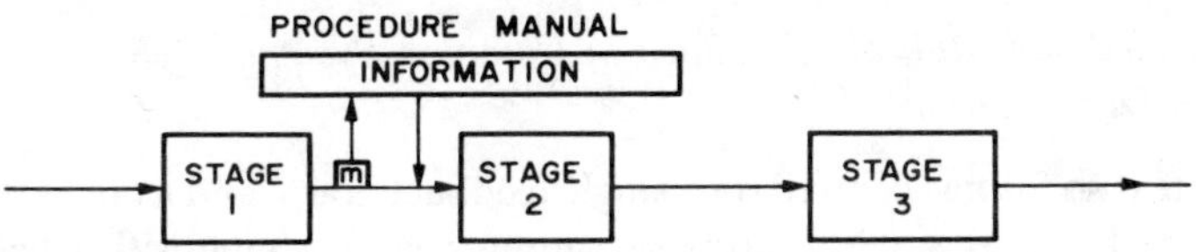

Fig. 6.2. Predetermined information available to meet future decision requirements.

(ii) The necessary corrective action for each type of disturbance is determined in advance.

(iii) The feedforward loop works without fault, that is that there are no mistakes in diagnosis of the disturbances and no failure in the application of the predetermined corrective action. As feed-forward does not pass through the system again, there is often no way of checking that the feedforward loop is in fact working.

In the feedforward planning situation (3), a series of previously agreed required future states are projected forward at set time intervals and comparisons made with what is actually achieved before determining the next future state.

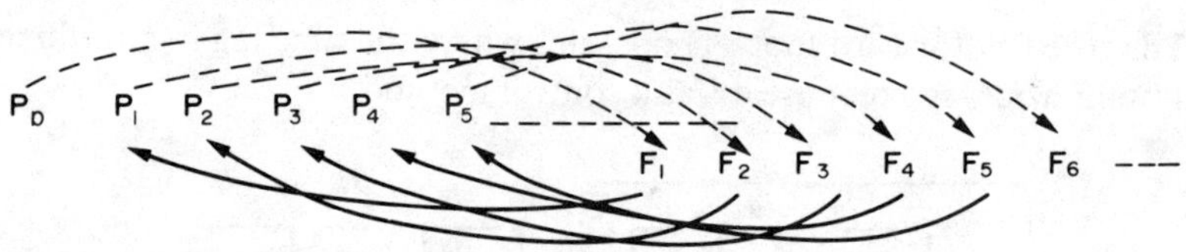

Fig. 6.3. Feedforward in time from present position to planned future position.

Feedback

Feedback controls are well established within an organization and indeed are required by law. The whole of the accounting and costing function together with verbal and written reporting, executive meetings and finally the annual general meeting reporting to members, represent the feedback control within an organization. The details of such controls are extremely well documented in many books and will not be repeated here.

Extended and Multiple Feedback in Complex Systems such as an Organization

The text so far has centred on a single feedback loop, and a consideration of whether that single loop is providing negative or positive feedback information. Single-loop feedback will apply only where very simple systems are being dealt with—for example, the ballcock and tap that fills the water cistern regulated by the feed-back information of the level of water already existing in the tank—or the manipulation of large systems in general terms—for example, where the overall demand for a product shows growth but we do not analyse this increasing demand into a growing demand in some areas and declining in others.

When a complex system, particularly organizational systems, is analysed in some detail it can be seen that there are several, often many, feedback loops; that some of these feedback loops are greatly extended in time and pass through other systems before the control information returns to the input stage of the system under review and is available to alter input parameters. The overall *dominance* of all loops taken together may be positive, negative or again the dominance may shift between positive and negative as time flows.

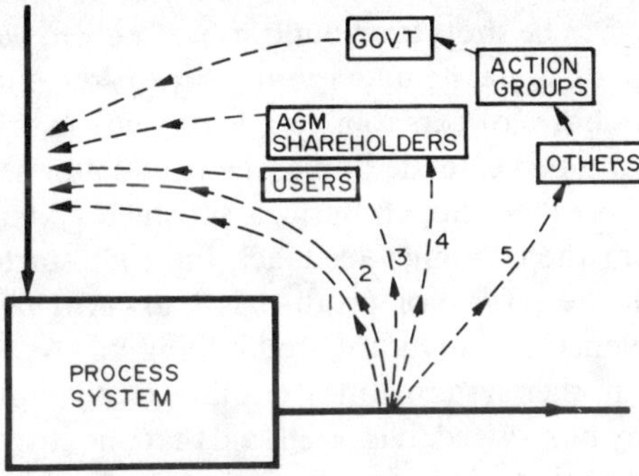

Fig. 6.4. Multiple and extended feedback loops.

Take the case of an administrative unit providing a service or a production unit providing an article. The many feedback loops that are used by the overall manager to control the unit can be usefully analysed in, say, five main groups using a time scale. Of course each of these main groups could be further analysed into many separate and detailed feedback loops, but for present purposes let us take the main groupings.

1. *Day-to-day operational controls.* These ensure that the product or service is being provided as specified. Information is mainly statistical,

how many items dealt with or produced and various aspects of time, quantity, size, shape.

2. *Weekly/monthly operational controls.* Many of these are directed to seeing that the operational support systems are being kept up, e.g. that maintenance is carried out, that operators are being trained. On the operational side emphasis will shift towards *costs* of making the article and providing the service.
Information in these main loops 1 and 2 will be quantifiable. This information is, in the main, generated internally. Its production, timing and use is within the control of the unit requiring it.

3. The first group of feedback loops *to pass externally through another system* before returning to an organization are those of the users; customers of a production business, clients of a service industry. The feedback in this loop can be short term but is more likely to vary from several weeks in the case of someone undergoing, say, medical treatment, some months with purchases of cars to a couple of years in the case of a ship being built. During this extended time, the product or service continues to be provided to others hopefully in a satisfactory manner but until information from the customer feedback link has started to flow and satisfaction with the service or product is known, it could be that innumerable problems for the future are building up. As the information passes through another system it may not flow freely, not only may it be delayed but it may be reduced. It is often said that one customer complaint hides up to a dozen that are never reported.
Contacts with suppliers of resources can also be treated as falling in this group.

4. It is the pattern of business life to review operations *formally at least once a year*. A company reports to its shareholders, a school has a governors' meeting. At this meeting operations are viewed in the light of overall criteria and sometimes the criteria used and hence the policy flowing from these criteria change. The day-to-day operations may be perfectly satisfactorily carried out, but the shareholder may desire a higher return on investment that means activity may be directed into other channels unless day-to-day operations can be pitched to a

new, possibly arbitrary, cost level. Service provision may be altered because a new hypothesis has been accepted. This feedback channel is partially internal, partially external. Its operation is delayed, but decisions made within this loop may alter satisfactory day-to-day operations in what at that point appears to be an arbitrary way.

5. The General Public, Local Government and Central Government can all in the the long run influence the action of a producer or provider of a service. Central Government may impose new weights and measures, Central Government and Local Government may discuss between themselves for *a great length of time* and with much oscillation of information backwards and forwards between them, possible changes in land use, action groups of the general public may finally obtain action by government. Such activity may culminate in an extended feedback loop that passes through many systems before the information returns and influences input parameters of the actual production or service unit. In the United States car manufacturers have been given up to 4 years' notice that what at present is considered a suitable car exhaust system will then no longer be so. Sometimes the effects of information and decisions in an extended loop such as this may be fended off for 5, 10, 20 even 40 years by the expedient of making it oscillate backwards and forwards within the loop, often using the delays of court procedure until the information and decisions, when they do finally arrive, may be of no consequence as the time has passed.

Consider the position of the manager in charge of an operational unit, in a starting-up situation. His short-term controls (Groups 1 and 2) may tell him all is well. He has no information flow at all in the others (Groups 3, 4, 5). To take account of these loops he can only indulge in planning-style feedforward techniques. He may try to forecast his profit margin from information in Groups 1 and 2 and so control in advance the information that will subsequently flow in the Group 3 channel from the Annual General Meeting. Most astute managers attempt to control future events by this type of feedforward technique. It is partially successful. It may help him to control his output to a profit of, say, 12% which has been agreed, but the technique is powerless to help him if future discussion suddenly raises this to 18% without warning, and proceeds to judge his unit on that basis. Similar remarks apply to the extended feedback loops of Groups 3 and 5 except that in these the information is less likely to be quantified and probably flows as "words and sentences" which may require a different type of skill and personality to handle them; compare the cost accountant and the barrister.

Once time has elapsed and information starts to flow in all the feedback loops, the overall manager's skill consists in occasionally standing back from day-to-day operations and judging the different reports as they come in. He may be praised at the A.G.M. for last year's production figures yet know that he has present operator trouble that will give lower profit next year. Or his day-to-day work may be proceeding well yet he may suspect that the local authority is replanning the area and that he may have to move. Any manager has to be able to receive reports that affect several different timescales, be able to judge the weighting he should give to each and so weld the varying reports good and bad into a single overall approach to practical action.

No views can be expressed or problem solved or action carried out unless a standpoint is taken up and the views or action judged in the light of specific criteria. In the *time*-scale there is, for example, Discounted Cash Flow as an integrating concept though the technique tends to favour short-term criteria. In the *space*-scale a quantitative technique has not been satisfactorily developed and managers tend to use the concepts of private property and the nation state, heavily supported by the rule of law. Having considered all aspects and used what management techniques he understands, the manager will integrate the various aspects within his own person intuitively and make his decision.

Viewed in system terms, feedback loops in Groups 1 and 2 may contain straightforward negative feedback information. Because of the extension of the other loops (3, 4, 5), the fact that they pass through other systems with possible time-delays, these loops may contain positive *or* negative feedback. The loops may be non-linear shift from positive to negative feedback as time elapses and the overall dominance between each of the loops may shift from one to another. The manager must accept or reject the apparent shifting dominance of the various reports as they come in and follow a steady course. Otherwise a "stop-go" policy develops as each feedback report is acted on in sequence and such action is to nobody's benefit. The non-linearity of a loop may be epitomized by a reported decreasing profit which nevertheless elicits no action until in one time period a further only slight decrease in profit changes it to a loss when immediate and punitive decisions are taken. The difficulty there is in handling multiple and extended feedback loops in organizational systems accounts for a large amount of the management literature published.

The Behaviour of Complex Systems

One point the manager is not likely to know in advance is the interactions that are likely to flow from his decisions. Most decisions made intuitively tend to be based on experience, and most persons' experience tends to be limited to systems of negative feedback in *first*- and *second*-order systems only. Where higher-order systems are being considered it may become necessary to use simulation techniques to uncover outcomes. These outcomes are often complex and not what we might be led to expect.

The term complex systems when applied to socio-technical systems covers systems that are so differentiated in their parts that their feedback-system structure is of high order, multipleloop and non-linear. The socio-technical system just described had five groupings of feedback and begins to be of high order. Once separate loops are distinguished within each group this system is certainly of high order. The complexity of a system can relate to the system itself as it exists, or the model we make of it. Frequently a simple model of a complex system is made because we can understand the simple model that is made and this gives us confidence. Our own experience relates to the simple working of the simple model. Unfortunately when a prediction is made using the simple model, the prediction frequently does not fit with what subsequently occurs in the actual situation. Simple models do not often explain complex situations.

Professor Forrester at Massachusetts Institute of Technology has made studies of the behaviour of complex systems using complex computer simulations and out of these empirical studies certain system characteristics of complex systems have been discerned. The behaviour of complex systems is found by him to:

(i) *Be counterintuitive*. Such complex systems do not behave in a manner we might expect from our own stored experience against which we judge performances. In most situations a person is concerned with first-order negative feedback systems and with cause and effect that are proximate in time. In the complex system conditions are likely to be different. The feedback is of high order and may change its overall dominant mode of working, as also the interaction between the various feedback loops. Cause and effect may become "uncoupled" so that they are no longer closely related in time and space, as our Kantian upbringing might lead us to expect. We are left with interacting processes that are difficult to map out with static control techniques.

(ii) *React in the long run in the opposite way to the short run*, e.g. increased food production may provide more food for each person, but in some complex situation the additional food may mean more births so in the long run less food per person.

(iii) *Tend towards low performance*. Because the true remedial policies required are counterintuitive, many remedial policies introduced into socio-technical systems to solve problems are often short-term solutions that in the long run make matters worse. We are beginning to understand this problem, e.g. to realize that additional wage awards solve the immediate strike problem but produce inflationary problems within a short time and possibly more strikes with more short-term solutions that further aggravate the problem. Such knowledge will precipitate a confrontation between the existentialist (the short-term view) and the planner (the longer-term view).

(iv) *Be insensitive to most input parameter changes* and resist policy changes. Input parameters can be changed within wide limits without much effect on output. Similarly this countering action applies to policy changes. The complex system will internally generate countering action that attempts to restore the *status quo* when any new policy is introduced. Resistance to change is very strong and appears to relate to past mental images and desires that do not easily become obliterated, e.g. where a new bonus wagescale is introduced, it is quite likely to be so manipulated that before long the equivalent output is being made to produce the same wages as before. Sensitivity analysis is now a management tool.

(v) *Have some influence points*, both in parameters and structure, that are highly sensitive to change. These may not be self-evident. The classical example is of the Bank wiring room at the Hawthorne plant where it was considered that improved working conditions were improving output whereas it was subsequently discovered that improved output was more closely related to improved interest in the employees as persons.

Forrester argues that the influence points must be found by careful analysis of system behaviour examining on output graphs the interaction of the numerous variables along a timescale. Examining the output lines not only for changes in parameter values but also for differing structures which in a model means changing the equations that describe the structure.

Mutual Causality

The concept of mutual causality is not so much new but rather it gives a new emphasis to a concept basic to the understanding of systems. Mutual causality emphasizes the interdependence of parts rather than their connection in a unidirectional causal chain. The concept of mutual causality goes beyond the concept "A causes B" ($A \rightarrow B$) to point out the interdependence of the two parts "A influences and so causes B, but also B reflects back into and so causes and reinforces A" ($A \leftrightarrow B$).

What we may at first have seen as a causal chain,

$$A \rightarrow B \rightarrow C \rightarrow D \rightarrow E,$$

may be possible of examination as a closed system of interacting subsystems. This is not to say that the concept of causality is superseded, but that for some purposes the concept of mutual causality may produce

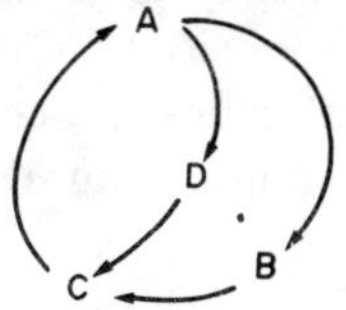

more useful solutions. The interacting sub-systems may be in a state of equilibrium or more likely the continued circularity effect will be generating deviation from an initial condition (state t_1) of the system to a new level of equilibrium (state t_2).

Because of the circulating effect a small initial kick in some direction may be amplified and reamplified throughout the system until it attains a magnitude far beyond the originating force. In such a system the direction of an initial kick, which may be an accidental kick, assumes great importance.

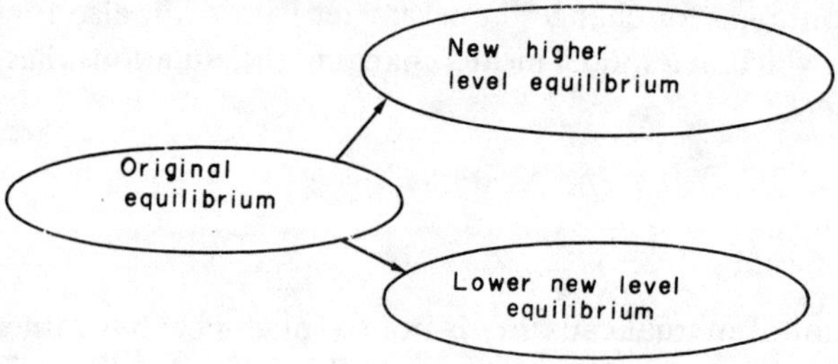

The first greeting given to one's wife on returning from work may set the tone for the whole evening. If the initial "kick" and her response is cheerful, a mutually reinforcing set of sub-systems may lift the level of discourse and produce an exhilarating evening. If, on the other hand, the first greeting is a grunt, the effect may be entirely deflationary and the conversation may degenerate into a vicious circle of mutual recriminations. In either case the initial "kick" will generate movement which will circulate and build up until the system gradually settles to a new equilibrium level as forces counteracting the initial "kick" come into play. Here the system will remain until a further "kick" is given in some direction.

The connections between the sub-systems can be regarded as feedback loops, some negative, some positive. Quoting Maruyama,[1] "The deviation-*counteracting* mutual causal process is called 'morphostasis' while the deviation-*amplifying* mutual causal process is called 'morphogenesis'."

[1] "The second cybernetics", *American Scientist*, Vol. 51(2), 1963.

Where the deviation-counteracting (negative feedback) morphostatic forces predominate, the system is likely to stay at the same level of operation, e.g. small organizations stay small.

Where the deviation-amplifying (positive feedback) morphogenetic forces prevail, the system is likely to move to new levels of working as previously described, once an organization has made some return which it retains it may be able to self-finance growth at an increasing rate. In any analysis the situation is likely to be complicated in that feedback loops can change from deviation-counteracting to deviation-amplifying. As previously mentioned, the position is non-linear. It is the deviation-amplifying processes that are interesting here, for these are the ones that produce growth and decay. The classical example quoted by both Maruyama and Forrester is the homogeneous agricultural plain. All the land is similar as regards agriculture. At some spot a farmer starts to farm. This is the initial small almost accidental "kick", from which much differentiation develops due to the action of deviation-amplifying processes. Other farmers start up farming near him for friendship and protection. For mutual benefit one or two shops open and gradually a village develops. The village is used as a market-place so more farmers start to farm nearby and gradually a city develops. The choice of the first spot was in theory accidental and in practice any possible specific reasons would relate to agriculture and not to the advantages of the location for a city. The build-up to a city comes about through a series of mutually interacting and amplifying processes. In spite of the fact that the position may be totally unsuited to the location of a city and the last place one might choose if planning a city from the start, yet the process once started continues to build up and differentiate and cannot be stopped. In this analysis it is the mutually interacting causal *process* that has caused the city, not the initial choice of site by the first farmer.

Deviation-amplifying mutual causal processes cause an increase in differentiation. From the same beginnings, very different end-results may occur, due to the action of specific deviation-amplifying mutual causal processes. We may compare this concept with the principle of *equifinality*, that a system can achieve a given end-state in many ways, which principle relates to open systems where homeostatic (deviation-counteracting) principles are stressed.

Models are frequently used to examine the outcome of mutually interacting processes. In building a model of mutually interacting systems we usually employ the concept of a "closed boundary". All the interactions in which we are interested are enclosed within the boundary of the interacting systems. Then the dynamic behaviour of the enclosed model will generate characteristic modes of behaviour which we can investigate.

The earlier models were analytic, attempting to calculate values for each variable in the model for each time period. The present tendency is to use computer simulation models giving emphasis to the interaction *pattern* of the variables and secondarily to the values the variables achieve. These model patterns can give us very useful long-term information and help to determine policies. The world viewed from this longer-term consists of interacting processes.

System Boundaries

The need to spend considerable time maintaining socio-technical systems as viable units, stresses the need to consider such systems as open ones that are continually "trading" with their environment. In earlier chapters, the input to a system was shown as raw materials, energy and information. These are the process inputs. Additionally there are *maintenance* system inputs to keep the physical assets and human parts of the system going, to counteract "wear and tear".

The process inputs and outputs and the maintenance systems' inputs all cross the system boundary, which requires to be a distinct skin so that the service or production unit is controllable, yet at the same time this skin should be permeable so that inputs and outputs can cross the boundary without too much loss through friction (Fig. 6.5). The open-systems manager will appreciate that he needs knowledge of his environment and will be concerned with market research, public relations, contact with suppliers and users and with being a good neighbour locally. The permeability of the system boundary requires his consideration; for security reasons it may require to be closed apart from a few distinct access points, for other reasons it may require to be easy to cross at many points. Different parts of a system may require differing boundary permeabilities. Few studies are available in the literature so

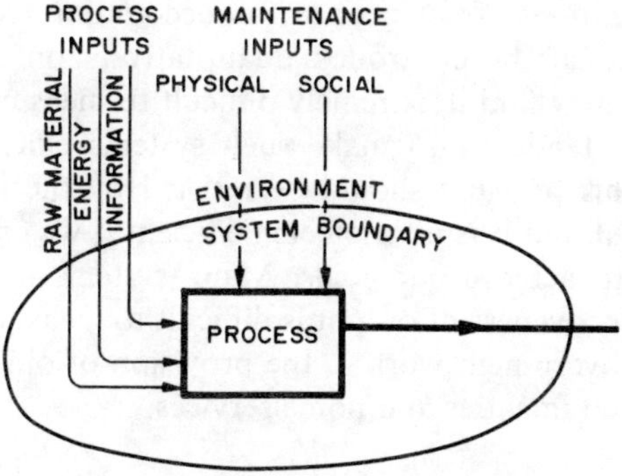

Fig. 6.5. System boundary permeability.

far on the effect of varying boundary permeability on effective achievement of goals.

The open system exists in a state of negative entropy. It is a tension point. The systems manager must control the inflow and outflow across his system's boundary, balancing them and always retaining a reservoir of energy within the system. He imports selectively, raw materials, energy and labour, and information. He exports his service or finished product. His success in Western-type culture is measured not by the physical flow; but by the cash values presently attached to the physical flows, expressed through the techniques of financial and management accounting. A systems trained manager would be particularly interested in cash flow statements in addition to the traditional balance-sheet and profit and loss accounts. Indeed in some quarters of the accountancy world there is a call to make cash-flow accounting part of the statutory system.

Accounting is the technique by which, in many systems, the amount of build-up of tension retained in the system is measured. Techniques of negative feedback are used to control input and output in great detail and should these fail or work badly trouble arises, "when a system's negative feedback discontinues, its steady state vanishes, and at the same time its boundary disappears and the system terminates".[2]

[2] D. Katz and R. L. Kahn, *The Social Psychology of Organization*, John Wiley, quoting J. G. Miller, *American Psychologist*, Vol. 10 (1955).

Not all organizations are subject to full accounting techniques. Many service systems can be controlled quantitatively on input, but their administrators may find it extremely difficult to measure output. There may then be a tendency to make such systems efficient rather than effective and this pressure should be resisted by the manager. To be efficient is useful, but it is no use being efficient if we are not also effective and able to achieve our goals. Many systems having qualitative goals where effectiveness of output is difficult to measure quantitatively arise in local government work in the provision of old persons homes, local recreational facilities and home services.

The Manager and his Goals

The manager will find the overall limits of his organization stated in the Articles of Association or the constitution of his society, but these are overall permissive goals often couched in legalistic terms and as such hardly a target by which his performance may be measured or motivation gained. The goals of any system require restating at the several system and sub-system levels: at the operational (tactical) level, the strategic level and at the top policy level.

It is at the operational level that goals are most easily stated. The operational goals of a "hard" technological system can be stated as "*x* units of output per hour", clearly stated in words and quantities. The operator is motivated to achieve these goals by his need to tend the machine and by his need for access to money. At this level it is fashionable to dictate inputs, goals and outputs in behaviouristic terms, so that the system can be the more easily controlled in its operation. Such goals and targets and methods of working can be laid down in manuals and agreements. As we move from the "hard" technological system of making a product to the business level, the setting of goals becomes more difficult. Products may be engineered, organizations seldom are, they just grow. As a constructed system, the organization that the manager or administrator is in charge of will have distinct goals that can be stated.[3] But additionally it will have an aspect of "continuing" drive or viability, an

[3] Not that this stating in words is an easy matter, See A. Donald "On the Stating of Goals", *Systems Engineering*, Vol. 4.2. (1976).

aspect of its working that bears little relationship to its stated goals. For example, with the advance in technology and with the advance towards an all-embracing money economy, an individual finds he needs to be a member of some unit in order to achieve work by joint effort and hence to obtain access to money wages. He may or may not be interested in the goals of the organization of which he is a member and may or may not be interested in doing much work. Other unstated goals will be imposed on an organization by the general cultural context in which it operates. To a person who has always lived in one country such pressures may be unnoticed, they soon become of importance when a business operates in the international sphere. Such goals may take the form of constraints: how a thing can be done and how it may not be done; such approaches to working may be entirely unstated verbally, but may be conveyed by general conventions of behaviour. At this strategic and policy level, not all goals are stated in words and those that are stated are not always the important ones. The manager may find he requires to exercise much skill to find out what the goals set for him really are.

Within this context the manager of an organization agrees his goals with his policy-makers, no doubt using some such technique as Management by Objectives so that managers at all levels are involved and motivated.

In relation to constructed systems, the systems approach stresses the need for stated goals. This one point is perhaps the most difficult of all the requirements in systems management. Nobody cares to state the problem outright; it is extraordinarily difficult to state goals.[4] There can be overall goals "to land a man on the moon within five years and bring him back safely", "to broadcast to the nation between 12 noon and 12 midnight daily", "to make a profit of 8% p.a. on share capital".

[4] Professor Checkland at the University of Lancaster admits this difficulty in relation to "soft" systems (as opposed to "hard" technological systems) in which "objectives are difficult to define, decision-taking is uncertain, measures of performance are at best qualitative and human behaviour is irrational". For the last decade he has been refining a methodology to use in these apparently unstructured areas. Rather than stated goals, the "root definitions" of the relevant systems are uncovered. The "root definition" attempts to define the basic nature of the system. (Ref. P. B. Checkland, "Towards a systems-based methodology for realworld problem solving", *Systems Engineering*, Vol. 3.2.)

Strangely enough the first-mentioned goal appeared to become the one most easy of achievement, perhaps because of its large technical content and because even the human content became one of psychotechnology; the broadcast goal masks the difficult normative problem of what to broadcast once technical competence has been achieved, even the last goal may become difficult to pin down as there are many categories of share capital and issues may be made from time to time.

Overall goals can then be broken down into multitudinous detailed goals, but the main problem for the system manager is twofold:

1. A main goal may have many aspects.
2. He may be asked to achieve a multiplicity of goals and be given no rank order.

The systems manager can press for more detailed instructions as to which aspect is paramount or which rank order to aim for; at the risk of losing his job because he lacks "flair". It is a human problem and none the less so because viewed in system terms. Yet the systems approach familiarizes individuals with the idea that it is reasonable to objectivize goals and targets in advance for constructed systems. The goal may be focused on a single point of achievement in time, e.g. to construct a bridge, but better perhaps on a continuing achievement, e.g. to provide a service. The danger is that emphasis may be put onto the achievement of goals rather than the process, the manner in which resources are being used towards achieving goals and the need to achieve minimum threshold values in many areas whilst aiming towards the target.

In natural systems there are no goals and hence no problems, only interacting processes. In constructed systems the setting up of goals creates objective problems, which may or may not be solved when the goal is reached. It is often stated that we are a problem-solving society. Rather more perhaps are we a problem-creating society.

The Parts of his System

Once his goals are known, the manager can look towards the parts of his system, the resources with which he is to achieve these goals, to see how they are interrelated. The parts of a system will be specific to that system, for a small shop the parts might be distinguished as:

Building: Repairs. Leases
Procurement of materials for sale
Display and advertising
Labour employed
Cash control
Customer area facilities
Outside deliveries
Legal and Safety requirements

The Manager will be concerned with *control* relationships, specifically over cash and the safety of stock, and the safety of persons working within the building. He will be concerned with *representational* relationships, with the union to which his employees belong, to the co-operative perhaps from which he buys some of his stock. He will be concerned with *advisory* relationships regarding, perhaps, materials for sale and display and advertising.

The systems manager will then require to know what processes take place within the system. These will be physical processes. The movement of stock into the shop, its exchange for money, its delivery to the customers, the items that were wrongly delivered, etc.

If the system is of any size the manager will not be able to examine all these processes by keeping a constant watch on all that occurs, but will require his assistants to raise a flow of information by writing down what work they carry out, from this information flow he will construct his models.

The Manager and his Models

In his daily life, the manager becomes less and less in contact with physical processes and more and more concerned with interpreting the physical processes, controlling their daily operation and planning their futures, by what he discerns from his models of the situation.

A model epitomizes a situation. It is a simplification of what is taking place. It is generally abstract, a conglomeration of words and numerical symbols and graphs. It purports to represent the essential parts of the real-life situation. These essentials are extracted in order to see their interaction in simplified form to manipulate them, and to predict from this manipulation what will actually occur in real-life terms. A trained person can handle perhaps half a dozen variables in his mind, a computer model say one or two hundred. The real-life company situation may be said to comprise several thousand variables. To extract *all* these and put them into a computer program tends not to be useful. It tends to re-create the complex real-life situation, whereas the purpose of the model is to extract the relevant variables for the particular purpose in hand. Following this argument it would appear that the clue to good modelling is to produce a series of interlinked models covering specific areas rather than attempt a single overall model for the organization. The battle between total corporate models and partial models is not yet finalized. It depends on how computers develop and how successful we are in linking together smaller models. Here a series of models is developed; it is essential that they interlock in some aspects and are not developed in total isolation of each other.

A Static Framework

The manager's first requirement is to develop a framework of the areas within which to collect information, to locate himself at a particular position in time/space and to examine events from a distinct point of view. Within limits, the point of view is open to his choosing and because of this choice organizations that one might expect to develop in similar ways, do in practice develop in very different if not opposing ways.

Environmental Framework

(i) *Technological* analysis. What technologies are open to him at present and how they are likely to develop within the medium-term future.

(ii) *Economic* analysis. The markets for his product, the costs of and availability of his inputs; raw materials energy and labour.

(iii) *Social* analysis. Industrial relations. His employees as customers for his product. Needs and markets. Work as one of the activities in which human society engages. Includes the consideration of social mores embodied as law. The political power-structure within the company.

(iv) *Environmental* analysis. The effect of his possible activities on other than the business sphere. Whether the activity meets social needs or is a mutually-causal deviation-amplifying process, existing to create and satisfy imposed needs. Consideration whether the social and economic infrastructures are adequate to cope with technical growth.

In making these analyses, the manager may well decide to split his total environment, the world, into two parts:

(i) that part of the environment considered outside the scope of influence of the organization,

(ii) the more immediate environment within his sphere of influence.

The fourfold analysis of the environment will require a synthesis which, together with the introduction of certain value judgements, will represent the standpoint from which the organization carries out its dealings with others: other organizations, other businesses, governments, the public. This framework begins to structure the manager's thought. It is not a framework that cannot be altered, but it alters slowly and for short-term decisions is fixed, value judgements are capable of much quicker change and possibly will do so if the manager himself changes. This model operates simultaneously at the highest and lowest levels of the organization's model-building framework. It operates at the highest point to develop the *attitude* of the organization, sometimes called its "ethic", it operates at the operational level to give information regarding the availability of resources and of markets for the products or clients for the service offered.

Within this environmental framework, a more dynamic model of the organization's input/conversion/output processes, its operational trading with its environment as an open system, will be developed. Traditionally these horizontal divisions of the organization's activity, the process flow are dealt with by separate models covering procurement, conversions and marketing (see Table 5).

TABLE 5

	Procurement	Conversion	Marketing
Sources and costs	Raw materials Energy Information Personnel Plant—maintenance new items	Conversion rates Efficiency ratios	Stocks: Levels and rates of flow
Stocks: Levels and rates of flow			Products and markets

Information is carried statistically and in money amounts. Problems arise when this detailed information written as figures on paper is examined in static mode for its interacting effect; in budgets, trading accounts, profit-and-loss accounts and balance-sheets. There would appear to be little technical problem (other than costs) to combine all this process-flow information into a single model. Such an information model would control the present flows and cumulate information for period statements of levels (balance-sheets) and rates of flow (trading a/c profit & loss a/c). Were it practicable to integrate the process information in this manner and, strangely enough, make control more flexible, the manager might spend his time more usefully in intervening to *guide* the process system *away* from undesirable states and *towards* desirable states instead of the rather fruitless effort of continuous control to achieve a particular state agreed upon some 6 months or more previously, which state is not always found to be presently desirable when with much effort it has been achieved.

A duplicate of the same model could be used for the "What if" question so often used in planning at the operational level. "What would be the effect on markets and profits if we made twice as much of *X* and half as much of *Y*?"

The model of the lateral process flow follows in symbols what is actually taking place, or rather what is thought to be taking place as recorded by certain selected measurements, at the operational level. To operate as a control feedback loop, decision points must be introduced into this lateral flow.

Because at present we have many levels of management, the decision process involves a *vertical flow of information* between the lower level controllers and the Chief Executive. This is the vertical managerial apparatus of line management that makes decisions in relation to some objective, initiates action, motivates and at the lowest vertical point the decision enters the lateral process flow as a control action. The information in this vertical flow is subject to much selection and continued sophisticated processing so that in the end only a few control figures arrive on the top manager's desk. Information on an individual case is subsumed in and exchanged for an insight into overall pattern-change. Data handlers, accountants and company secretaries have devoted whole lifetimes over many generations to ensure that the resulting extracted figures are the pertinent ones. The figures provided do not always fall into this classification. As with the lateral-process flow, in addition to the vertical decision/control structure a duplicate planning model, a "what if" model is required relating to different decisions in regard to strategic planning and policy planning, so that the organization's strategic goals and policy objectives, its entrepreneurial activity, may be continuously under review. At the very top of this model a continuous realization of the organization's attitude to society is introduced, e.g. are we in business to make a profit, to make cars or to provide transportation, or both?

To recapitulate, five model areas have been distinguished.

(i) *Environmental model.* The technological, economic and social environments that act as a life-support system to the organization and which it in turn affects.

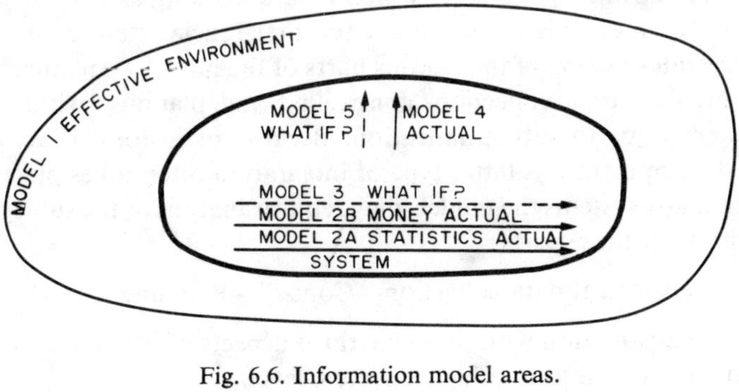

Fig. 6.6. Information model areas.

(ii) *Lateral* process *control* model. A feedback flow of information from the process flow with decision points where the vertical decision model impinges.

(iii) *Lateral* process *planning* model. The "what-if" model to monitor possible changes under existing goals and strategies.

(iv) *Vertical* management *decisional* model. The managerial model that decides what control is to be exercised in the lateral process flow.

(v) *Vertical* management *planning* model. The "what-if" model that considers the effects of changed strategic goals and policy objectives and which at the very top connects with the environmental model to keep under review the attitude of the undertaking to the rest of society and the physical environment.

For reasons of economy an attempt is often made to review all these aspects of the situation within one "jumbled-up" information system covering

Collection of historical data,
Control of present process,
Planning of future processes.

This procedure is all right if the manager can sort it out and knows what he is doing at any particular moment. From a model-building viewpoint it greatly helps if the three functions are kept distinctly separate, being examined sequentially with an awareness of the mode, historical data collector, controller, planner, in which we are working at any particular moment of time. This separation is the first crucial step towards the necessary interlocking of the various parts of the models. An integration which involves data collection, controlling and planning within each sub-system leads to sub-optimization. Because of historical factors in model development this latter type of integration often takes place and hence in many systems the models may require analysis at the sub-system level into their three parts:

Historical data collection—Control—Planning

then an amalgamation with the same three aspects of other sub-systems to produce a synthesis at a higher system level.

It is not the intention here to go into the detailed working of specific models. Many books are available on this subject, each book treating of one or more of the available models economic, accounting, inventory, production, marketing, etc., so that it is in fact necessary to read half a dozen books or more to obtain sufficient information in this area. Less perhaps is written on how to integrate these many models. At the moment the economic models, budgets, the trading and profit and loss accounts and the balance-sheet, appear to be used as one of the main integrating frameworks.

Information Flow

A fully integrated information flow will change the existing system of reporting to management. There will be the need to understand and gain experience in "real-time control". This might better be called "current-activity control"; the control of current activities as each event is occurring, not a week or month later when the events have been batched. At present this "current-activity" type of control is best seen in an operations room controlling, say, aircraft. A very similar situation may also be seen in certain sharebrokers' offices. Whilst work is in progress, it will necessitate continual attendance by some level of management, not necessarily top management, authorized to make decisions as information is received and needs to be dealt with.

Information input, for example sales orders, tends to be randomized in the time scale, and so, as well as controlling each event, selected trends important to the particular business will need to be cumulated and watched. This operation becomes more feasible with the greatly reduced cost of micro-processors with visual display units.

Many of the operational decisions, production, acceptance of orders, ordering of raw material, will not require reference to top management, and as experience is gained many of these will be automated decisions, the computer being programmed to print out for top management decision only those occurrences which are outside the prescribed limits. This will extend the principle of "management by exception" already used by top management.

As well as the exceptions, some well-digested and easy-to-read figures will be printed out on paper for presentation to management. During discussions, detail on the current situation can be obtained by dialling or typing a preset code number on a line linked with the computer handling the information flow. This facility, which is already available in hardware, is called random access. The computer will have been programmed to supply the information on twenty or thirty important questions, and the up-to-the-minute figures on each of these current activities is found and immediately printed out on the typewriter at the place where the discussion is in progress.

Level of Information Feedback

"Where to put the feedback?" At what level should the processed information be fed back into the system, should details of an operation be fed back first to the operator and later to his manager? Or should the information be given to his manager only, who is then allowed to make what use he thinks fit of it?

Before the advent of the computer, information was fed up the organization. At each stage an operator or manager would process his information and pass it on to the next higher level, taking note of the information before he passed it on and to that extent exercising control over the information he processed (Fig. 6.7). Current computer practice is now to capture data as near to its source as possible, process it and then feed it back in. Where the information is fed in at a high level of management it may subsequently flow down the organization, thus reversing its

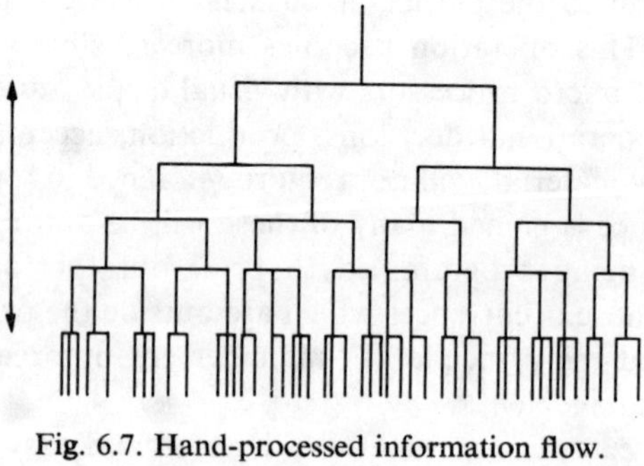

Fig. 6.7. Hand-processed information flow.

traditional flow and having a considerable impact on the way management is organized. As control of information correlates with the wielding of power, a shift in the power structure within the company is likely when decisions are made to alter the level at which information feedback re-enters the line management system from the information system (Fig. 6.8).

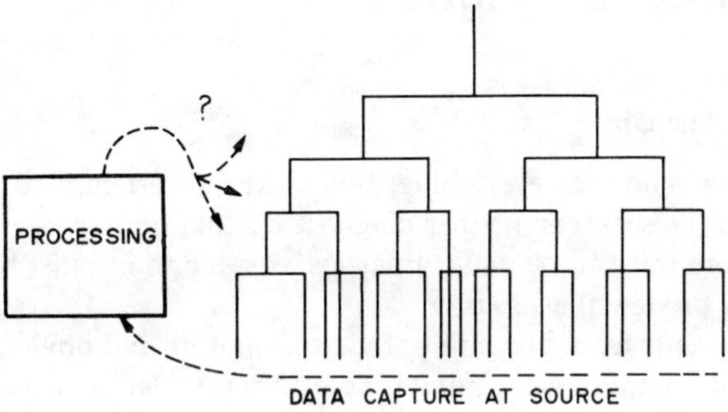

Fig. 6.8. What level of information feedback input?

CHAPTER 7

Obtaining Information

Patterns of Thought

The observer who sees everything, but makes no attempt to order or classify what he sees, can neither diagnose a situation nor take effective action. Before this can be done, a particular standpoint must be chosen from which to view the situation.

To look at events from one point of view is limiting and obviously gives a "one-sided" point of view, but it is necessary for effective action. What is important is that our frame of reference should be sufficiently inclusive to enable us to classify events effectively, and so give reasonable decisions at the level at which we are operating.

Building up a conceptual framework is the basis of all education and training. When we are considering the effectiveness of an adult person and wish to know his pattern of thinking, we can try to discover the answer, in the case of a particular person, to Fisher's classificatory questions.[1]

(i) What events does Mr. Jones classify? What seems important to him, and what events is he capable of classifiying?

(ii) How, and how well, does he classify them?

(iii) What does he classify them as? Different persons may regard the same event in vastly different ways.

(iv) How does he classify them as such?

(v) How does he come to classify them in this way? To what extent has his framework developed?

[1] G. H. Fisher, *Psychology Today*, Dept. of Psychology, University of Newcastle, 1964.

The answers will depend on Mr. Jones's culture, the level of training available to him within that culture and his individual ability to make effective use of the training to which he has been exposed. Should it be considered that his conceptual framework is not satisfactory, further questions may be asked:

(vi) How can we harness Mr. Jones's developing classifying systems in order to educate him? and

(vii) How can we change the ways in which Mr. Jones's classifying systems operate?

The answers fall into the category of training, of redirecting a person's manner of thinking, of developing the way in which he constructs models of the outside world to anticipate the results of his possible actions. At the present moment many people have a "mechanical linkage" model of the world, and so in order to enlarge their conceptual framework, many articles and books are being written to present to them the newer "cybernetic" feedback model as a more useful conception. Conceptual frameworks can only be changed slowly, and an individual seldom completely outgrows his initial training, however desirable this might prove in an era of change. Change in technology often greatly affects and influences our patterns of thought. The factory system has brought a new conception of time. The coming of automation has changed our model of mechanical linkages to a "feedback" model and in policy, technology has effected a change from the aristocratic group supported by the common folk to the concept of an educated mass society and industrial democracy.

A person is effective to the extent that he can build more and more inclusive models within his conceptual framework. Sometimes he may find it impossible to relate one of his models to another and so they exist side by side, and one can never be certain what action a particular stimulus may elicit. A person may have one mode of action for Sundays and one for the rest of the week and be unable to integrate the two in any way. The roles we play—businessman, father, husband, committee man—in which we behave in a manner suited to the activity in which we are involved, also tend to emphasize that we have separate models existing side by side, and sometimes we may not be happy in the roles our social system sets out for us to play and may wish to change them because they are not effective for us.

In communicating with a manager or a competitor we must realize that his pattern of thought is built up from his background and experience. Background can be analysed into the culture of his country, the culture of his group or class, his individual approach, his role and the status he has achieved in life; experience consists of his particular education, training and business positions. To communicate effectively with someone of a completely different culture, it is necessary to have some acquaintance with the other person's conceptual frameworks in order to influence them or even be influenced by them. As already stated, a person's conceptual framework changes slowly. It is within his *existing* thought patterns that an executive takes his decisions, modified by the sociological and psychological pressures under which he is working. Decisions rest on facts and the relationship of facts within the framework. Where decisions have to be made in the absence of some facts, the gaps will be filled with data consistent with the executive's preconceived ideas.

The Use of Facts

Facts imply information. Data considered relevant is gathered, processed from a particular point of view to obtain factual information which in turn is related to other facts. In the following sections we consider the logic of valid argument, the computer as a tool with which to process information and some of the techniques now used for relating one set of facts to another.

Most thinking, including creative thinking, tends to take place within our existing conceptual framework and in a logical manner. But where this logical step-by-step pattern becomes sterile, it may be possible to break through it by an emotional or illogical approach, often termed "brainstorming", where any idea that comes into a person's head is written down and considered no matter how unrelated to the situation it may at first sight appear. This is a source of ideas when logical extension of known facts cannot produce further ideas. The ideas produced in this manner will then be tested logically before any action is taken on them.

Knowledge, and what passes for knowledge in the world today, comes from various sources:

Scientific facts, as revealed by scientific method, in experiments that can be repeated by anyone who has the facilities and takes the trouble. Scientific fact is limited to knowledge that can be verified by experimental means.

Direct intuition entails personal knowledge where subject and object, the observer and observed, become interrelated. Understanding so gained is almost impossible to communicate to others. This applies even in a scientific laboratory of physical sciences, and is an inevitable part of much social investigation.

Metaphysical discussion is concerned with the ordering of abstract concepts and with the ultimates of value judgements.

Revelation, as revealed by God and the prophets in religion, is a matter of belief rather than proof.

Opinions and beliefs. The lifetime's accumulation of knowledge by an individual which constitute his personal beliefs and viewpoint and which, because he is but one individual, will be biased by his own past experiences, associations and thoughts. Opinions and belief often exert a strong influence on others.

Logic

It may seem a far cry from the Aristotelian syllogism studied at school.

All men are mortal	Soldiers are patriotic
Socrates is a man	Sailors are patriotic
Therefore Socrates is mortal	Therefore sailors are soldiers
(Valid reasoning)	(Invalid conclusion)

to the statement that the computer that graces our office is in its operation a logical machine. Nevertheless, there is a direct connection.

To the manager some understanding of logic is useful as a tool—firstly to trace the validity of argument in the written reports he handles and in discussion, and secondly as a general explanation of how the computer works on which he depends for his data processing.

Logic in speech and writing. Aristotle the Greek who lived in the fourth century B.C. developed the logic of *terms* and in particular the syllogism as a means of determining the validity of argument, and it is within this framework of logic laid down by Aristotle that most of European philosophical and scientific thought took place until the last hundred years. Logic is concerned with the way the argument progresses, the validity or invalidity of reasoning, not with the truth or falsity of the propositions being dealt with. It is the province of Scientific Method to establish empirically whether the propositions are true or false. Whether men are in fact mortal, and whether soldiers are in fact patriotic is the province of Scientific Method to discover.

Symbolic logic. Just as we made no real progress in arithmetic until we forsook Roman numerals for the Arabic ones with their significance dependent on position, so no step forward occurred in logic until symbols were substituted for writing out our argument in full in words. One advantage of the newer method is that we know how to manipulate symbols easily and quickly. With the coming of Boolean algebra and symbolic logic we are now able to express our thoughts precisely and in symbols, so obviating the necessary inexactness of every-day language, and enabling us to manipulate these symbols to see the full development of the argument; often these developments of the argument are too unwieldly to visualize when full sentences are used. Thus was started the logic of *propositions* from which truth tables can be set up.
An example of symbolic logic is provided in greater detail in Appendix III. Here it is possible to compare the conventional language statements with the corresponding symbols arranged in truth tables, to study the equivalent Boolean arithmetic and Venn diagrams, and to appreciate how logical steps are performed by an electronic computer. A description of the capabilities of computers now follows, to enable understanding of how these machines can assist management in the processing of data and its logical analysis to provide effective information.

Computers

The electronic computer is a logical machine, very quick at the four basic operations of arithmetic, also having the ability to choose a course of action, depending on whether a particular number it is dealing with is less than, equal to, or greater than some other number about which it has information and with which it is making comparison. In addition it has a "memory" in the form of a storage on which it can draw when determining a course of action. The electronic computer's particular advantages over mental computing or clerical computing are accuracy, speed of calculation and ability to handle large numbers of variables. This is the type of calculation in which the human brain does not excel. The computer is thus of great help to man in processing information containing large amounts of data and many variables with which he could not otherwise cope. It does not at the moment excel in the recognition of patterns or in seeking out relationships; here the human brain shows to greater advantage.

The electronic computer handles data according to the instructions given to it on the program input. Because there is storage, some machines are able to modify their original program instructions according to the empirical results they have achieved during previous working. This puts them in the class of adaptive machines, using their programs in the way that a person who learns from past experience uses a set of rules, flexibly, to meet a given situation. Because they are machines and their memories work efficiently as long as there is no machine breakdown, computers may beat man at such competitive activities as games of chess.

Computers greatly extend man's reasoning and intellectual capabilities in the same way that mechanical machines have extended his muscles. The electronic computer excels primarily in its speed of operation. There are no moving parts inside the electronic computer apart from input and output mechanisms. Unlike electrical machines where electricity drives mechanically moving parts, the basis of the computer is the flow of electricity, representing the information being processed, round fixed circuits. Only the current moves and this it does at the speed of light. Secondly, it provides unique storage facilities. Instead of being able to hold only a few totals, large amounts of quantitative information can be stored inside the computer itself, in subsidiary machines or fed in quickly by tape or punched cards.

There are basically two "genus" of computer: analogue and digital. The former sets out to be a representation of the system of which it is an analogue. The digital computer works simply on numbers, digits.

The analogue computer. These can be special-purpose machines built as a model to represent the working of a particular system. How the system reacts to a change in input, or a modification in the system itself can then be examined quickly, cheaply and without damage to full-scale equipment or loss of life. For example, the working of the electricity grid can be simulated and the effect traced of cutting off the supply from certain generating stations for maintenance or other reasons. Other uses for analogue computers are in ground training for pilots, scientific and engineering problems, and programming of construction work at minimum cost. Large general-purpose analogue computers also exist. On these, any of a number of different problems can be simulated. They incorporate, in effect, basic building blocks and basic operations which can be combined in any way to simulate the problem in hand. The analogue computer works on the basis of varying current within a circuit. Because of this there is a rounding-off effect at the end of each stage of calculation and consequently some small loss of accuracy, but this can be confined within acceptable limits.

Digital computers. In these there is no loss of accuracy as either there is a digit or there is not. The current in the circuit either flows or does not; there is no varying in the size of the current. Digital computers are used wherever a general purpose machine is required to solve problems that can be presented to it digitally. Even here there is specialization. If the machine is to be used primarily for accounting data processing, a different model is likely to be bought than if it is to be used solely for engineering calculation. In the first case there is much input and output and comparatively little processing. In the second case there is small amount of input, but much processing of the data.

Hardware. So much literature is now available describing in detail the various types of machines available that such detail need not be repeated here but certain information, basic to all types of digital computer, is worth mentioning. In the digital computer the clock frequency at which the computer works, the basic frequency at which the pulses carrying the information are driven through the machine and processed, needs to be sufficiently high to ensure high computing speed. Access and cycle times in relation to storage are important, as also is size of the store. It is generally possible to increase the store capacity by supplementary storage units. Input may consist of punched cards, paper or magnetic tape or direct reading of special ink characters. Very often the speed of the input does not correspond with the speed attainable by the processing unit and it may be possible to resort to parallel input and multi-processing to increase efficiency in the use of the computer itself.

Output may be in the form of punched cards, paper or magnetic tape or direct printing by means of typewriter (single character at a time) or line printer (one whole line at a time) linked to the processing unit. Where internal and output speeds do not correspond it may be useful to punch up tape or cards as well as direct printing. The cards or tape can subsequently be printed out on an "off-line" printer if required.

At present many organizations are at the stage of having computerized small aspects of their technical control or their information control. Computers are used "on line" to control a process, say a fractioning column, in real time, and as such are built into the technical process. Where computers are used entirely for data processing they can be regarded as "on line" to the informational system, as opposed to a computer used *ad hoc* to solve engineering or other specific problems.

With the advent of cheap mini-processors many new modes of use are rapidly opening up.

Having considered means of processing information it is now necessary to examine how effectively this information can be communicated.

Communication and Information Technology

We communicate by using symbols, patterns having a specific meaning, words, letters or numbers, and whether the communication be spoken, written or the visual recognition of shapes, there will be four aspects to it:

(i)	(ii)	(iii)	(iv)
The choice of symbols to be used; selective information.	The problem of conveying the symbols used. The technical problems of speech, TV, telephone. Chalk and blackboard, etc.	The meaning behind the symbols that they are intended to convey.	In what way the communication as received affects behaviour. The meaning as interpreted and the motivation of the recipient.

When using language as a means of communication, these four aspects may be more closely defined as follows:

(i)	(ii)	(iii)	(iv)
Letters and words.	Syntax (rules of grammar) Phonetics (sounds).	Semantics. Linguistic analysis of the meaning	Pragmatics (the effect on actions).

The purpose of communication in industry is, we hope, to promote better understanding. A piece of information in one person's head has to be transmitted to other persons for their information or for their action. This seemingly simple operation is beset with pitfalls, the more so when the communication is between two groups rather than two individuals.

Before even considering the effectiveness of the communication we must consider why the communication has arisen; what has motivated a particular person to endeavour to communicate with another. Certain communications are demanded by the organization and, through the "official channels", information may be expected to flow up and down and across the company. But this is only a fraction of the total communication taking place within the company. Persons tend to communicate voluntarily with those nearest to them spatially, and after that to those in the group who have had a similar training and hence have a similar outlook to themselves—for example, sub-groups of accountants, salesmen, engineers, chemists. In this way individuals build up a feeling of solidarity and from that a feeling of security. People also tend to make the best of what they have to say, to show themselves up in the best possible light under the circumstances, particularly when speaking to superiors. Thus whilst ostensibly communicating about a problem connected with production, a person may often include in the communication overtones of his own personal aims. This may even be carried to such an extent that a communication couched as a work problem may really be intended to convey a status problem. It is always useful on receiving a communication to sit back and consider what it is this person is intending to convey.

The message. Let us now take a case where it is intended to convey a straightforward message, and as far as possible only that message is to be conveyed. The managers wish to inform section heads that, "Overtime is now permissible"; this in a factory where the order book is filling up, and where for the last year there has been a management ban on working overtime. A four-fold analysis may help us to make the meaning clear and to avoid misrepresentation. The choice of words for the message is important as each sentence may convey different shades of meaning.

Overtime can be worked.

Overtime may be worked.

Overtime is now permissible.

Overtime should be worked as necessary.

What does "overtime" mean? Does it mean working late on weekdays, does it include Saturdays or Sundays? What about early starts? Next, the sentence itself; is it to be construed to mean that overtime may be worked if need for it is shown and volunteers are found, or does it mean that an employee must work overtime if directed and is liable to dismissal if he refuses? Or has it some other meaning?

Communicating the message. Having agreed on the message and drafted out a form of words that appear to convey the meaning intended, the next step is to decide on the method of communication. Shall it be by written memo, by word of mouth from the manager, by both means together, by display on the notice-board, by broadcast over a loudspeaker system? This is a simple message and there should be no loss of information in its transmission, though a total failure might occur and one department not be informed. This possible failure can very often be obviated by using the principle of redundancy; that is, the use of more than one channel of communication so that if one channel fails the message gets through on another. Notice particularly that the information and the medium that carries the information (speech, paper, sight, pulses in a computer) are separate and distinct. There may be interaction between the message and its carrying medium and certain types of carrier may be best for specific types of information. In this case, both written and verbal formal messages may fail, but the message may get through informally during a tea-break.

Languages themselves carry internal information; and the spelling mistake in the second message "Overtime" is corrected automatically whilst being read. Communication engineers are concerned to see how many mistakes can be made before a message becomes meaningless. The internal information in a series of numbers is not so great, and messages containing numbers need to be more carefully transmitted than those consisting solely of alphabetic information grouped as words.

In our example, were the message passed to be a longer one, say "Overtime is permissible as from next month" there may be partial failure of the communication due to "noise" in the system. Typist errors, crackling in a telephone receiver, the banging down of a teacup may cause the message to be received as "Overtime is permissible as from next (week)". The lost word is filled in by contextual implication and by the word most desired, as explained earlier in the patterns of thought action. Loss of message due to noise in the communication system is the special study of communication undertaken under "information theory", particularly where it is related to wireless, telephonic and similar means of communication.

Behaviour. The behaviour of the recipient of a communication may not be what the sender expected. On receipt of the message, "Overtime is now permissible", employees may make arrangements to work slowly during the day and then work the maximum overtime hours allowed. Again, whilst passing on a message, a manager might, by voice, dress or manner, so antagonize the recipient that in order to "get equal" again, the recipient ignores the message as far as he dare. In other cases there may be no antagonism but the exhortation may be outside the "terms of reference" of the recipient and meaningless to him. To a manager it may make much sense to call for greater production and reduced costs, explaining that the organization must "export or die"; but to particular employees who have never studied economics, even if they have been abroad, this may seem absolute nonsense, as it refers to ideas outside their normal daily routine. Hence the exhortation is received as, "The boss has another bee in his bonnet, let's try to humour him and do what he wants, *up to a point*". Often a sound scheme is put forward by management only to be found to be totally unacceptable, not because there is a failure in communication and not because the scheme itself is bad, but because the existing power structure is unacceptable to the employees, and so their behaviour on receiving the communication is to reject the scheme.

To enlarge the conceptual framework of the those to whom communications are directed will take time and energy. Mass communications such as TV are forces in the gradual extension of the nation's conceptual framework, and no doubt an organization will make some special effort in regard to its own employees; but whilst this is taking effect, it is also necessary to draft communications within already acceptable frames of reference if the communication is to achieve its objective.

Common language. Most of the specialized professions in industry, such as engineers, accountants, lawyers, have developed their own specialized language, and no doubt can put forward a very good reason why this should be so. These specialized vocabularies can become a barrier to efficiency, however, making us unable to communicate with each other fluently about the task in hand. There is no doubt that there is need for a common language in industry that all participants can understand. This common language might come about more quickly where industries are product-oriented and efforts directed to the completion of the product rather than the efficiency of departments.

A move in this direction is discerned in the management technique of value analysis, which on an *ad hoc* basis or even sometimes on a full-time basis, brings together a senior member of each department to study the firm's end product and how it can be improved, while still fulfilling its original function. Thus purchasing officers, designers, engineers, production engineers, cost accountants, lawyers and salesmen will be meeting together for a specified time for the purpose of discussing the same product and explaining to each other their attitude to it.

Classification of information covers two aspects of its use:

(i) classification for immediate use,

(ii) classification for storage, subsequent retrieval and future use.

How we classify our data for *immediate use* depends on the questions we wish to ask and answer. How we classify our information for *storage* depends on the type of information we expect to have to answer in the future. Perhaps it is the second aspect that it is the more difficult to achieve, for we ought to know what kind of questions we wish to ask at present, whereas in the future there may be changes in the type of questions asked. How to classify information prior to storage presents a problem, unless we store each item at random. If we do this, there will have to be a complete search through all items of information whenever a question is asked. This search may take some time and will certainly cost money. Information is usually stored already classified in some way, in which case it can be retrieved more easily, but will only be useful for answering questions framed in a particular way. Keay[1] has pointed out that the type of questions we are asking has tended to alter. To date, questions have been asked about particular items of information. Most libraries keep their information classified in this manner, e.g. details about each king of England. If, for instance, we wished to examine not the specific items "Kings of England" but a physical feature itself, e.g. how many kings of any country were fairheaded, then we would have to search through all the information classified under kings of each country and reanalyse it. Transformed into a production situation, *item* classification would tell us that specific items were held in a particular store, *feature* classification would tell us in which of many stores particular items could be found. The problem of classification and reanalysis of information is nothing new to a sales manager who requires his sales analysis in at least three different ways, by salesmen, by geographical area, by product. Each analysis will require a complete run through of all items of the information in order to reclassify them. Even if a sophisticated computer program manages to carry out the three analyses in one run, this in no way cuts out the analysis work that has been necessary, it has simply been carried out inside the computer. Computers have enabled us to handle information more quickly and therefore to be able to ask different kinds of questions, but the amount of reanalysis work to be done still remains as also do the costs involved in doing it, though as computing techniques advance these costs may be expected to fall.

[1] F. Keay, *The Numerate Manager*, Allan & Unwin Ltd., 1969.

Scientific method. Scientific method has been with us in embryo at least since the time of the Greeks, and made a great leap forward at the time of the Renaissance. As regards scientific enquiry into management and work, this can only be said really to have started with the work of F. W. Taylor in the 1890s. In order fully to appreciate the meaning of scientific method and to relate it to the day-to-day task of the manager in shaping his thought and guiding his decisions, it is useful to study the various stages through which the scientific approach has passed in the natural sciences. It can then be related to those areas in which the manager works, such as the economic situation and the social context. By appreciating the similarities and differences, the usefulness of scientific method to the manager can be seen and pitfalls in its use avoided.

In the very early stages of development of a science there will be a recognition that individual items have certain properties in common and can be given class names, e.g. "house", "bird", and, a modern example, "feedback circuit". In other languages and culture patterns different classifications may be developed from ours. This reflects the grouping that the particular society considers important, and it also makes for difficulties of translation and communication.

At a later stage in development of the embryo science comes the discovery of causal uniformities, e.g. "Wind causes waves", expressed in general terms as "A causes B". As this concept of cause becomes precise, difficulties begin to arise over a unit of measurement, and no progress can be made to the next stage until these have been overcome. The entities involved here have qualitative properties, and in some way these qualitative properties have to be measured quantitatively before progress in the science can be made. No longer must the wind be regarded as the irate puffing of some god, but as the movement of a mass of air at a measurable speed and in a measurable direction over a measurable length of time.

Once a satisfactory unit of measurement is found, the causal concepts can be expressed as a functional dependence between quantitative variables. The notion of cause then disappears[2] and the law takes the form of a mathematical formula describing properties not things. There is an

[2] Compare this position with the concept of Mutual Causality, p. 87.

invariant relationship between the properties such that the constituents of the equation can be moved around,

e.g. Ohm's law $I = \frac{E}{R}$ where I = current, E = e.m.f. (volts), R = resistance

which can also be expressed:

$$E = I.R. \quad \text{or} \quad R = \frac{E}{I}.$$

Whilst these individual developments are progressing, other scientists will be working on universal theories to link together in one general pattern several existing minor theories. Such are Newton's Law of Gravity and Einstein's Theory of Relativity.

In developing a science any or all of the following methods will probably have been used where suitable:

Reasoning from analogy.

Induction by simple enumeration (counting things).

The method of hypothesis.

The probability concept, and statistics.

Analogy is argument based on resemblances. Where a set of items have a common property, they are said to be analogous as concerns that property. Analogy can be a dangerous method, particularly when used quickly in conversation. Because two objects or situations are alike in *some* respects, it is dangerous to talk as if they will be alike in *all* respects. Yet the transfer of modes of thought from one study to another often leads to new insights. Reasoning by analogy is one of the oldest methods and was in use by the Greeks, yet it is frequently used to good effect in our new approach to problem-solving, Operations Research.

Induction by simple enumeration consists of counting the properties of a certain number of instances, and from this forming a general law inferring that all future instances will have this property. For example, we may count the frequency of the property, redness, of 1000 roses and find all 1000 are red. From this we might infer (wrongly) that all roses are red. The next 50 might be white, and prove our first hypothesis as wrong or inadequate.

There is a basic problem in the use of scientific method. Can we form a conclusion from observing some instances, which will enable us to predict other instances, including future cases, with reliability?

Perhaps not, but when we have been examining a specific occurrence for many years, say, the boiling-point of water at sea level, and the answer is always the same, we become more and more sure that future occurrences will not be different. The observed facts can then be taken as a law.

The method of hypothesis develops the inductive method a stage further. It consists of an attempt to order facts and so reveal the pattern. In using this method we

Pinpoint the problem demanding solution.

Collect data.

Form an hypothesis.

Test the hypothesis.

Must, if the hypothesis does not pass the given test, reformulate the hypothesis and gather further data, if necessary.

Test reformulated hypothesis, and accept it if it passes the tests.

It is not an easy job to formulate problems that require solution, and that will also bear fruitfully in the solution of allied problems. As well as factual knowledge, deep insight into the problem, akin to intuition, is required. Research team leaders are valuable men, and it requires scientific genius to ask the significant question. Problems are seldom self-evident in the data itself, and it often requires a break in the continuity of thought—the intuitive "leap in the dark"—before progress to a solution can be made.

The probability concept and statistics are concerned not so much with the event itself as with the evidence as to whether or not the event will occur.

We must make sure that all relevant evidence is available to us and that we interpret it correctly.

"The probability that Australia will win this test is 0.7."

With the convention that 1 represents that the event will occur and 0 that it will not, the phrase means that on the evidence we had at the time the statement was made, the probability of Australia's winning was greater than England's. We may not have had all the evidence, we may not have interpreted it correctly and even if we have, we have not precluded the possibility of England winning, merely said it is less likely, 3:7.

Much management information falls into this category and the statistician needs to be able to explain to the management team that many management decisions are made under conditions of uncertainty. Management require ability to handle and make decisions on such information as

> "If stock can be replenished only once per day, £800 of line X will be 85% sufficient to meet daily sales. If 90% certainty of meeting all daily sales is required, then £870 must be carried . . . etc."

understanding what this implies and not complaining when the occasional "stockout" (which is to be expected) occurs.

Scientific Method and the Social Sciences

In the category of Social Sciences we can include economics, social theories and investigations into management theory, practice and control, as pertinent to our study.

Three differences between the Natural Sciences and the Social Sciences become apparent:

Firstly, the facts under investigation tend to be very numerous and often very difficult to isolate. We can seldom carry out laboratory experiments on the human situation in controlled conditions akin to those in the physical sciences. There is, for instance, a laboratory at Bethel, U.S.A., carrying out experiments on human reactions under the heading of "group dynamics", but this is well removed from what a scientist would call a laboratory experiment where he attempts to alter only one variable, keeping the others unchanged. The activities of the Common Cold Research Unit near Salisbury, where the common cold is studied under controlled conditions, might be more nearly so. There is a difficulty in carrying out controlled experiments on human beings either individually or in large groups; frequently it requires the co-operation of the individual as in the Hawthorn experiments, and often the mere fact of investigation alters the situation and so affects the results obtained. Often coercion would be necessary and this is considered morally wrong.

Secondly, in the social sciences the effects of a given cause are often delayed, thus giving time for the remainder of the variables in the situation, which one is endeavouring to hold constant, to alter. The situation in the social sciences is usually a complex one and it is not possible to isolate or control the variables affecting the situation so easily.

Thirdly, there is the distinction between laws of nature and normative laws. Whereas laws of nature are probabilities we accept, e.g. "Men have two hands", normative laws are laws based on decisions made by man. These laws must be within the limits set by nature, but can vary widely within these limits and are changeable. In the social sciences we are dealing very often with normative situations. It is important to remember that these are changeable, often being based on an ethical, moral or religious code.

> "Men do not live past 100 years of age"
> is a law of nature seldom broken;
>
> "that men in this company retire at 63"
> is a normative law and can be changed.

But it must change within the context of the law of nature; it would be useless to state:

> "That men in this company must retire at 125."

In spite of these difficulties scientific methods are making progress in the social sciences and giving us much knowledge about ourselves. Some of the new social sciences in the development stage have enormous difficulties of semantics, not so much from lack of agreement as from lack of clarity of concepts. It takes time for a science to work out the exact meaning of the words it uses. In the social sciences, including management, new words are constantly being invented and those that are well known are used in different ways by different authors. In reading any book in this subject area it is imperative to ask what meaning the author is giving to the words he uses. Communication is no less a problem for those who preach management, than for those who practise it!

CHAPTER 8

Information for Control

Perception of Data

Viewed then from a systems standpoint, what is information and why do we require it in the control or planning of systems?

> "Any system uses its sense organs to extract relevant data from its environment, processes that data into useful information and uses that information to help it to continue as a viable system in the mode of working decided upon."

This is a description of the feedback link as used by most living, social and constructed systems to control their actions and in the long run to modify their responses. Static systems and open-loop systems do not take account of information in this manner.

From the flux of phenomena, the system's perceptors will select only those events that they are capable of sensing. A human being has the main five senses of sight, hearing, touch, smell, taste and will act according to the data he can extract with these sense organs and his instinctual and trained abilities to process this data into useful information. Such sense organs might, for example, lead an individual to attempt to rescue persons he thought might be in a burning building. Another person in possession of a radio that effectively extended his sense organs might take no action because he might have already have heard that the building was empty. Yet another person who happened to have a geiger-counter handy might actively try to stop others coming to the area because he could tell that dangerous radiation was apparent. The latter two's sense organs have been extended by technical artefacts so that they perceive a wider range of data.

Action taken will depend not only on data perceived and the information that has been extracted from that data. The information will be related to an existing *framework* according to the present mode of being or in the case of a socio-technical system in relation to current policy. When relating current data to the existing framework, the accepted ethic or current organization philosophy will play a large part in deciding what type of action should flow from a knowledge of the new information.

A person might be concerned with his own safety or be concerned in helping others at any cost to himself. An organization may be in a state of expansion, contraction or stability and view information accordingly. In our sophisticated world the final decision whether or not to take action may depend not so much on the intrinsic worth of the action itself as on the effects the action will have when judged in money terms. For most living systems the overall criteria is viability, continued existence as a system, measured in either real or money terms depending on circumstances. A business may supply a particular item at a financial loss in order to keep its good name. The business may continue to do this for a little while. Finally it may refuse to supply any longer and risk the consequences. Such consequences could be drastic leading to final rundown of the company.

Loss of viability can come about through action in real terms (the non-supply of an article of production because of a fire at the works) or action in money terms (non-supply because insufficient profit will be made on the article). Either may come first. The relationship between money terms and real terms is difficult to assess and certainly non-linear. For a business the final test of viability is always in money terms.

Information

What is it that flows in a control loop?

In the simple mechanical system control information and the medium that carries it may be of the same order as the main process. As previously mentioned, in a steam engine the governor will be made of metal and consist of a series of mechanical linkages of a similar nature to the main engine itself. The main engine in its operation will activate the governor which is so adjusted that at a certain speed the linkages will act to reduce the input of steam to the main system and so control to a predetermined speed or level. The mechanical governor has "sampled" conditions of operation and fed the information back in the same physical medium. In more advanced systems the control loop is not of the same order as the main process itself, but originates in perceptors that sample the output of the process. The data collected by the perceptors is carried in some medium and is processed into "information" on which decisions are made to alter input parameters and sometimes in the case of constructed systems to alter the structure of the system itself. The control loop tells us *about* the process. In more sophisticated systems the control loop collects descriptive data about the process it purports to control. Such data may be in the form of:

words,

numbers used as labels,

numbers on the ratio scale that can be operated on mathematically.

After processing and examination, the decisions taken have to be translated back into a form of action that can affect the process and its input parameters. An integral part of the problem of handling data in a control loop is the decision regarding what medium it shall be carried in:

an individual's head (brain),

a group of people's heads (necessitating talking),

on paper (necessitating the ability to read and write),

on tape, magnetic or paper (necessitating some type of visual or aural output),

by wire, using a code (necessitating the understanding of the code),

by radio; through water, etc., and in many other ways.

The effectiveness of a control loop and hence the effectiveness of the system it controls may well be as much dependent on the effectiveness of the carrying medium as of the data that is carried. Frequently loss of control in a system can be attributed to failure of the carrying medium

TABLE 6

Information flow in some feedback loops with emphasis on perception and its effects

	Individual's perception in a given situation (e.g. burning building)		Business information (e.g. perception of production)
	(without equipment)	(with equipment)	
Sense organs	Sight Hearing Touch Smell Taste	Human sense organs plus additional perception provided by equipment	Employees who fill out data sheets Automatic recording
Data	Sees building with several doors and windows Hears noise going on	As individual sees the same situation	Quantitative reports covering 1. Quantities of items 2. Measurement of attributes i.e. Quality Written reports where no units of measurement
Processing	Reference to existing framework of knowledge. Decides it is important to know what is happening inside building	Decides to use equipment to find out what is happening inside building	Data processed using chosen management technique Information related to budget and policy

Mode of working	Enquiring Concerned with personal safety Concerned with helping others	Enquiring	Expansion Stable state Contraction
Information	Appears to be a fire Others may need help Need to confirm above (decision point)	Equipment shows no one present but dangerous radiation (decision point)	New large market located (decision point)
Action	1. Locates door, walks through investigates Action completed *or* 2. Walks through Smells burning, retreats back through door, rings fire alarm	Warns others to keep away	Consideration of plans to exploit market
Money value of action	In this case No money value attached to expenditure of time	Cost of using equipment and subsequent warning action taken	Although goods needed, cannot manufacture at price market can bear. No further action taken. Enquiry costs written off

rather than ineffectiveness of the data. The result may be the same, loss of control in the process, but the system designer in carrying out "repairs" needs to distinguish clearly between the two: lack of information (an information problem), breakdown in the carrying medium (a technical problem). Table 6 gives some examples of the way in which information is perceived, flows through information loops containing decision points, and finally influences action in the physical world.

Organization of Information

How do we organize data collection and subsequent information in a constructed socio-technical system for it to be of use in decision making?
Table 7 shows how this may be done taking the information through several stages.

Collection	Collection of data.
Processing	Selection of processing technique. Processing of the data. Reference to existing framework.
Decision-making	Listing of alternative courses of action and the probabilities of stated consequences. Selection of a consequence and its related course of action, in the light of the policy of the organization and according to some value-system.
Implementation	Action to implement; decision returned to existing framework to act as precedent.

Almost as important as the data itself in its effect on the type of action finally taken is the choice of processing technique. For example, viewed

TABLE 7

Information flow in feedback loop with emphasis on selection of alternatives

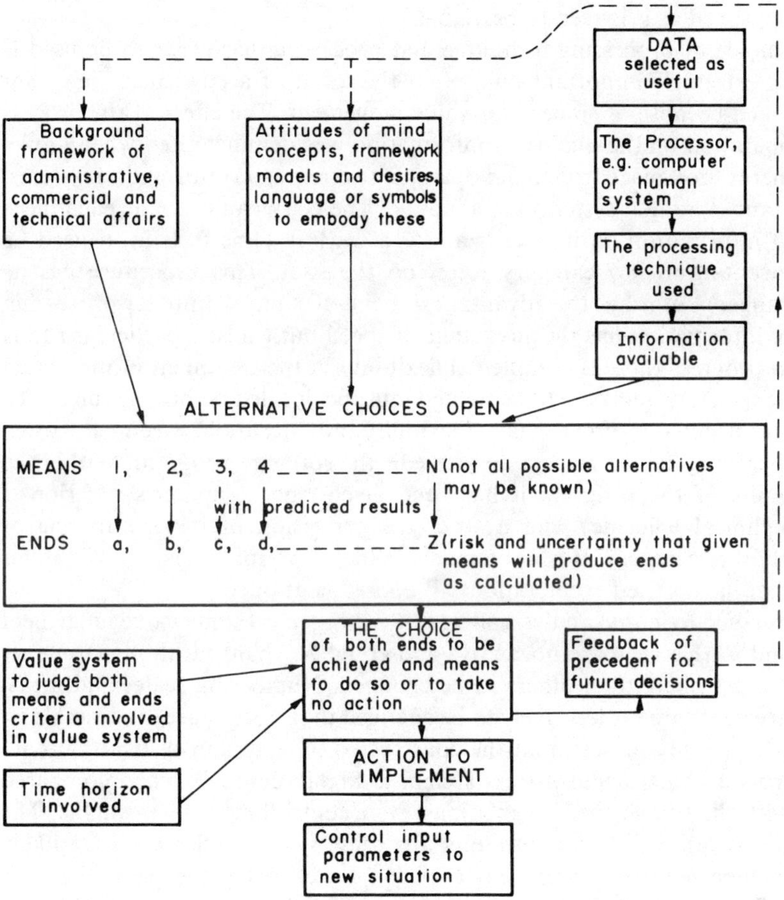

ITERATION MAY BE REQUIRED OF THE EARLIER STAGES before a final choice can be made.

on pure financial terms, costs and income, the building of the Victoria Underground line in London did not at first take place as costs involved were said to far outweigh likely income over many years. Widen the base and examine the proposition on cost/benefit terms taking in third-party interests and the cost of congestion, then the proposition is approved as it is seen to be viable.

Choice of processing technique and processing hardwear to be used is an extremely important one, often the result of a particular viewpoint taken because of some prior value judgement. The effect of the process operation on the quality of information was demonstrated when movements took place from hand operated to computers information systems. Hand-operated systems are adaptive. The clerk can examine each piece of information on its merits and deal with it as he feels fit, if need be inventing a new category for it on the spot. This procedure has its dangers but it has the advantage of being flexible. Computer processing of information has the advantage of speed but whilst a particular run is in progress there is complete inflexibility in the treatment of individual items. How items are to be treated must be decided before the run starts, and decided in great detail. Flexibility only occurs between runs when there may be the opportunity to edit the software program. Within the limits of the program it has been given, the computer's criterion is technical efficiency and a strict categorization of items into one or another category. It is not a machine that is useful in dealing with items that have varied connotations all operative at once.

Pursued to a final analysis all figures are based on some value judgement and in this view are normative and could be changed, though some are far less likely than others to be changed. Numbering scales and measurements are far less likely to be changed than cost figures and rankings. It can easily be seen that the constructed information system that controls a constructed process system is highly complex when compared with the simple speed regulating-device controlling a steam engine. The information system controlling a process system will more than likely include iterative procedures that could well delay the passage of the information and more than likely conflicting value systems will be introduced at various points of the information loop. Regarded in detail from a systems point of view it is a wonder such a control loop works at all. And of course sometimes it does not do so very satisfactorily.

Unit of Data

To be of value, the information we extract from our data

1. Must tell us something we need to know. It must tell us something new that we do not know already, or confirm our existing knowledge where we are not certain.
2. It must enable us to take a new course of action, or in some circumstances, such as local authority expenditure, it must confirm that our present course of action is correct.

The unit of data therefore is not an absolute unit, it is relative to the specific system that is being dealt with. For that system the unit of data will be the smallest incremental item of change we *decide* to take notice of. The decision to take note of such data is because by doing so and collecting it, it is found that the data builds up into a data base from which relevant information can be extracted on which to base decisions that will control the system. Where the control loop is extrinsic to the system it controls, that is, external to it and man-constructed, continual thought will have to be given to the question "Is the right data being collected in order to control this system effectively?" In practice the size of the data unit will be related to the costs of collecting it. Also the triviality or importance to the system of specific data will be related to the costs of collecting and processing.

Value of Information

Collection and processing of information and subsequent action should lead to some type of benefit to the main system. If this does not occur then any socio-technical system, being an open system existing through trading with its environment, will gradually lose its "tension", run down and cease to be viable. At the very least the cost of supply an information system to act as a feedback link to a constructed system should be less than the benefits its use induces. As the process and relevant information system are often already in existence when the effectiveness calculation is made, the proposition is best stated at the margin; will the increased expenditure on an information system be more than offset by the increased benefits that accrue from its use?

This is a difficult calculation, for whereas the costs can always be minutely calculated, the benefits accrue not from the efficiency with which the information is collected, processed and presented but on the effective use to which such information is subsequently put. Although vital to the viability and continued existence of the management information system itself, the persons operating this system have little control over the subsequent use of the information they produce. They are only one link in the overall information feedback chain.

Biased Information

Once the designers of a constructed system have decided the way in which the feedback loop of their process system is to handle information and the type of questions it will be set up to answer, the collected information must be placed into the categories agreed upon. These categories act like screens or filters through which the information must pass (Fig. 8.1). What information passes depends on the shape of the holes, that is the categories and classifications.

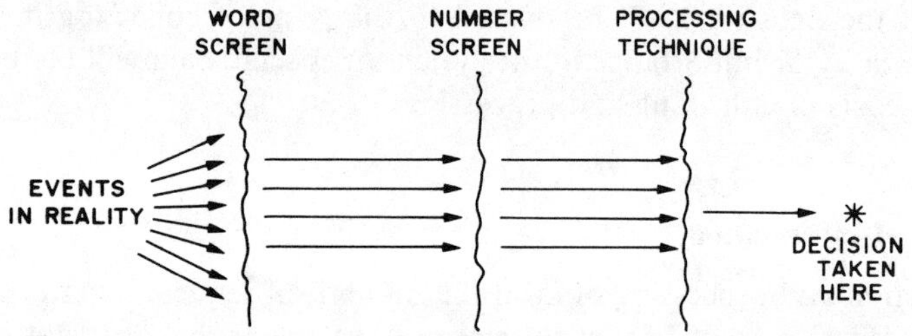

Fig. 8.1. Classificatory screens.

There is then a danger of the information becoming biased as it is forced into given categories. The computer or even hand-operated information systems, become based on quantitative data supported by a few written statements. Information that cannot be expressed in this manner is unable to pass along the information loop and is not available for consideration in the decision-making process, so that managers making decisions may not have available to them the key information pertinent to their decision. The irrational influences of emotion, morale and mood are nearly always missing in an information system. Many constructors of systems would say that they omit these aspects on purpose as the system must be rational, whereas in fact they may do it simply because they are unskilled in taking account of irrational elements present in any human situation. The idea of introducing irrational elements into an information loop may appal the reader. This is probably because he has been conditioned not to see the need. Where irrational elements are not included the end result is to make decisions on information not in accordance with the reality of the situation. The missing elements finally show themselves, perhaps in the form of strikes that could have been averted if attention had been focused and the problem identified at an earlier stage.

Management Information System

What is a management information system? This descriptive phrase tells us about the boundaries and functions of a specific type of system but the phrase does not specify anything about the properties of such a system, for instance whether it is working in realtime or whether the information is processed in monthly batches; whether the system is deterministic as in a computer information system or to some extent adaptive as in a clerical information system. What the phrase does convey is that it is a system to collect information about some process in which we are interested.

The process itself about which information is collected may be a technical production system, a service of some kind or an administrative task. It will be a constructed process system needing a constructed information system to control it. The Institute of Cost and Management Accountants defines a management information system as a system "in which defined data are collected, processed and communicated to assist those responsible for the use of resources". The situation so far can be represented as shown in Fig. 8.2.

Information is not always collected for immediate use. Take the case of a library where much of the information may be stored in case it is ever needed. Some information might possibly not be used for a hundred

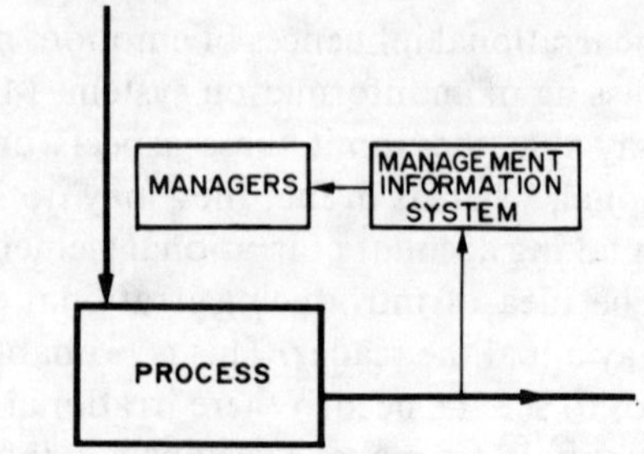

Fig. 8.2. Management information system places information on the desk of manager.

years. But information collected about a constructed process system is presumably collected in order that decisions may be made about that process and alterations made to the input parameters. The objective then is to collect data and produce information about the process so that sooner or later the input to the process or less frequently the structure of the process can be altered.

Viewed in this light the management information system is a part of the feedback link controlling a main process. The feedback link is completed when (Fig. 8.3)

1. The managers take *decisions* on the basis of the information provided.

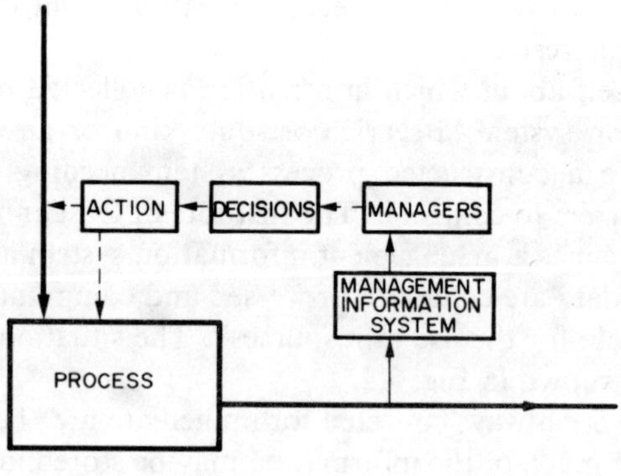

Fig. 8.3. Manager completes the feedback loop.

2. The managers take *action* to initiate change
   (i) in the input parameters of the existing process system,
   (ii) in the structure of the process system,
   or (iii) decide on the basis of incoming information that no change is necessary.

It is perhaps unfortunate that we have no word in common use to describe the information/decision/action feedback link. Such a description might emphasize that this link is an extrinsic one that has to be constantly monitored to see that it is working. Information by itself is only of potential use. It is "information in action" that creates results and either

(i) controls the main process to its existing limits,

(ii) creates new limits by taking divergent action to alter the existing goals,

or

(iii) alters the process structure the better to achieve new or existing goals.

A management information system considered as a system by itself is frequently an open-loop system, its end product is information, not information in action, and it is extremely difficult to place a value on this information it produces. This problem will be further considered in the chapter on evaluation. Meanwhile it is sufficient to state here that the final criterion of evaluation of many management information systems is the effectiveness in controlling the main process system in money value, rather than in real output. This requirement adds a further dimension of difficulty, relating money input to money output. Taking the previous example, it is only in libraries of very specific kinds that the final criterion could be the minimum cost of collecting and storing information for future use, relating money input to the amount of information stored. The management information system of an organization is frequently classed as a separate sub-system and shown as such in administrative charts. The idea is here submitted for consideration and it would clarify thinking if the information system was not given this separate emphasis but was always considered as part of the information feedback loop of the main process. In any constructed system, there is a need to integrate the information channels as part of the main system rather than to isolate them into separate sub-systems.

Information for Control

Figure 4.13 adapted the basic model to the situation where budgetary control is in operation. Typically, we shall find many departmental managers, each one measuring and controlling the input to his own department, comparing its output with standard and taking departmental action. This may be so even if the data is prepared by a central processing unit; central processing does not necessarily imply integrated interpretation. In this model of the operational situation the standard is represented by the budget. The budget is generally built to have limited flexibility only in one main aspect: "volume" of sales and hence production; in other respects the parameters are rigidly controlled. Points to watch in such a system of control are:

1. The rigidity of the control structure. If the budget is subject to annual review and if the only variable is volume, *then* after several months working, the balance of interactions between departments may well have shifted and the action of a departmental head, in trying to keep to his laid-down budget, may optimize his own results, but his success may be more than offset by the detrimental effect on other departments.
2. The effect, sometimes considerable, that the collection of data may have on the process system. Often almost identical data may be collected by different departments, because if the information system is not integrated, the communication channels may not allow such information to flow between departments.

Where departure from the budget exceeds certain set limits the matter will be referred to the Chief Executive, probably on the "management by exception" principle, and he may have authority to alter the budgets. This may ease the rigidity of the structure somewhat, but control is nevertheless departmentalized, and the full implications for the total system (organization) of the shift in relationship between the various parameters are not always considered. In certain cases the *ad hoc* alteration of a budget may merely serve to extend the life of a budget that requires radical alteration. Where alteration is made to the standard, this implies the use in two ways of the information collected, for control and as a basis for decision-taking.

Particular Conventionalized Information Systems

Quantitative reporting to management at the present time covers many aspects of the undertaking, past, present and future. With emphasis placed on reporting the past state of the company annually to shareholders, information had been collected primarily in a way suited to this report, subsequently being adapted to meet the requirements of other reports. These other reports have widely different ends in view, and to "bend" information in this manner, using it for purposes for which it was never intended, has been the cause of much bad decision-making in the past. Information should ideally be collected and presented in a way appropriate to each separate purpose.

Purpose may vary considerably (Fig. 8.4).

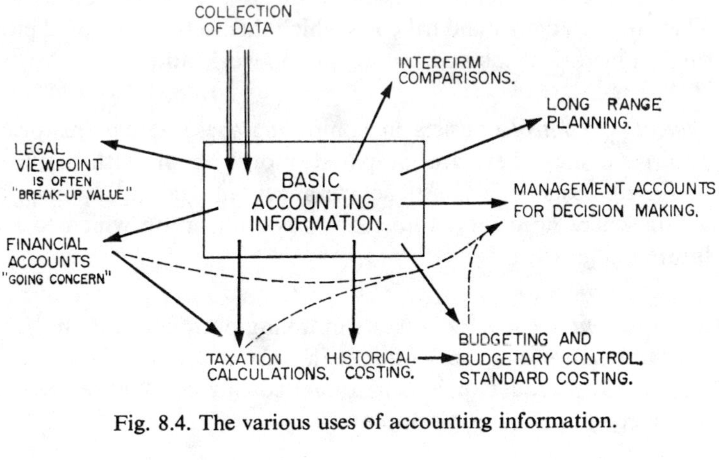

Fig. 8.4. The various uses of accounting information.

The *published accounts* stress external accountability; they are historical, "after the event", must be accurate and show the organizations position as a going concern in relation to shareholders, debtors and creditors. In the profit and loss account they give an overall view of the operating and trading position. In the balance-sheet the depreciation on long-lasting items is calculated on a conventional basis and it is frequently necessary to "go behind" the figures to see their true worth.

The legal approach is, in the main, concerned with ownership of property and consequently concentrates on the balance-sheet, interpreting it in a specific way. There is a tendency to view an organization at a "break-up" value rather than as a going concern.

The taxation position is normally derived by taking the financially calculated profit figure as a starting-point and then calculating the liability to tax by means of a separate set of rules.

The *historical costing system* gives a detailed account of how labour, materials and overheads have been expended in the operations of the organization.

Budgets are short-term plans projecting the organization as it is. They are based on standard costs which themselves are based either on past historical costs or, better still, on work study.

Budgetary control consists in comparing these actual (historical) cost results as they are prepared month by month with the budgeted costs, analysing the variances and taking appropriate action where necessary. Information is built up on which to base future budgets.

Management accounting consists in taking both financial and costing information and presenting it in a form suitable for decision-making. Techniques such as marginal costing or other approaches of the economist may be employed.

Speed of preparation is important. The information to be discussed at a weekly or monthly management meeting is of little use if it does not arrive in time for consideration. Consequently, reasonable estimates may be used where definite figures are not available in time.

Interfirm comparisons may be of cost or financial data. All undertakings need to compare on the same basis to make the exercise meaningful. As it is unlikely that all organizations taking part analyse their figures in the required way, special analyses will be necessary. If the comparisons are to be continuous then it may be worth while adopting the particular analyses as permanent features.

Long-range forecasting involves consideration of change and the use of assets in different ways, the disposal of capital into different assets, the replacement of assets. The exercise requires its own particular approach often nearer to that of the economist than that of the accountant. There is much in the way of new techniques being developed in this field. Because they cover the future, reports dealing with long-range plans tend to cut across present organization and data may have to be reorganized. A factor that concerns all long-range reporting is the erosion of the money unit. Pounds sterling (or other currencies) may always look the same, but suffer devaluation. A 1938 £, a 1948 £ and a 1978 £ may look the same but they are not: to add them together would not produce any useful total.

Integrated Accounting

Rather than attempt to use information collected with a "financial" bias to answer problems in all these areas, it would appear to be a better approach to collect all basic information and then to examine this basic information in the way required by each specific problem. Integrated accounting is an attempt to do this.

In integrated accounting the basic data is first analysed and presented in a format suitable for management decisions which will be made at weekly or monthly intervals. The control of the present situation is our first concern. Later the same data is analysed in other forms to prepare the shareholders' accounts, the taxation returns, and comparisons. Special reports such as legal valuations, reorganizations of capital and long-range planning combine specialized external information with that received from the day-to-day flow. Such reports are required at random intervals and may be regarded as "off-line" as regards the data flow. They change rather than control the present situation.

Many books have been written on the various fields of accounting and the reader is referred to the book of his choice for specific aspects. Our purpose here is to realize that the subject has diversified, because knowledge of operating in each field has required a specific training and this has tended to emphasize the different approaches. Accounting information has become departmentalized within the accounting function and the problem is to reintegrate it, so that accounting information of all types flows freely and quickly within the organization. Integrated data-processing systems are helping us to achieve this position. Traditional methods of double-entry book-keeping, relatively unchanged since the fourteenth century, are being examined to see if they can be improved and in many cases changes in approach are taking place. As long as the basic integrity of the system is maintained, there is no reason why these moves should not be welcomed.

Auditing. Auditing involves scrutiny of the recorded information to verify the accuracy of recording and the legality of the analysis. It is often carried out on a sampling basis, say 15% of items checked, in order to keep down costs. In checking the recorded quantitative information, reading documents and asking questions, the auditors do more than merely find past inaccuracies, they impress on others the necessity that the system should record correct data. This scrutiny has significance for the future, as recorders of information will tend to be more accurate if they know their work is likely to be checked. The audit also has an effect on the difficult-to-control ethical situation, as many of the questions asked will be to ensure that all legal requirements have been carried out; for example, company auditors in their report on the balance-sheet categorically state that all is in order as far as they have been able to discover. If this is not so, they mention it.

AUDITORS' REPORT

We have examined the accounts which have been prepared under the historical cost convention as modified by revaluations of the premises and of the investments.

In our opinion they give, under that convention, a true and fair view of the state of affairs of the XYZ Company Ltd. at the 31 March 1978 and of the profit and source and application of funds for the year ended on that date.

We have also examined the current cost statement together with the notes thereon for the year ended 31 March 1978. In our opinion the statement has been properly prepared, in accordance with the methods set out in the notes, to give the information set out in the Accounting Standards Committee's interim recommendation on inflation accounting of November 1977.

Certified Accountants

June 1978

Internal audit. Auditing is based on the principle of independent checking. The original work of one person is checked by a second and possibly a third. None of these should be in a position of authority over the other. Auditing takes time and much of it is "after-the-event". For this reason the organization itself often checks much of its own work, by means of an internal audit. This function does not relieve the external auditor of his responsibility, but it lightens his load and he will obviously take note that it is being carried out. The internal audit is carried out continuously throughout the year. It may consist of spot checks, say, on cash balances or regular running checks, for example, perpetual inventory control. Although working within the company, the internal audit team must be a distinct and separate part of it to work efficiently. Audit may be carried out in many areas where the statutory audit is not required, such as management efficiency audit, organization audit or methods audit. Care should be taken that auditing does not unduly impede the information flow.

Proposed Control System

A control system which overcomes many of the faults discussed in this chapter is indicated in Fig. 4.14. Here all information is processed and interpreted centrally in relation to the budget, before being issued to the various departments for effective action. This structure will at least in theory produce a much better control, for each item of information can be studied in relation to all other information and the optimum solution for the overall situation arrived at. This interpretive function would be presided over by "the controller" of the organization. It includes integrative, analytical and decisional aspects, both to control the ongoing process and to build up information which at discrete intervals of time will be used in deciding what changes to make in the standard. Integration of the departmental data attempts to obviate suboptimization so that control action will be for the benefit of the whole. Theoretically this is sound; the practical danger is the amount of time involved in extracting the needed information if the data are numerous. At this level control action works basically on "exception" data and the size of the "exception" will have to be determined. The higher and lower "action" limits require to be reasonably spaced, so that the system is not frustrated by continually undergoing correction in opposite directions, as could occur if the limits are placed very near to each other.

Much control is achieved merely by summation of data and comparison with standard, but in many other cases the data will need to be analysed and interpreted by mathematical techniques. Such analyses build up information on which future changes in standard will be based. This does not necessarily imply monolithic centralized control, although there could be dangers of that occurring if this method of control were wrongly used. The departments should have some representation on the interpretive function, being trained to understand that it is the good of the organization that is being sought rather than departmental success. This stresses the need at all levels of management to know and accept whatever "good", i.e. goal, is being sought for the organization as a whole. With the processing of more information more quickly we are, in effect, able to reconsider the budget at each meeting and thus there can be more flexibility in the relationship of the input parameters. One reason for the rigidity of budgetary control so far has been our limited ability successfully to control many input parameters at once, and so we tend to hold them rigid and only vary one or two.

The practical difficulties to this approach are the amount of information to be considered and the time involved. These limit the level at which optimization can take place. The computer is our tool of control in the information field and once programmed it can work very rapidly. So far data tend to be processed on an historical basis, i.e. "after the event", though the time intervals are getting shorter. The ultimate in computer control of an information system will be "real-time" control. Each event as it occurs will feed itself into the system and be immediately combined with all the other information existing in the system and its effects worked out, so that cumulative effects and trends may become more important than absolute limits. Our problem then becomes one of input, effective action on the output without too long a time-lag, and the human problems of motivation if no decision-making is allowed at lower levels.

Diagnosis of Poor Working of the System

Efficient control should not allow a system to arrive at this state, but where deterioration in operation has occurred it may be traced to three groups of causes.

(a) Control has been not fully present and this absence has allowed the situation to deteriorate, i.e. *slacken*.

(b) The plan standard is no longer capable of achievement. Possibly due to *change in the external environment* and a new standard is required immediately.

(c) The process being controlled has changed or deteriorated, and it is time for a system analysis of the process with a view to introducing a new system.

Information for Change

A diagnosis of this sort prompts us to state our objectives in obtaining information and define in greater detail our concept of "control". As already explained, control in a system is not limited to maintaining a static situation in equilibrium, it also embraces the dynamic role of harnessing change. This is particularly true for the organization viewed as a system. The homeostatic controls must not preclude growth (and in some cases decay); but it must be controlled growth or otherwise growth may become a weakness.

Continued growth in size may not always be beneficial for the organization. There comes a point within any particular state of technology and management organization where economies of scale and strengths of differentiation are offset by difficulties of control and communication in the larger unit. But the state of technology and our knowledge of management organization are continually improving, and for this reason the point of balance at which a particular organization reaches efficiency will undergo change with a tendency towards increase in size.

Growth in size is not the only form of growth. Limitation of size may mean size of labour force, size of plant, size of site, size of capital, size of organizational capacity. Organizations limited in size for any reason may yet grow in quality, improving the quality and efficiency of such assets as they do have.

Some smaller organizations may be considered to be entirely at the mercy of the market. When they lose their equilibrium, for example by giving poor quality or wrong delivery dates or charging too high a price, they soon meet the "corrective" action of external market forces.

But many modern organizations and particularly the larger ones are not at the mercy of the market in quite the same way. The attempt to obtain some monopoly control over their particular market is often quite successful even if only limited and somewhat temporary. This may, for example, be as a result of advertising branded goods or building up a public image. Where this happens and the organization is able to influence its environment to some extent, the direct play of market forces is mitigated and their effect is often delayed. Thus many former external decisions become internal decisions decided on by the organization as a matter of policy and not forced on them by direct market forces. It is then vital to have an efficient information and control system, as the results of wrong or poor decision may not show up for some considerable time. When these poor decisions are eventually revealed as such, it may be quite difficult by then to initiate corrective policy. It is necessary, therefore, to the continuance of the organization that sufficiently reliable and up-to-date information on which to base decisions is available at all times.

Change

"Change" is one of the basic philosophical concepts supporting Western society. In such a dynamic society, part of the executive's task is to seek change, to progress, to alter his production or administrative system for the better. To be "better" implies to be more effective, as measured in terms of the materials and effort to which we attach an economic significance. A manager innovates to stay in business. The static society or organization is prone to fossilization and may perish.

"Change" can occur in the resources used, the administrative and technical processes or in the service provided and final product made (Fig. 8.5). To reach a position where change is possible a manager will need to be in possession of new knowledge and ideas and these he may have gained from accidental discovery, deliberate decision to experiment in order to achieve a particular purpose or by obtaining new knowledge from elsewhere. In every organization there should be a department, or at least one person, whose prime concern is the consideration of change; firstly considering what may be possible and then

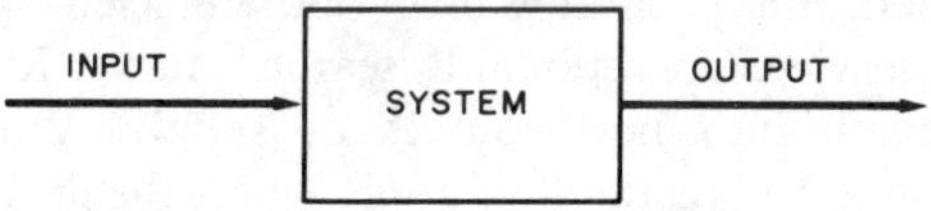

Fig. 8.5. Change in a process system.

Input	System	Output
New sources of material	New combination of material, skill and energy	Changes imposed by the price system (supply and demand) as constrained by law, morals, rationing, etc.
New types of material	New discoveries in the technology	(i) Fashion changes (ii) Better products due to change in technology
New skills		(iii) Consumer demand changes. Different products demanded due to changes in aims and values of society

how and when it may be introduced. Although it may be assumed that any company at the moment making its way has at least one good selling line, this line may not, or rather will not, last for ever. Attention therefore must be paid to research and development and also to the question of patents.

Only management themselves can decide when is the time to think about change, though a decision may be thrust upon them by an attempted take-over bid or dangerous drop in turnover. The division of managers into "thrusters and sleepers" is quite appropriate. Some organizations look for change at every possible corner—it is budgeted for when planning. Some are content to let others do the spade-work and then try to take over the new ideas. Change is not directly related to profits, and too much change as well as too little may cause a fall in present profits. What is looked for is change that does not adversely affect present profits and at the same time strengthens the future position. In his approach to change there are many factors that can help the manager, but most important is the attitude of those holding positions of authority. Once having made the decision, which is an interaction of personal and company personality, to be a thruster rather than a sleeper, he may decide to tackle "change" at many points; the type of raw material used and the source of supply, the operational methods used in production and to provide the service, and through market and design research the volume and type of service or product produced. Value analysis will help him to see that the changed product will in fact benefit him profitably or by more efficient use of resources in the case of a service. Operational Research, Market Research, Design Research, research into new sources of supply, Work Study and Systems Analysis are all methods of approaching the problem of change. With an existing product it may be sufficient to apply the specific tool of change to the specific area felt to be in need of tightening up. With a new product in mind it will be necessary to have a team co-ordinating all aspects of the research and change, not necessarily a full-time team, but one that meets fairly frequently so that continuity is preserved.

What is said above applies equally to non-profit making social organizations. A club, for example, may for years make no change in the services it provides and so imperceptibly over the years become completely out of touch with what its members require.

Research and development can be distinguished at the levels of pure research, applied research and product development. Pure research consists of the pursuit of knowledge for its own sake; this kind of research, which is expensive and shows no immediate cash returns, will normally be undertaken by government research establishments and universities.

Applied research will take place within a definite field with the object of advancing the industry, being carried out in research association establishments with Department of Industry and industrial support. Product development is mostly carried out at the level of the individual organization or group, although there may be a routine for referring specific problems of general interest to the trade association research establishments. It behoves the manager to know what progress is being made in each area relevant to the organization for which he works, and in the short term he will be most vitally concerned with product development. All research and product development costs money but it is essential that some takes place if the organization is to remain viable and continue to exist.

In the life of each product, four stages can be distinguished:

(i) A period of research and development prior to its being placed on the market. This is a time of heavy expense.

(ii) The initial selling period when it is hoped that the development costs will be fully recovered.

(iii) The period of profit after initial development costs have been recovered. It may then be possible to drop the price a little. Novelty is still promoting sales and patents are still inhibiting competitors.

(iv) The decline when the product is no longer new. Better, or at least different ones, are challenging it. The patents may have run out, or be no longer worth keeping up.

In administrative units, social research may show new needs to be met, at once or as funds become available, and technical research within the units will show more efficient forms of organization to carry out the administration.

It is necessary to understand and be in sympathy with the rhythm of change within local and world markets and work with it, not against it. Outdated products and services do not sell and very advanced products do not sell without a lot of effort and customer-education, which is expensive and needs large capital. For many organizations it will probably suffice to aim to be just slightly ahead of current products and product design; so that the organization has a reputation of leadership with all the advantages that entails, yet at the same time is very much in present-day markets. Change consists in leading on from one product to a slightly different one and showing the need for it. Only occasionally can complete breaks occur in the type of artefact made and the means of production used, which is as well, for the general public can only assimilate change at a definite pace. Social outlook is the main control; in general social and mental attitudes change much more slowly than the corresponding technological processes.

"Fashion" is variation on a particular theme. The basic need is there and accepted; the way it is met can vary, and those organizations not meeting the need in the current mood, which they themselves can affect (possibly even control, by advertising), find sales dropping. Where fashion changes become rapid, profit margins are higher but unfashionable stocks, though they may meet the basic need, are virtually unsaleable.

Introducing Change in the System

Where in the overall production or administrative system does one make an initial attack? At this point the so-called Pareto[1] principle can be of great use. By listing the points requiring attention, then sorting into order of the effect they are likely to achieve, the important few can be distinguished from the unimportant many. Out of, say, a possible 15 points that appear to require attention, three may constitute 85% of the task. It will be necessary to allocate persons to carry out this review of the situation. Docs onc introduce a new team, such as a peripatetic operational research team, or does one use existing personnel? The problem is always there. Existing managers who might be willing to accept the change in relation to problems they have worked out for

[1] J. M. Juran, *Managerial Break-through*, McGraw-Hill, 1964.

themselves will be fully occupied. A research team will have the time to make investigations, but there is no guarantee that their findings will be accepted by line management. Alternatively higher authority may seek to impose the research team's recommendations on line managers and this will cause conflict. If it can be arranged without too much strain on the structure of the organization or the manager's personality, the manager should be involved in the research whilst still retaining line authority. For what is under review is both methods of operation and attitudes. If a link can be forged to lead on from the old to the new, so much the better socially and from the point of view of the image of the organization. If not, breakdown in the organization will occur and individuals will suffer unless a formula of change, e.g. transfer to another area, covers the break.

Once a new course of action has been shown to be technically possible, the next stage will be a review of the financial situation to be expected when the resultant change has taken place. There may be an accountant on the research team. The proposed change must be inspected financially in three ways. Firstly as a project standing on its own, secondly by evaluating the effects of introducing the change into the existing structure, thirdly in relation to other feasible changes the organization might introduce, since resources are probably limited.

The change will no doubt bring in profit but it will generally necessitate capital outlay. Calculations will take place as to the profitability, using the techniques of pay-back period, discounted cash flow, rate of return and other methods. The decision to implement becomes bound up with sources of funds and financial considerations. The techniques mentioned above are purely techniques and give answers which are no more reliable than the input. As forecasts are being made on conditions up to 10 years ahead, there is much scope for discussion of what may occur in the future and this will widely affect the calculated profit. The arguments in favour of change may largely be conjectural. But expenditure of capital outlay occurs in the present, and the decision to implement *now* depends on availability of funds. Where new capital is not readily available it becomes doubly important that the upheaval incidental to change should not too adversely affect the "bread-and-butter" profit. This is the real argument of the "sleepers". It is a sound argument and must be answered in detail and thoroughly if progress is to be made. The change must be shown to be technically possible, to give future advantages, to affect present operations not too unfavourably and to take place at an assimilable rate. It must also be shown that the present situation cannot continue to exist unaltered and that it will tend to deteriorate. Consultants help as they bring the experience of one organization to bear on another. The published accounts of other organizations may point to the desirability of change. The spur of change is improved effectiveness, reduction in costs and prices, profit and growth and, in the long run, power and expansion. The decision to change is based on the manager's attitude towards the benefits that are expected from the new discovery compared with the losses due to changing the existing situation. To make the correct decision, to control and guide the system in the required direction, the manager must have the relevant information. Having discussed the types of information that can be made available, we must now examine how effectively this information reaches the manager.

CHAPTER 9

Processing the Information

Summation, averaging and comparison may not of themselves extract all available information lying within a given amount of data.
More sophisticated techniques embodying statistical inference and various mathematical modelling and programming techniques may reveal patterns that are not at first apparent when looking at unprocessed data. In using such techniques, information about the individual item may sometimes be lost but information about the overall pattern is gained. Processed information is needed as a base for management decisions. Without it the manager is swamped in detail.

Statistics

One approach in scientific method is to proceed by induction from simple enumeration. Statistics can be described as a set of techniques for making more meaningful the things we count, or the data we collect. Operations are carried out on the data, tabulating, classifying, averaging and comparing, to put them into a form which will help us in our decision-making. We operate on the data in accordance with mathematical concepts or models, and it is important to make sure that the concept being used is suitable for the particular data, otherwise "nonsense" answers will result. For example, the nominal scale of numbering is suitable merely to describe items, the ordinal scale to describe in a definite order, the interval scale to describe where there are distinct intervals of the same size and the ratio scale to describe data with intervals starting from zero. The arithmetic mean which is relative to the interval scale would be useless to obtain the average size shoes worn by a sample of 100 people. It might work out at 8.643 which is "nonsense" and the mode or most frequently found item, which is the central tendency for the nominal scale, is what is required here; this might be size $8\frac{1}{2}$ or 9.

Much of the work carried out by businesses on accountancy, costing, labour returns, sales analysis, etc., can be classed as statistics; the object being to reduce data to forms, such as averages, ranges, totals, etc., which make the data both easier to understand and to manipulate. In industry a further branch of statistics, statistical *inference*, becomes very important as a means of saving time and money. We can easily find out the characteristics of a sample. Then, by statistical inference we can discover with what accuracy we can draw conclusions about the bulk of population from which the sample was taken, and how big a sample we need to take.

Tests of significance are important too. We need to test whether the difference between two samples means they have been drawn from different bulks or whether the difference could arise by chance in sampling from one single bulk. Finally, the concept of probability is tending to be given more and more prominence in our decision-making processes as a method to be used when dealing with conditions of uncertainty.

The normal curve. Many industrial statistical techniques depend on the properties of the normal curve. This is a mathematical curve of distribution. It is regular and a great deal is known about it. Most distributions in actual life are not so regular, being "skewed" one way or another or following a different pattern such as the binomial or the Poisson distributions. Nevertheless, many distributions approximate sufficiently closely to the normal curve to let us apply the known properties of normal curves to the actual distribution under review. From Fig. 9.1 it can be seen how items are spread about the centre point. Measurements are expressed in terms of "standard deviations".

The standard deviation. This is a measure of how items are distributed about an average. It is calculated as seen in Table 8.

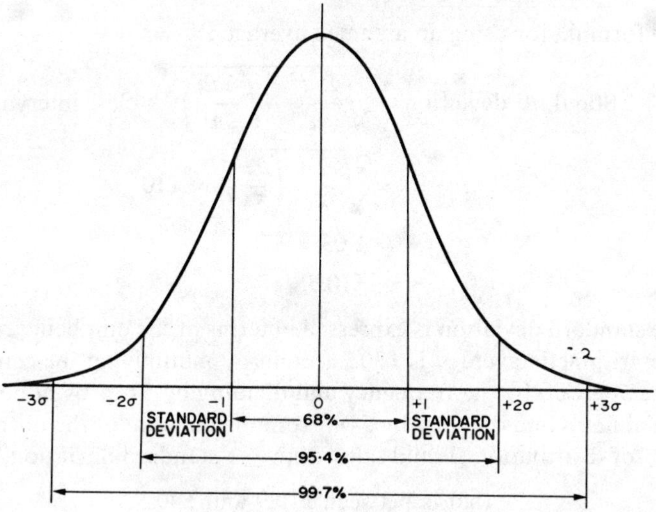

Fig. 9.1. The normal curve.

TABLE 8

Measurement £	Average of class	Frequency of occurrence (f)	Deviation from an assumed average £25 by class intervals of £10 (d)	$f \times d$	$f + d^2$
Up to £10	£5	2	−2	−4	8
Over £10 but under £20	£15	6	−1	−6	6
Over £20 but under £30	£25	18	0	0	0
Over £30 but under £40	£35	18	+1	+18	18
Over £40 but under £50	£45	10	+2	+20	40
		54 (number of items)		+28 (Σfd)	72 (Σfd^2)

The formula for using an assumed average is

$$\text{Standard deviation} = \sqrt{\frac{\Sigma fd^2}{n} - \left(\frac{\Sigma fd}{n}\right)^2} \times \text{class interval}$$

$$= \sqrt{\frac{72}{54} - \left(\frac{28}{54}\right)^2} \times £10$$

$$= 1.03 \times £10$$

$$£10.3.$$

The standard deviation is expressed in terms of the unit being measured. The arithmetic average is £30.2 (found by multiplying the centre point of each group by the frequency and dividing by 54 or by adding up the actual items and dividing by 54). From the diagram of the normal curve 68 % of distribution should fall within ±1 standard deviation,

that is between £19.9 and £40.5;

95 % of distribution should fall within ±2 standard deviations,

that is between £9.6 and £50.8.

In the example, the pattern of our measurement follows the normal curve reasonably well but is not a complete fit.

Statistical quality control. The aim is not only to detect rejects but also to prevent them occurring. Control of a single dimension is carried out on two charts, the mean and the range. The machine is set to make the part to the correct dimension, the first few made are measured and the process average worked out. This may be slightly away from the measurement set, but not sufficient to require the machine to be reset. Applying the theory of the normal curve, it is decided what number of defects can be accepted due to chance variations in the setting of the machine, say 1 in 1000 (±3.09 standard deviations) and the outer control limits of the mean chart are calculated from the samples. Inner warning limits (1 in 40, ±1.96 standard deviations) are also calculated. It is important at this stage to check that the control limits calculated fall within the tolerance limits of the design.

As the process proceeds, small samples are taken from each batch and the mean and range calculated. Where the machine tends to go off its correct setting (out of control) this can be seen on the chart (Fig. 9.2), as a sequence of plots moving towards one of the limits; the machine can be stopped and reset *before* defectives are made. The range in the sample is similarly plotted on the range chart and gives additional information.

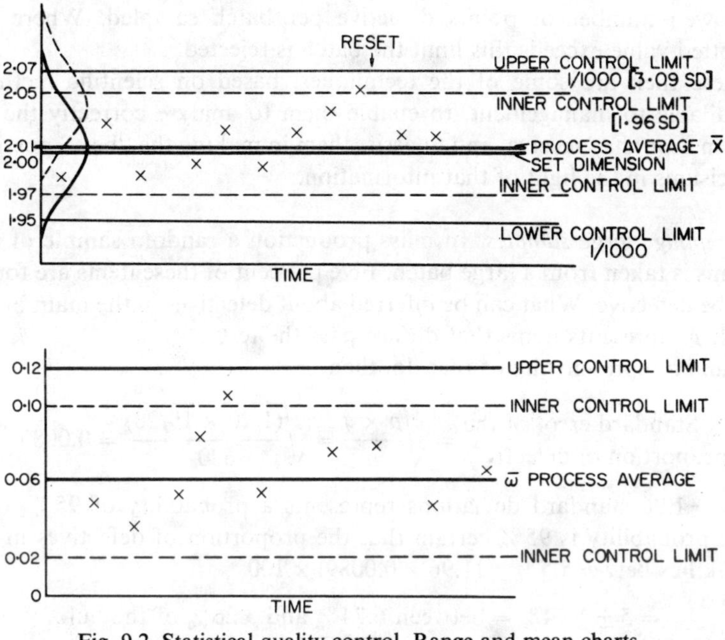

Fig. 9.2. Statistical quality control. Range and mean charts.

Tolerance limits and design. It may be that the control limits calculated statistically fall outside the specified tolerance limits. This means that the particular machine is incapable of making consistently accurate parts to the dimensions required. Even if the machine remains on its setting, some defectives will be made. The only courses of action if defectives are to be avoided is to buy a more accurate machine or question whether the tolerances can be greater than those laid down. It may frequently be found that alterations are possible on the design, both as to tolerance limits and to parts of the design itself, causing easier and cheaper manufacture.

Where three or four separate measurements have to be made on a small part it may not be economical to control each dimension separately. Statistical quality control is then carried out on a "points" system and a part rejected will count 1 point for each wrong measurement up to, say, 4 points in all. A line is drawn on the control chart to show the allowed number of points defective per batch sampled. Where the plotted value exceeds this limit the batch is rejected.

These then are some of the techniques, based on scientific method, available to management, to enable them to analyse correctly the information they receive, and to assist them in making the "best" possible decisions in the light of that information.

Sampling: large samples. In mass production a random sample of 600 items is taken from a large batch. Five per cent of these items are found to be defective. What can be inferred about defectives in the main bulk?

If p represents items that do not pass the test
and q represents items that do, then

$$\text{Standard error of the proportion of defectives} = \sqrt{\frac{p \times q}{n}} = \sqrt{\frac{(1/20 \times 19/20)}{600}} = 0.0089.$$

As ± 1.96 standard deviations represents a probability of 95%, then the probability is 95% certain that the proportion of defectives in the bulk lies between $5\% \pm (1.96 \times 0.0089) \times 100$

$$= 5 \pm 1.74\% = \text{between } 6.74\% \text{ and } 3.26\% \text{ of the bulk.}$$

Regardless of the size of the bulk, if large, it is the size of the sample worked on that gives information; the larger the sample worked on, the more likely it is to approximate to the whole population. If we wish to alter our level of certainty, say to 99.7%, then we would multiply by ± 3 standard deviations.

If the sample is doubled,

$$\text{S.e.p.} = \frac{(1/20 \times 19/20)}{1200} = 0.0063$$

at same level of certainty 95%.

We can be sure with 95% certainty the bulk has

$$5\% \pm (1.96 \times 0.0063) \times 100 = 5\% \pm 1.23\% = \text{between } 6.23\% \text{ and } 3.77\% \text{ defectives.}$$

We can never tell the exact number of defectives in a batch by statistical methods. To do this we would need to examine each item which would cost a lot of money and we would probably even then make mistakes, but if we are prepared to accept the statistical approach to the problem, we can save a lot of money and time.

Correlation. The technique enables the relationship between two sets of data to be made apparent. Multivariate analysis extends this to many sets of data. In the area of data reduction the "law-like" relationships developed by Ehrenberg[1] are particularly interesting.

Modelling

When using the scientific approach to organizational problem solution, exemplified by Systems Engineering and Operational Research, we frequently set up a model of the situation as an aid in understanding both the problem and its possible solution.

Models in use. Often an approach to a solution may be made in the first instance by analogy and this may prove to be very useful as long as we are quite certain that the analogy is justified. A scientific analogy may be used as long as there is found equivalence between it and the problem under review. The two things, the scientific analogy and the problem, may not look the same, nevertheless the former can be used to explain the problem as long as there is identity of underlying structure. When there is, then the scientific analogy may be called a model, e.g. the flow of water in pipes may represent flow of traffic for the solving of some traffic problems.
The definition of a model and the problem it represents may thus be given as "formal equivalence between two externally different manifestations, based on an underlying structural identity"; a working

[1] A. S. C. Ehrenberg, *Data Reduction*, John Wiley, 1975.

situation can be simulated. Results are apparent much more quickly on a model and different working conditions can be quickly run through to choose the best.

Static scale models of buildings and plant are frequently constructed to examine working situations and solve such problems as manning in steel mills, refineries, etc. Mechanically working scale models of engines, ships, planes are often made to examine their working before going ahead with the cost of a full-scale prototype.

An analogue computer may be used to simulate the actual physical conditions and so becomes an electronic model of the situation being studied. It is relatively easy to operate and the man in charge of a plant could learn to use it to run through all possible input changes and possible plant changes, in order to determine which of these it would be worthwhile putting into effect.

Mathematical Models and Analyses

Allocation models are used for those problems that arise where there are a number of activities to be performed and alternate way of doing them, and also when resources are not available for performing each activity in the most effective way. For example, limited capacity or materials have to be used to accomplish the required work in the most economical manner. The methods which can be used are linear programming and related procedures, activity analysis and other methods of mathematical programming.

Inventory models are used for fixing such schedules as the amount and time when goods should be ordered, taking into account cost of ordering and holding costs.

Waiting time models—These problems arise when either the facilities or the units requiring service stand idle, that is, wait. There are two main types:

1. Queuing models deal with arrivals that are randomly spaced, number of service units and service policy, and queue discipline or how the units are served, and the standard of service provided,

2. Sequencing models deal with the time of arrival of customers at fixed facilities.

Replacement models are concerned with situations where the equipment deteriorates or becomes obsolete (e.g. machine tools) and where the equipment is liable to complete failure (e.g. light bulbs).

Competitive models deal with external conflict due to competition and show how the effectiveness of decisions by one party depends on decisions by another party. Models cover the "Theory of games" where all players strive to win the game, but only one can achieve it, and bidding models where businesses bid against other firms for rights or opportunities.

Operation research is not necessarily mathematical in its outlook, but mathematics does produce some very powerful models and there is no doubt that operations research uses these mathematical techniques to great advantage.

The solution of operations research problems will often put accepted practices and methods in a critical light, sometimes openly, sometimes implicitly. Such criticism needs always to be constructive and delivered with patience and tact. For example, the labour difficulties that very often have to be faced before the new solution is accepted are part of the data of the problem and should be included in the calculation.

So far, operations research as a means of bringing scientific method to industry appears to have been applied somewhat piecemeal. There is no reason in principle why operational research should not be applied to the working of the organization as a whole unit, and in a continuous manner instead of being applied to the solution of *ad hoc* problems only.

Programming Techniques

These mathematical methods arrange and integrate the known data so that an optimum solution to a problem can be arrived at. Hitherto the manager has had to make decisions on inadequate information, often supplying an estimate of the gaps from his past experience and carrying out the integrating process in his own mind. In employing mathematical techniques, the manager requires to know sufficient of the mathematical approach to be able to state his problem in a manner that the mathematician can understand and work on. Apart from facts known in detail, some of the input to the problem may be subject to uncertainty and here the manager must be able to assign a numerical possibility, using, if necessary, some of the better known statistical techniques. Where it is difficult to measure the input of a particular variable it is nevertheless better to assign some value (perhaps one of rank) rather than to ignore it.

Management problems are complex, and although mathematics as a tool for managers is developing rapidly, still it is able to cope with only a limited number of variables. Where the number of variables involved goes beyond a certain point, the technique of simulation may well be of more use than programming.

Linear programming. As its name implies, this technique can be used in cases where the variables bear a linear or direct relationship to each other, and the linear programming approach assumes that the system being examined is static, stable and linear. Many industrial and management problems although not entirely of this type, approach this situation fairly closely, and linear programming as one of the simpler techniques can often supply a good working solution to such problems as:

> location of factories and distribution points;
> the most profitable product mix;
> the lowest cost manufacturing schedules.

The technique involves setting up the data in a matrix and operation on that matrix until the optimum solution is found. The problem will require a definition of what unit is to be considered to give the optimum answer. Mathematically any solution, e.g. *lowest* cost or *maximum* production regardless of cost, could be regarded as optimum, and the manager must state objectively what he regards as his criteria. This statement in itself is a very important decision and we may ask on what criteria or value-judgement it is made. The figures are then worked on by a process called iteration, within the matrix until the optimum solution is found.

The transportation problem deals with the most efficient routing from several origins to several destinations.

Example of Transportation Method of Linear Programming

A manufacturer has three factories, one at Blackburn, one at Portsmouth and one on the Continent at Antwerp. He has at the moment orders from six customers. Fixed and variable manufacturing costs for each factory are known, as also distribution charges from each factory and the prices at which sales were closed. A production schedule is required of accepted orders to show maximum profit. Selling prices being fixed, this now means minimizing costs (see Table 9). (The fixed

TABLE 9

Data available

Factory	Variable cost of manufacturing one unit	Factory capacity per period
	£	
Blackburn	50	2800 units
Portsmouth	53	1900 units
Antwerp	equivalent of 48	2900 units
		—
		7600 units

Sales	Units	Sales contract price*
		£
A (Brussels)	1000	147
B (London)	1200	128
C (Canterbury)	400	150
D (Glasgow)	800	148
E (Paris)	1400	152
F (Lyons)	1600	153
Unused capacity	1200	
	—	
	7600 units	

* N.B. Price data, and hence relative profitability, is relevant only if demand exceeds supply.

costs, being sunk, do not enter into this management decision as we are dealing with the short-term use of existing production facilities.)

Distribution charges. These cover transport, insurance, customs duties and all other charges incurred by the company in putting the goods into the hands of customer (Table 10).

TABLE 10

Blackburn to	£	Portsmouth to	£	Antwerp to	£
Customer A	39	Customer A	41	Customer A	20
B	24	B	22	B	34
C	26	C	25	C	35
D	22	D	28	D	36
E	41	E	35	E	24
F	43	F	38	F	26

An information matrix is set up showing the cost to fulfil an order, that is variable production cost plus distribution charges (Table 11).

TABLE 11

	A	B	C	D	E	F	Slack	Total factory production
Blackburn	89	74	76	72	91	93	0	2800
Portsmouth	94	75	78	81	88	91	0	1900
Antwerp	68	82	83	84	72	74	0	2900
Orders taken	1000	1200	400	800	1400	1600	1200	7600

A quick method to arrive at a first solution is to allocate orders to the cheapest filling point and to calculate what under- and over-capacities this gives (Table 12).

TABLE 12

	A	B	C	D	E	F	Total	Over Under
Blackburn		1200	400	800			2800	−400
Portsmouth							1900	−1900
Antwerp	1000				1400	1600	2900	+1100
	1000	1200	400	800	1400	1600		

Then move the over-capacities into those places requiring production which show the least cost increases (Table 13).

TABLE 13

	A	B	C	D	E	F	Slack	Factory capacity
Blackburn		1200	400	800			400	2800
Portsmouth					1100		800	1900
Antwerp	1000				300	1600		2900
Orders taken	1000	1200	400	800	1400	1600	1200	7600

Antwerp's over-capacity has been moved to Portsmouth and the spare capacity filled in.

Note that the number of squares occupied (9) is one fewer than the sum of the rows (3 factory capacity restraints) and the columns (7 customer requirement restraints). This is purely fortuitous in a "rule-of-thumb" solution of this kind, but is an essential condition if a formal mathematical approach is to be applied, since there must be at least one overlap, but no more than one overlap between each row and between each column. When this is not the case it is impossible to derive comparative costs for all the unoccupied squares, and the correct number of occupied squares must be achieved by consolidating quantities, or more likely, by inserting small fictitious values which can be ignored in the final solution.

Here the short-cut method has given a final answer; in more complicated situations it will give a good starting position but may not always give the final minimum cost solution. It is then necessary to evaluate each unused route to see if its use would increase or decrease costs. The formal approach will determine which unoccupied box it will prove most advantageous to use, and indicate how many units may be transferred into it. As restraints must still be complied with, this entails at least a rectangular shift, sometimes a more complicated one, of items round the matrix. This process is repeated until no further cost reductions can be achieved by transferring items from one to another, and the optimum solution is clearly demonstrated to have been reached. For a fuller treatment of this technique and others described briefly in this book, readers are referred to standard texts on operations research.

Simplex Method of Linear Programming

The simplex method also uses the matrix form, but the operation within it is different. Basically there is a set of equations which contain more unknowns than there are equations and so the answer cannot be obtained by "school" algebra. We can, however, determine the more significant factors and calculate the maximum and minimum positions, proceeding from zero to maximum by the quickest possible route.

Setting up the matrix. A factor assembles two types of radio receivers. The standard model (B) requires one of the basic circuits and a standard speaker and case. The more expensive model (A) requires two circuits; a different speaker and case is used and this model takes half as long again to assemble and test as the standard model. Production facilities are sufficient to make 3600 per week if all production is of the standard model. At the present moment the supply of circuits is 2600 per week, and of cases 1800 of type A and 2500 type B could be made available. The profit, or strictly speaking the marginal contribution, is £2.50 for type A, £1.50 for type B. What is the most profitable mix? For prestige purposes, at least 250 per period of the expensive model are required by the sales force.

Set down the "inequalities" from the information given:

(Time)	$1\frac{1}{2}A + B \leqq 3600$ units (*less than or equal to*)
(Main material—circuits)	$2A + B \leqq 2600$ units
(Cases type A)	$A \leqq 1800$ units
(Cases type B)	$B \leqq 2500$ units
(Sales)	$A \geqq 250$ units (*greater than or equal to*)

and by introducing "slack variables", fictitious products, transfer these inequalities into true equations.

(Time)	$1\frac{1}{2}A + B - X_1$	$= 3600$
(Main material—circuits)	$2A + B \quad +X_2$	$= 2600$
(Cases type A)	$A \quad +X_3$	$= 1800$
(Cases type B)	$B \quad +X^4$	$= 2500$
(Sales)	$A \quad -X_5$	$= 250$

It is now possible to solve these equations for the minimum or maximum position. If all fictitious products are programmed the profit is assumed to be 0. We proceed from this position to the position of maximum profit by a process called iteration.

In the body of the second column in Table 14 is placed the programme representing the fictitious products and in column 1 their profit, which is 0.

TABLE 14

Columns											
1	2	3	4	5	6	7	8	9	10		
			$2\frac{1}{2}$	$1\frac{1}{2}$	0	0	0	0	0		
	Schedule	Availability	A	B	x_1	x_2	x_3	x_4	x_5	Ratio	
0	x_1	3600	$1\frac{1}{2}$	1	1	0	0	0	0	$\frac{3600}{1\frac{1}{2}}$	2400
0	x_2	2600	2	1	0	1	0	0	0	$\frac{2600}{2}$	1300
0	x_3	1800	1	0	0	0	1	0	0	$\frac{1800}{1}$	1800
0	x_4	2500	0	1	0	0	0	1	0	$\frac{2500}{0}$	∞
0	x_5	250	1	0	0	0	0	0	−1	$\frac{250}{1}$	250
	Profit	£ 0	$-2\frac{1}{2}$	$-1\frac{1}{2}$	0	0	0	0	0		

Column 3 shows units, at first limiting units but as iteration proceeds the units to be made take their place, cols 4–9 the values of the items forming the equations. In the top row is placed the profit relating to the items produced and in the bottom row the solution box is the product of col. 3 × col. 1, the rest being a repeat of the top row with signs reversed. The bottom row shows the increase to be obtained per unit if that item is introduced into the schedule, e.g. A $2\frac{1}{2}$ B $1\frac{1}{2}$ (Table 14).

The "more than" item for x_5 requires the addition of an artificial variable x_6. The columns are resorted to obtain the identity matrix (Table 15).

First Matrix

TABLE 15

Columns													
1	2	3	4	5	6	7	8	9	11	10		
			$2\frac{1}{2}$	$1\frac{1}{2}$	0	0	0	0	0	0		
	Schedule	Availability	A	B	x_1	x_2	x_3	x_4	x_6	x_5	Ratio	
0	x_1	3600	$1\frac{1}{2}$	1	1	0	0	0	0	0	$\frac{3600}{1\frac{1}{2}}$	2400
0	x_2	2600	2	1	0	1	0	0	0	0	$\frac{2600}{2}$	1300
0	x_3	1800	1	0	0	0	1	0	0	0	$\frac{1800}{1}$	1800
0	x_4	2500	1	1	0	0	0	1	0	0	$\frac{2500}{0}$	∞
0	x_5	250	①	0	0	0	0	0	1	−1	$\frac{250}{1}$	250→
	Profit	£ 0	$-2\frac{1}{2}$	$-1\frac{1}{2}$	0	0	0	0	0	0		
			Entering ↑									

Operations on the matrix

Choose the largest minus item in the bottom row (A) and arrow that column.
Divide each "production availability" by the corresponding item in the chosen column and work out the ratio.
Choose the row that has the smallest positive ratio (x_5) Row x_5 leaves the matrix, Row A enters.
Where the column and row intersect, ring the key number.

Second Matrix

To calculate the second matrix divide the key number by that amount necessary to reduce it to 1 (it already is).
Divide the rest of the row by this number.
Then deduct the necessary times the key line from each other line in turn and place the result in the matrix.
Again calculate the ratios, choose the row with the smallest positive ratio (x_2), and the column with the largest minus item in the bottom row. (B) Row x_2 leaves the matrix, Row B enters. Where column and row intersect, ring the key number. Strictly speaking x_5, having the

TABLE 16

Columns												
1	2	3	4 A	5 B	6 x_1	7 x_2	8 x_3	9 x_4	11 x_6	10 x_5		
0	x_1	3225	0	1	1	0	0	0	$-1\frac{1}{2}$	$1\frac{1}{2}$	$\frac{3225}{1}$	3225
0	x_2	2100	0	①	0	1	0	0	-2	2	$\frac{2100}{1}$	→ 2100
0	x_3	1550	0	0	0	0	1	0	-1	1	$\frac{1550}{0}$	∞
0	x_4	2500	0	1	0	0	0	1	0	0	$\frac{2500}{1}$	2500
$2\frac{1}{2}$	A	250	1	0	0	0	0	0	1	-1	$\frac{250}{0}$	∞
	Profit	£ 625	0	$-1\frac{1}{2}$ ↑	0	0	0	0	$2\frac{1}{2}$	$-2\frac{1}{2}$		

largest negative number in the base row, should be introduced at this point. If this is done, the same answer; £3775, is finally arrived at but a further iteration is required. Knowing that only A and B, the "structural variables", are of use in the practical situation, B can be introduced at once rather than x_5. The artificial variable (col. 11) may also now be dropped out.

Calculate the third matrix by dividing by the key number, etc., as in moving from matrix 1 to 2 (Table 17).

Third Matrix

TABLE 17

Columns									
1	2	3	4	5	6	7	8	9	10
0	x_1	1125	0	0	1	−1	0	0	$-\frac{1}{2}$
$1\frac{1}{2}$	B	2100	0	1	0	1	0	0	2
0	x_3	1550	0	0	0	0	1	0	1
0	x_4	400	0	0	0	−1	0	1	−2
$2\frac{1}{2}$	A	250	1	0	0	0	0	0	−1
	Profit	£3775	0	0	0	$1\frac{1}{2}$	0	0	$\frac{1}{2}$

Results

Subject to the restraints given,
Maximum profit will result from,

250 units of A @ £2.50 = £625
2100 units of B @ £1.50 = £3150

£3775

It will be noted that this solution is bounded by two restrictions only, the number of circuits available (2600) and the minimum sales requirement of A (250).

The slack variables x_2 (as to circuits) and x_5 (as to sales requirements) have dropped out of the schedule, in other words their value is nil, or at least to consider them as nil will not radically affect the results. The remaining slack variables x_1 (spare production time), x_3 and x_4 (excess availability of cases A + B) remain in the schedule, as an indication that they have a positive value. The restrictions on production time and availability of cases have therefore not affected the optimum result: the amount of these items still available can be read from the matrix (col. 3).

Some of the linear programming terminology is of general interest, and it is instructive to relate the expressions found in O.R. to the management concepts which they can be used to represent (Table 18).

TABLE 18

Management terms	Mathematical terms
Competing products	Structural variables (up to 3 may be shown graphically)
Limiting factors	Constraints (one equation per constraint)
"Best" or "optimum" achievement goal (such as marginal contribution or minimum cost)	Objective function (maximize or minimize)
Surplus capacity (time or materials)	Slack variables (inequalities are changed into equations by introducing slack variables)

Convex or quadratic programming. By no means all the problems with which management has to deal bear a linear relationship, and quadratic programming can be used where the relationship if graphed would follow a curve rather than a straight line. This might, for example, be the case in studying the relationship between direct costs per unit of volume and total output. Quadratic programming will give a more accurate answer but the calculations are considerably more involved than linear programming; the decision to use quadratic in preference to linear programming therefore depends on whether the greater accuracy of the answer obtained offsets the extra costs involved.

Dynamic programming takes into account time intervals. The decisions governing one stage of the problem become the conditions governing the next stage. This is unlike the previous forms of programming discussed where the variables are considered as interacting with each other at the *same* time.

Dynamic programming is potentially of great use in management but is not yet fully developed. Examples would be in problems of determining finished goods stocks in relation to production and sales, and in long-range capital planning.

Game Theory

The theories developed in the study of wagering have been adapted to the business world and within their limits can throw some very useful light on competitive situations. The approach most fully developed is the "Two person, zero sum" game. This implies that there is a fixed field in which to operate and that what part one person loses, another will gain. This is often true of a short-term situation in which an organization finds itself. The mathematics of the approach is also limited to two persons at the moment, but where there are more than two competitors involved in a situation, it is possible to lump all one's opposing forces together calling them "The Rest" or "Nature".

Each organization knows what strategies of play are open to it in a given situation, say as regards marketing policies for a given product, Where there are only a few contestants and where information is good, the organization would also be able to calculate what possible strategies are open to its opponent. It is assumed that both decide on policy simultaneously. By market research, values are attached to these possible strategies. For each of one's own possible strategies one puts oneself in one's opponent's shoes and sees how he would attempt to counter it.

It is taken that both organizations involved are trying to obtain the largest share of sales in the given market and to prevent the other obtaining it. Also, that both know what is at stake. To adopt this approach against an ill-informed business that chooses its policy at random may, of course, not prove satisfactory.

The results of different competing strategies are plotted in a matrix on a percentage basis as follows:

		Y's strategies				
		1	2	3	4	5
X's strategies	1	15	80	40	15	10
	2	80	35	90	5	80
	3	85	25	40	20	65
	4	65	70	50	45	80

When X plays strategy 1, at best he gains 80% of market, at worst 10%.

When X plays strategy 2, at best he gains 90% of market, at worst 5%.

When X plays strategy 3, at best he gains 85% of market, at worst 20%.

When X plays strategy 4, at best he gains 80% of market, at worst 45%.

Knowing that Y is well informed and will do everything possible to counter his moves, X will choose strategy 4, which does not show the biggest gain but assures him of the biggest minimum amount. He maximizes his minimum payoff.

Subtracting all figures in X's matrix from 100, Y's payoff matrix will be

		Y's strategy 1	2	3	4	5
X's strategy	1	85	20	60	85	90
	2	20	65	10	95	20
	3	15	75	60	80	35
	4	35	30	50	55	20

When Y plays strategy 1, at best he gains 85%, at worst 15% of market.

When Y plays strategy 2, at best he gains 75%, at worst 20% of market.

When Y plays strategy 3, at best he gains 60%, at worst 10% of market.

When Y plays strategy 4, at best he gains 95%, at worst 55% of market.

When Y plays strategy 5, at best he gains 90%, at worst 20% of market.

Y will therefore play strategy 4, and if they are both informed of the true situation, there is nothing X can do to stop this. In this case, this corresponds with X's choice. This position is called the *saddle-point*; if the situation were graphed three-dimensionally it appears like an animal's back with a dip at this point where the saddle occurs. Not all situations have a clearly defined saddle-point, there may be more than one saddle-point in some situations.

Where one is playing against an ill-informed organization which chooses its strategy at random, it may prove better to go all out for one's own maximum position and hope one's opponent misses his chance through lack of information.

Simulation

Where it is not possible to obtain all the data, or where the relationships cannot be formulated mathematically, simulation is often employed to solve industrial and commercial problems. If the techniques of mathematics available are not powerful enough to produce the *best* answer, simulation can be used to run through all the possible combinations of the variables and hence to select an answer that, whilst perhaps not the optimum, is suitable and which is probably much nearer the optimum than a "guess" would be.

The logic diagram representing the situation is first drafted out and for this purpose a flow chart may be useful. The logic diagram can show possible events, decision points and the assumptions involved.

A model of the situation can be fed into the computer and the whole cycle of events simulated. One variable at a time is then altered and the result of each change noted on an experimental basis. Thus by a type of "trial and error", which is inexpensive because it is carried out on a computer and not in real life, a good solution can be found.

"Monte Carlo" methods are resorted to frequently in simulation experiments. For instance, in a study of the reorganization of a loading bay,[2] lorry arrivals over 1 week only could be studied. It was known other weeks would have a similar *total* of lorries received, but it was necessary to know the exact *time* of their arrival so that delays in servicing could be calculated. Random number tables were used to derive times of

[2] "Simulation applied to a loading bay", DSIR Industrial Operations Unit pamphlet.

arrival of lorries in the second week, and these values processed on the mathematical model which had been set up.

Choice of Simulation Model

Where the manager has decided to use a simulation model, he has the choice of two basic types:

1. Time-oriented simulation, such as Industrial Dynamics.
2. Event-oriented simulation, such as GPSS—General Purpose System Simulation.

Both types of model have a timebase, but the approach to time intervals is different.

Industrial dynamics, developed at Massachusetts Institute of Technology by Jay W. Forrester over the past 20 years, employs a fixed time increment. The simulation equations are based on "Levels" and "Rates of flow". A special compiler "Dynamo" was developed by Alexander Pugh III for use originally with an IBM 7090 computer, now adapted for IBM 360 and other current computer configurations. These digital computer programs give a printout in the form of a number of sets of similar letters of the alphabet whose change in their spatial position is printed out at each fixed time interval. Subsequently each set of similar letters is joined up to produce smooth graph lines. The interaction of these lines is then studied.

The output in its original form is not a continuous line, but a series of points which can also be listed as numerical values.

Choice of the length of time period is important as all events simulated to take place during a time period are treated as if they take place at the beginning of that period. Where a long period is chosen the output information tends to be smoothed by the programme itself and some interactions between variables may not then be apparent.

GPSS is a simulation model with a variable time-increment. After one event has been processed, the simulation moves onto the next event regardless of the varying length of time interval involved. Choice of the next timepoint is made by the "sequencing set". A block diagram is used to describe the simulation with such activities as Generate: Seize: Release: Transfer: Terminate. The computer program is available for an IBM 360 and later configurations.

Generate—originates the time elements.

Seize—occupies a facility.

Release—move forward, leaving facility free for occupation.

Transfer—selection of a choice of paths.

Terminate—finish simulation.

After all the input data has worked through the model, the results of the simulation are listed numerically by the computer, ready for examination. Large and complex simulations can be handled in this way. For specific problems *Analogue Simulation* models working on the basis of varying current may be useful to simulate specific physical processes to determine operating conditions, e.g. a simulation of an electricity network or simulated aircraft trainer. Where it is needed for this one specific purpose, analogue simulation can be cheaper than digital. General purpose analogue computers also exist but are unable to handle complex simulation. For large and complex simulation, digital computers are now used.

Network Analysis

Network analysis came into prominence as a management planning, co-ordination and control tool with the development of P.E.R.T (Program evaluation and review technique) to control weapon systems. Developing at the same time were two aspects likely to be of most interest to the manager: Critical Path Scheduling (to control time aspects) and Minimum Cost Estimating (to control cost aspects) of a project. Network analysis is essentially a dynamic control tool. It is concerned with the planning and control aspects of a project. The method has been applied to constructional projects with particular effect but it is by no means limited to these; it could equally be applied to the cycle of work involved in the payment of invoices by a head office for a group of companies.

The network stresses the *interaction* of the parts of a project.

Network analysis could be regarded as a development of the Gantt chart. There are two distinct parts to the development of a network:

The planning of the detailed interaction of jobs and hence the logical network.

The attaching of time and/or money values to each event for the subsequent calculation of the critical path or minimum cost.

The technique requires a detailed technical knowledge of the work involved in each step of the specific project under review; which job can be undertaken concurrently with other jobs, which jobs must be completed before further progress can be made.

CHAPTER 10

Evaluation and Change

Evaluation

Evaluation of systems is of concern mainly in relation to *constructed* systems, where evaluation can take place in regard to stated goals. Natural systems do not have such man-stated goals and can only be examined for the efficiency and effectiveness with which their processes interact. To posit a goal for a natural system is a human construct imposing boundaries and human thought onto a process where interaction of parts is discerned.

It is frequently easy to read into natural interaction some teleological meaning or end purpose. For example, the millions of eggs laid by a fish or the many seeds produced by a plant seem without doubt a process designed to ensure that the species continues. The goal is not stated in words, but it would appear to be very firmly stated by contextual implication. So also can we see the inner drive of living matter to continue to exist. But whether the natural goal of a species of grass is to continue to exist for itself or to exist as a food for some animal is a question that could only be answered by applying thought constructs. The natural processes by themselves do not give an answer. Natural processes appear simply to contain the inner drive to continue to exist and, if possible, expand. This situation leads us to notice a difference in apparent operational values between natural systems and humanly constructed systems. The natural system is often profligate in its use of resources. From many seeds or eggs only a very few reach full reproductive maturity. By contrast, humanly constructed systems go to great length to make the utmost possible use of all input resources. The possible answer to this may be that whilst each natural process appears to have only a single end in view, humanly constructed systems are required to meet the whole spectrum of human needs and desires. Fully stimulated human needs and desires can become endless, far outweighing the capacity of the available resources to satisfy them, and this recognition of the multiplicity of end goals for humanly constructed systems leads us to conserve our input resources jealously.

Evaluation in Relation to Constructed Systems

Before any type of evaluation can take place, there must be an overt stating of goals and purposes. Change and process interaction is a condition of life but at stated points in time a congealment of this fluidity is needed. The goal itself need not necessarily be possible of attainment. It is fixed as a positional reference point. At a minimum of two points in time, attributes of the system under review are measured so that changes within the system and its output can be calculated in relation to the overtly stated goal.

Evaluation can take place in:

(i) Systems and Sub-systems

The qualitative overall goals of large socio-technical systems are split down to quantitative targets at operational level. This dimension is covered in many textbooks on management and will not be repeated here except to stress the difficulty of crossing the interface between word descriptions and figure descriptions.

(ii) A further relevant dimension of analysis

(i) *Means* Evaluating the operational processes and decisional techniques as sub-systems as well as in relation to overall goals.

(ii) *Ends* The stated goals.

(iii) *Standpoint of observer*. Internal or external to the system under review.

Means. The evaluation of means is frequently based on some form of measurement. Three stages of evaluation can be distinguished.

(a) Those that are concerned with input resources and the efficiency of conversion to final product. Evaluation of input resources has advanced because it is these items that are most frequently bought at a definite price and to a defined technical specification. The same availability of data applies to conversion factors within the system.

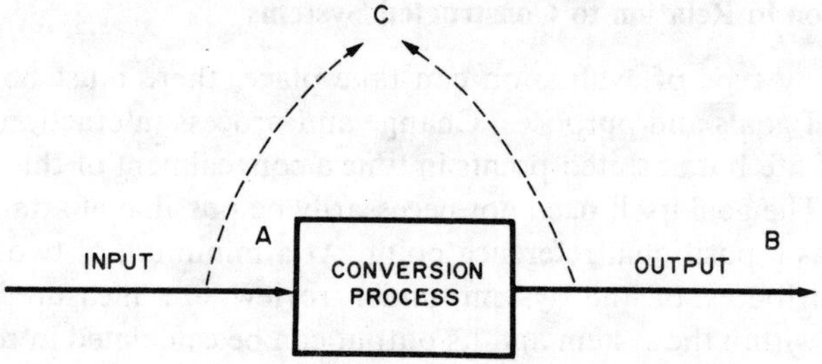

Fig. 10.1 Stages of evaluation.

(b) The second stage of evaluation is of the output in relation to the environment that absorbs it. In trading companies this simply means the need to sell the product at a good price in the market. To do this keeps the system viable. In other spheres the output evaluation problem is far more difficult as no units of measurement may exist. Such particularly is the case in social work. It may be possible to evaluate a "meals on wheels" service to old persons by an indirect method such as the cost to a local authority if such persons were not provided with meals, could not manage for themselves, and had to be taken into homes. But to evaluate the service directly is almost impossible. Much research work is at present being done in this area of output evaluation.

(c) The third stage in this approach to evaluation of a system relates

(i) the output achieved to the input used. This is a measurement of the system's conversion efficiency;

(ii) the input used in relation to the effectiveness *in use* of the output achieved. This is a measurement of the effectiveness of the system as a whole, but also highlights the benefits obtained by using resources in the given way and by implication highlights their opportunity-cost in that the inputs are scarce and once used are not available for other purposes.

Ends. It is frequently mentioned that the goals of a constructed system must be stated. Such goals may be stated for several purposes:

to attract attention that the system exists,

to be attained (within a reasonable timespan),

to motivate,

to facilitate evaluation of activity, internal and external.

The need to state goals in advance of operations carried out to achieve that goal admits a time problem. Stated goals are always "in arrear". Their validity may change. What may have been seen as a useful goal at the beginning of the year and stated, may become an embarrassment as time goes by. It is often said that the strength of the British Constitution is that it is not written down and certainly when the expenditure of effort required to make necessary changes to the written constitution of the U.S.A. is examined, the point may have strength. Systems theorists have been criticized for taking the stating of goals as an easy task. It is not so in socio-technical systems and often may only be achieved as the end-result of much intersub-system conflict in a power context. Certainly the validity of stated goals may be challenged and certainly systems may be evaluated in relation to goals other than those laid down. Yet whenever an evaluation of the effectiveness in operation of a system is made, the evaluation in relation to WHAT must be determined at the time of the evaluation and stated.

Standpoint. The stated goal of a system is often the formalized one, stated by those who are in charge of the system and to that extent outside it. The concept has developed, particularly in business, that a manager creates a system, states its goals and measures the efficiency of his system towards these goals. This places his standpoint outside and above the system he is controlling. In other spheres, for example, the king is now constitutionally *within* the system and not above it, army officers *within* the military system, the final control of the military machine being civilian. It is curious that the controllers of many of our newly created systems place themselves outside the system they manage and hence increase alienation of those within. Goals appear very different to those within and those outside a system, and consequently evaluation takes place from completely different standpoints. The evaluation of goals from different standpoints will be likely to pose problems for systems engineers as movement takes place from the construction of hard technological problems about which most people are agreed to "soft" areas.

Evaluation of a Specific System

The evaluation of a computerized management information system will serve us as an example (see Table 19).

In evaluating the information provided within a socio-technical constructed system, the most important first point of evaluation we consider is whether the information system is in balance and adequate in relationship to the other systems, the technical system, the organization system, the psychological (human) systems, the marketing systems. It is to be expected that the information system as developed will have been considered in relationship to these parallel systems. The new information system may well have been introduced because a new technical system demands the provision of information at a particular level of efficiency. In accepting the configuration of a new information system an organization will have had to trade-off the cost of each item of equipment and operational costs against its effectiveness in operation until an acceptable configuration has evolved. For instance, speed of system response may be a desirable factor, but the organization may be under a severe overall cost constraint and the cost of installations begin to increase rapidly in a non-linear manner as increasingly sophisticated real-time systems are considered. The cost constraint will extend through to the program writing stage and to ease the cost constraint in one direction means that it will apply more stringently at another point. The cost

TABLE 19

Operational evaluation of a management information system

Operational Evaluation

I. *Input and conversion efficiency*

(i) of installation	(ii) of hardware operation and firmwave	(iii) of basic soft ware
(iv) of particular programmes	(v) of documentation and organization	(vi) of support and maintenance facilities
(vii) of staff training and effectiveness in operation		

Techniques: (i) Total measurement (ii) Marginal measurement, i.e. evaluation by comparison of marginal change

Units of measurement,
Quantities: of throughput, errors, time taken, downtime, etc.
Money values attached to above in total
Money values attached per given unit of quantity

II. *Technical working efficiency*, from the standpoint of line management. Have the input and conversion sub-systems, whether they worked efficiently as sub-systems or not, combined to produce the information programme as agreed?

III. *Use-in-action evaluation.* Does the agreed programme provide information in a manner that satisfies a need of the organization and so more than "pays for itself"?

constraint will limit the amount of data that can be dealt with within a unit time period.

Some little time after the installation of a system should come the more detailed evaluation stage. This evaluation may not always occur as the individuals concerned with designing and installing systems may be more interested to go forward to new work than have their past partial successes brought before them for examination. For this reason it is useful to write appraisal/evaluation sessions into the time schedules as routine and necessary periods that cannot be avoided. Where such sessions are regarded as routine rather than special recrimination sessions, they may well be most interesting to all concerned and be treated as an occasion when questions may be asked and much learning for future occasions achieved. Under evaluation will be:

Was the choice of configuration a good one?

Has it led to a viable information system?

Broken down to

(i) Does the system provide information of sufficient quality within the agreed time limit?

(ii) Is the cost of providing this information satisfactory and within budget?

And, perhaps a little later in time,

(iii) Is the information as requested by the line manager proving useful? Is it "paying for itself?"

A two-stage evaluation process requiring several meetings would be necessary:

1. With the information system personnel.
2. With the line managers using the information, including meetings jointly attended by system personnel and line managers.

Within the information sub-systems at operational level technical efficiency will be a main criterion, the cost and efficient use of input resources to achieve the accepted goal.

(i) Was the installation handed over on time. Had all installation been affected by that date?

(ii) Has the installation run as expected? An analysis of machine downtime and its related cost.

(iii) Has the basic software provided by the installing company been successfully loaded onto the system?

And specifically from the organization's point of view:

(iv) Has the operation of its own particular programs proceeded to schedule?

(v) Have the organization and documentation systems effectively helped the running of the installation?

(vi) Has the supply of stationary, tapes, cards, etc., been organized satisfactorily?

(vii) Have the support and maintenance facilities been organized as planned? Air conditioning, space, storage, fire precautions, acoustic and thermal installation, etc.

(viii) Has staff training been carried out?

(ix) Has staff training reflected into effectiveness in operation?

Having considered and evaluated its own position regarding its efficiency, the information systems department will be ready to discuss the effectiveness of its output with the user, the line manager.

Has the information been received as planned, both from a point of view of time and quality? If so, can improvements be suggested that are within the capabilities of the information systems department as it at present exists?

The line manager will have had meetings both within his own department and possibly with line managers of other departments at their operational level. Within the constraints of the existing configuration of the information system, suggestions may be put forward querying the usefulness of the information as at present presented and suggesting improvements. Supposing this evaluation proves the present information worthless. There is no reflection on the efficiency of the information systems department's operational capacity as they provide the information as requested. They do, however, have an important secondary role, that of giving advice and so are interested in this evaluation for they must help to locate and find ways of presenting more useful information If they cannot, then however efficient they may be, they run the risk of being swept away as their own sub-system goals of efficiency in providing (useless) information will no longer be relevant to the organization. At the top policy level there may be evaluation of the "use-in-action" of the information provided. This high-level evaluation may result in a seen need for much better quality information and hence a further expansion of the information system or as sometimes happens its complete rejection. Whatever may be the results of this evaluation the efficiency in operation of the information systems department is not in question, yet this system will be dependent on evaluations made at a higher system level which can question its very existence. Perhaps it is because of this insecurity and dependence on higher levels for decision that such information systems will tend to develop their advisory function into a homeostatic technique, making sure that the need for the system is appreciated at all levels.

The conclusion of this example may give the impression that evaluation contains a political element, and so it does: the choice of the reference point in relation to which evaluation is made. Following Garbutt (1972): "it is axiomatic that study of the system as such should not be conducted by parties who are playing a particular role in that system. In contrast the monitoring of the system performance and state should always be the basis of its management, and must be conducted by the components involved in the total system".

Who sets the goals in constructed systems, goals for achievement and goals for evaluation is a very important point for consideration and may greatly affect the outcome and evaluation sessions.

Change

The areas of system design and systems engineering cover a field of ever-growing importance in modern living. The conscious design of systems has now entered a vast spectrum of industry, business, agriculture and social living and the increase in this aspect of systems modelling and planning is likely to continue. Such constructed systems are obviously to be classed as normative; they consist of such parts as their designer and constructor decide that they should. The designer may be guided by "best practice", a study of what systems have been successful in the past and what systems have not, but designers are not limited by such studies and within bounds of safety, within the limits of their ability to convince committees and practical men, are encouraged to plan and design such new systems as they are able with the resources available at present or likely to be available in the near future.

Together with an emphasis on the "putting together of parts" is an equally important emphasis on interfaces, the points where various parts link together, such interfaces can often be the weak points in any constructed system. Because of this nature of constructed systems, the analytical approach to construction and subsequently to improving effectiveness is frequently to be found useful. This alteration and improvement of parts of a constructed system does not lead so directly to

the imbalance frequently met when systems of long evolutionary development such as ecological systems are interfered with.
One can alter parts of a technological process or parts of a management information system without ill effects, possibly with good effects. But to introduce rabbits to Australia, where the animals entered a finely balanced ecological system, may well in the end leave the situation with more problems than it started with, even if the original single goal was achieved. The system constructor requires a sensitive feeling for the difference between a balanced system that has taken a long time period to evolve and an engineered system that can be constructed as quickly as possible to achieve a given or perhaps limited goal. He has also to be able to translate this "feeling" into a sound practical approach that can be made acceptable to those who will live within and operate his constructed system. When using an analytical approach to examining the parts of a constructed system we have to remember that the aim in view is the synthesis of the system. Does improvement of a part improve the functioning of the system as a whole? Being man-created the problem of cost effectiveness looms large here, so the question in practice becomes, "Does the outgoing cost involved in improving a part (capital cost and running cost) result in equal or greater incoming benefits in the use of the system as a whole?" Often it is very difficult to measure the costs and benefits in money terms and the technique of cost/benefit analysis is being developed as a tool to answer this problem.

Systems Engineering

The systems approach to problem solution and the subsequent construction and introduction of the recommended system passes through distinct stages:

(i) Identification of needs and definition of problem.

(ii) Appreciation of benefits to be obtained by the introduction of a new system and decision to proceed.

(iii) Design of the new or replacement system.

(iv) Implementation of the designed system in "real life".

(v) Evaluation in operation.

To consider the above list in more detail gives problems of presentation. A diagram, say a matrix, is presented in two dimensions. Properly to consider the life-cycle of a constructed system at least three if not four dimensions are required and it is not easy to achieve such presentation on a printed page. An attempt is made in Table 20.

Problem Identification and Definition

Initial identification of a problem or a problem area will generally take place by operational line management who may report having trouble in a particular area. The reporting of such a problem may lead to an attempted *ad hoc* solution by line management itself or it may have involved the introduction of a systems engineering team to view the problem in its widest aspects and put forward an integrated solution. In other circumstances, the systems engineering team may be asked for a "green fields" solution to provide the necessary systems that could be needed when a new organization is commenced.

In most cases it is operating management or prospective management that call in the systems team. Having had indicated to them the problem area, the system team will be concerned with correct definition of the correct problem. A proferred solution to this problem will become the goals of the system the team will finally advocate. The right formulation of the problem for solution is thus extremely important, it is also often skipped over as line management may indicate along with the problem itself the type of solution they would expect, prefer and accept. Any movement outside the suggested solution area might be firmly rebutted. Having put into written form all the unstated assumptions regarding the situation that can be discerned, the systems team may usefully ask,

What is the problem?

Is the problem as now formulated likely to be the right problem?

In what parts of the system does the problem lie?

What is the nature of the mutual dependency of these problem parts of the system with other parts at the same level?

What is the nature of the mutual dependency of these problem parts of the system with the higher parts?

TABLE 20

Stages in cycle	Area of work	Responsibility
Ideas and concepts Identification of needs Definition of problem and relevant system	PLANNING	MAIN AREAS OF SYSTEM ENGINEERS' WORK
System analysis Presentation of alternatives		
Decision and choice		
System design Design of chosen alternative Development Pilot model Trial and development Production model	DEVELOPMENT	
Installation		LINE MANAGEMENT
Operation and use Input of resources Material Energy Information Support systems and renewals	OPERATIONAL USE	
Modifications and/or withdrawal	REAPPRAISAL/ DEVELOPMENT	LINE MANAGEMENT/ SYSTEM ENGINEERS

Procedure involved at each stage of systems work

- Analysis — Gather information; Agree criteria
- Synthesis — Develop model; Operate model to obtain alternative solutions
- Evaluation — Evaluate alternatives in light of criteria
- Decision — Choose one alternative and proceed to next stage

System engineering tools used

- Planning — The full range of management techniques available according to the current "state of the art" in the locality where the planning takes place
- Design — Depending on the type of system being engineered, the full range of management and physical process techniques according to the current "state of the art" in the locality where design takes place

Is an acceptable solution likely to bring in benefits?

Are these benefits likely sufficiently to outweight costs of introduction and interruptions to work flow to make introduction of a new system worthwhile?

Most of the questions are of an analytical nature.

The purpose of the investigation to date is to relate actual performance and possible performance to the *objectives* of the system, and to relate objectives of sub-systems to main systems. In the practical situation the approximate cost of achieving such objectives will bear much weight as we are dealing with a man-created normative system in which it is not so much the achievement of objectives that is important (as might possibly be said to be the case in some other systems, as to win a war regardless of cost in money or lives) but the achievement of objectives *at a given cost* that is important. A maximum acceptable threshold for that cost, whether stated in money or physical-effort terms, will determine whether the proffered type of solution is within an acceptable area. At this stage, there will be a report back and the team will await the go-ahead. One of the problems likely to worry operational management is the ranking of objectives where there are several or many objectives. Often the necessity to make a decision to rank objectives is blurred by allowing objectives to be taken sequentially, looking at them one at a time during a time-span such as the course of the year. This may be the only procedure possible but it will not lead to maximization of system performance. To obtain a maximum performance, objectives must be ranked. This may be by no means easy. In a business with profits as the overall criterion, there will be a pull between present profit and possible future profit. Little progress in the operation of a model can take place until criteria for sub-system and overall system performance are agreed.

Iteration. It is unlikely that a single sequential consideration of the points so far mentioned will achieve an acceptable solution. A cycling feedback procedure, interation, which entails going back and reconsidering analysis of earlier points in the light of subsequent information, now takes place. Within the imposed time constraints iteration can take place as often as is felt necessary. During this process some interlocking of the technical process systems, human systems, economic systems and organizational systems will take place towards a single overall socio-technical system. The stage of synthesis is being entered.

System design. Engineered systems may be of many types, perhaps information systems or systems of organization, or again the system may be physical processes to produce certain material goods. Analysis and design stages can be kept distinctly separate. How distinct they are kept may depend on the type of system. In the former case it is more likely that after the initial analytical consideration of the points so far mentioned, iteration will gradually move the team on from definition and analysis stages to design, and that although the team will be following their laid-down procedure there may be a gradual build up of the design content, rather than a complete dichotomy between analysis and design. Design starts in earnest when a single possible alternative has been chosen as the one to be proceeded with.

Where physical processes are involved, the design content may appear as a more distinct entity, involving the use of different tools to build a physical model of the process chosen.

In all probability the system being engineered will be a socio-technical one and hence an "open-system". Part of the information required to design such a system successfully is a description of the environment, at least the local environment in which it will be operating. Systems designed without taking into account the environment in which they will work are doomed to failure, or at least it will be pure luck if they do work. It is necessary to stress this point as it can be so frequently overlooked. A multinational company may transfer its systems of working from its home environment to some overseas subsidiary company's environment where its methods have never been encountered previously and hence are unacceptable. Strikes have frequently been the result.

The recommended solution system in the field of constructed socio-technical systems is likely to be interdisciplinary. A newly introduced system of agriculture, say a new method of undersowing different crops to give succeeding yields over several months, may not in fact alter the existing labour or machinery systems, but it might radically alter the financial system on which the farm is based. A newly devised way of cracking oil may not involve any extra finance than normal capital replacement, but it could alter dramatically the manning solutions and labour involved. Physical solutions are related to hard cash through the money system. But the money system itself is not a natural system. The monetary system is normative like any other social system, is "managed" on an international basis and is subject to political power systems. Fashions in socio-technological solutions change because of technological change and advances, but also because of normative decisions, generally of a political nature which are based on the sociological and economic infrastructure systems, to admit certain changes. For the last century, western socio-technical solutions have been based on an increasing use of energy to aid physical production. Solutions, therefore, have tended to be ones that increased the use of capital machinery and energy and lessened the labour ratio. These solutions are very successful. However, at the present time it becomes obvious that there is an overall limit to the possible increase in energy and that some thought may well have to be made soon to reintroducing the concept of the "dignity of labour" as a motivating force for less energy-dependent systems of production.

Design and Installation of the System

The core of the design phase involves Research, Development, Test and Evaluation. The chosen alternative decided upon at the system analysis stage will be developed through the stages of small-scale try-out to the full-scale operational model. In developing the various sub-systems that are to fit together to make the required system, tests for fit will be carried out in dimensions of compatibility, sensitivity and stability. Sub-systems that are of very different order are not likely to work together satisfactorily in practice. Particular attention would be paid to hardware/software (information)/liveware interfaces. Any items that are found to be working near their limits with normal input parameter values and hence liable to break down in the case of an overload should be redesigned. Installation of the finally agreed system is likely to be shared by the system engineer and user.

Operational use. The operational phase will be under control of line management. During this phase emphasis will be placed on operational reliability, the quality of the output and the relationship of output to input particularly as reflected by measurements of costs. Control of operations is given great importance as a means of exercising strict control over costs. Support systems will be required in order to keep the main system operational: systems of training for replacement of human personnel, systems of maintenance for the physical hardware. Towards the end of the operational use phase of the system it will probably become necessary to make a decision whether to carry out a full-scale overhaul of the system with modification of some of the parts or whether to replace the system with a new one. As an engineered system is one constructed from parts it is perfectly possible to redesign or modify some of these parts while the system is in operational use and install such parts over a short close-down period. If, however, it is felt that many parts of the system require replacement, then a full-scale new system will be called for, very often based on a cost calculation of the new "state of the art and of technology". The system engineering cycle is reiterated, begins again, and a second-generation system is developed.

Iteration of the complete design and use cycle, and iteration within each phase of the cycle becomes standard practice in systems engineering. The related costing of this whole operation has been given the name "terotechnology".

The systems engineer is a person who can see how different disciplines can be brought together for the purpose of solving one practical problem. His special technique born of system theory is to give as much weight to the *interaction* between parts as to the parts themselves. He may well be a specialist in his own right, but his systems engineering training will enable him to take a balanced approach, merging the human, technical, commercial, legal and organizational aspects, rather than the frequently met approach that it is possible to solve many problems by the application of one single management technique. We can see that the systems engineer will need to be able to build many models of his problem area, probably quantitative ones, and be skilled enough to be able to link these models together to obtain an overall solution. He will be part of a team and such teams are likely to exist on a full-time basis only in the largest organizations. Other organizations are likely to call in consultant systems engineers as the need arises or to tap the resources that exist in the systems engineering departments of universities and polytechnics.

Planning and Control of Policy

It is at top level that the broad experience of mature executives looking at the total situation will count most, as it always has done. As well as technical, financial and managerial knowledge, character is important. Under all political systems the businessmen are they into whose hands has been placed the greater part of the country's wealth and if they do not look after and increase that wealth, the country will suffer. This trust produces certain problems in the ethical system which should at least be kept in mind. These are problems which possibly cannot have a single "best" solution, but which undoubtedly must be kept within defined limits, and if these limits have been objectively defined, the task of creating policy is greatly facilitated.

We are back at the position discussed in Chapter 1. When framing policy, it has to be borne in mind that whereas the processes in the conversion of the product follow well-defined laws of nature, the social, legal and economic arrangements of the organization tend to follow normative laws which are susceptible to change and may well be different in one country from another, and different in the same country at one time from another. It is important that makers of top policy are sure that all members of their organization are cognizant of these normative laws and ethical norms and the effect of their impact on the organization.

The organization is carried on within the framework of government and as such must accept the laws passed by the government, though it should be able to contest them in a legal manner if it does not consider them in the best interests of business.

APPENDIX I

Controls in a Business Enterprise

Area of control	Control information	Action required
A. BUDGETS		
Overall budget	Variances from budget in use of all resources	Control at sectional level for particular budget volume. Complete recast of budget if uncontrollable external input greatly alters.
Detailed sectional budgets, based on standards obtained from work study or previous year's working.	Detailed cost variance reports by £ and p and quantity.	To keep within budget limits for volume achieved
B. FINANCIAL (ACCOUNTANCY) CONTROLS		
Current assets		
Raw material stocks	Amount invested in raw materials.	To keep within budgeted amounts—normally by speeding up the flow.
Work-in-progress	Amount invested in work-in-progress.	To keep within budgeted amounts—normally by speeding up the flow.
Finished goods stocks	Amount invested in finished goods.	To keep within budgeted amounts—normally by speeding up the flow.
Sundry debtors	Amount invested in credit allowed to customers.	To keep within budgeted amounts—normally by speeding up the flow.
Cash	Cash book/Bank statement.	To maintain sufficient liquidity.

Area of control	Control information	Action required
Current liabilities		
Sundry creditors	Credit taken from suppliers.	To make use of credit available without losing discounts.
Fixed assets		
Investments in Land Buildings Plant	Longer term reports, including figures, on present position and proposed changes.	To maintain overall balance of company for present and future working.
Capital		
Shares Loans Reserves	Longer term reports, with figures, on present position and proposed changes.	To maintain overall balance of company for present and future working.
Trading account		
Purchases	Amounts invoiced by product and amount. Variances from budget.	To follow budget particularly in relation to price and delivery
Sales	Amounts invoiced by product and amount. Variances from budget.	To follow budget and maintain product mix.

C. STATISTICAL CONTROLS
(by numbers, quantities, weights)

New business accepted.	Reports from sales dept.	To follow budget and maintain profitable product mix.
Production control	Details of orders completed and overdue.	To follow agreed production programme and ensure even economical flow from factory entrance to exit.
Labour	Detailed labour statistics.	To increase or decrease as required for economical working.
Quality control	Details of quality obtained and amounts of work rejected.	To keep quality within acceptance limits.

Area of control	Control information	Action required
D. QUALITATIVE CONTROLS (Reports)		
Methods	Reports on variances from standard methods.	To obtain efficiency and economical working.
Personnel and morale	Reports (frequently no objective information available).	To maintain "go-ahead" labour force.
Works layout	Reports on present position and proposed alterations.	To ensure efficiency and economical working.
Organization	Reports on present position and proposed alterations.	To ensure efficiency and economical working.

APPENDIX II

Some Systems in Outline

Scale	Process or system under observation	Possible objective discerned	Input to process	Output from process	Checking information fed back	Time scale of delays in feedback of control information
Small	Man/machine Typing a letter	To produce finished letter by specified time	Paper Information Keys struck	Typed characters in correct position	Visual check on output as it occurs with overall check at end	1 second
↓	Central heating system	To keep a particular airspace at a preset temperature	(a) Decisions at intervals by caretaker	Heat	(a) Spot decisions after looking outside and possibly visiting rooms	1–3 hourly
			(b) Thermostat in room controlling energy input to system Fuel	Heat	(b) Deviation from set temperature measured in room	Minutes

Material flow control	To ensure continued flow of raw materials as planned from receipt to finished goods without delays	Planning Dept. information on dates	Material flowing through works according to scheduled times	Progress Dept. visual and paper check Production protest when great excess or starvation of material	Hours/days
Control of product quality	To maintain predetermined quality	Inspection (includes all methods used)	Separation of good work from rejects and rectification	Measurement of 100% or sample (a) by inspectors (b) by automatic device	Hours/days Minutes
Performance of a specific department	To maintain departments output as specified in budget or revised budget and so play its part in optimizing company performance	Men Materials Plant Energy Information	Part product or service to specified quality by specified time at specified cost	Divergence from budget in quantity, quality, time or cost. Action to rectify	Days/weeks months
Budgetary control	A system to show departure from the budget as agreed—or budget as modified by events if a flexible budget, thus enabling appropriate action to be taken	Detailed budgeted figures Actual figures as they arise	Variances from budget	Cost accountants give details to line management for action	*To prepare information* 1 day after weekend to 3 weeks or more after month end *To take action* 2 hrs to days

Scale	Process or system under observation	Possible objective discerned	Input to process	Output from process	Checking information fed back	Time scale of delays in feedback of control information
⋮	Performance of the whole company	To make and sell a required product and so satisfy consumer, shareholder, employees	Men Materials Plant Energy Information	A saleable product at a satisfactory profit	Satisfaction/dissatisfaction of consumers, shareholders, employees	Months Yearly Days
→ Large	Performance of national economic system	Govt. policy (to increase N.P. 2%)	Taxation level of trade Productivity— Need to work Will Opportunity	Gross national product £'s	Semi-planned operation of free market	Govt. 5 yrs Budget 1 yr Special measures 3 months

APPENDIX III

Symbolic Logic, Boolean Arithmetic and Computer Circuits

In a closed logical deductive system the variables *p*, *q*......... are used to represent the propositions, which may be true or false; symbols are used for the constants: "$\sim$" not, "." and, "v" either.........or, "$\rightarrow$" if.........then.........Truth tables can then be set up to represent the following statements:

"Conjunction" truth table, with the proposition *p* ("it is snowing") and *q* ("the fields are white").

p statement	*q* statement	*p.q* statement
"It is snowing"	"The fields are white"	"It is snowing and the fields are white"
Actuality	Actuality	
True (It is snowing)	*True* (the fields are white)	Above joint statement *true*.
True (It is snowing)	*False* (the fields are not white)	Above joint statement *false*
False (It is not snowing)	*True* (the fields are white)	Above joint statement *false*
False (It is not snowing)	*False* (the fields are not white)	Above joint statement *false*

Likewise we can write out the following **"Inclusive disjunction"** truth table.

p statement	*q* statement	$p \vee q$ statement
"It is snowing"	"The fields are white"	"Either it is snowing *or* the fields are white *or* possibly both"
Actuality	Actuality	
True (It is snowing)	*True* (the fields are white)	Above joint statement *true* as it is snowing and the fields are white
True (It is snowing)	*False* (the fields are not white)	Above joint statement *true* as it is snowing
False (It is not snowing)	*True* (the fields are white)	Above joint statement *true* as the fields are white
False (It is not snowing)	*False* (the fields are not white)	Above joint statement *false* as the fields are not white and it is not snowing

The five basic truth tables are set out in the first column of Fig. III.1.

Boolean Algebra and Binary Arithmetic

In the second column of Fig. III.1 are set out the same tables using 1 to represent "True" and 0 to represent "False", giving Boolean multiplication and addition. One item needs comment, the first $p+q$ in the addition column. $T + T = T$ or $1 + 1 = 1$ can best be understood if we say everything + everything = everything, and this is the convention of Boolean arithmetic.

Binary arithmetic also has only two digits 1 and 0, but in this case counting proceeds into further columns and $1 + 1 = 10$. In other aspects of addition and multiplication, the two arithmetics are similar. An example of binary arithmetic is:

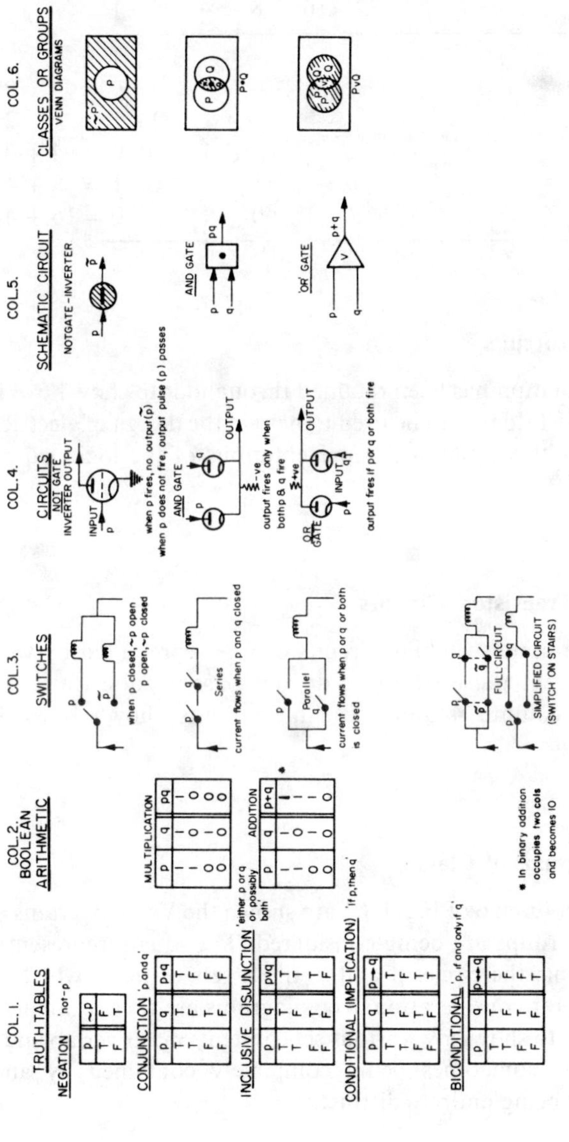

Fig. III.1. Logic and Computers I.

	2^n — — — —	2^5	2^4	2^3	2^2	2^1	2^0	
Decimal		32	16	8	4	2	1	
Binary examples							1	= 1
						1	0	2 + 0 = 2
						1	1	2 + 1 = 3
					1	0	0	= 4 + 0 + 0 = 4
				1	1	0	1	= 8 + 4 + 1 = 13
			1	0	1	1	0	= 16 + 4 + 2 = 22

Switching Circuits

The *p*, *q* notation has been retained throughout to show how, in column 3 of Fig. III.1, logic can be used to help in the design of electrical circuits These circuits are physical representations of the logic truth tables of column 1.

Valve (or Transistor) Circuits

Next these same switching circuits can be represented by valves which pass a current pulse (true) or do not pass a pulse (false). These are shown in column 4 and the same circuits shown schematically in column 5.

Venn Diagrams of Classes

Lastly, in column 6 of Fig. III.1 are shown the Venn diagrams used when classes or groups are being considered. The square represents the total environment; the circles *p* and *q*, those sets of items which have been abstracted for consideration. The diagrams are used as an aid to clarity of thought, to show how various sets of items may overlap and penetrate each other; sometimes being completely contained by another set, sometimes being entirely distinct.

Logical Build-up of Computer Circuits

The basic circuits described in Fig. III.1 are now combined in various ways to compose the logic circuits of the computer. As an example, Fig. III.2 shows first of all the basic "half adder" with the binary sum it is capable of achieving, and secondly, the combination required to make

ADDITION

p	q	CARRY pq	SUM $\bar{p}q+p\bar{q}$
1	1	1	0
1	0	0	1
0	1	0	1
0	0	0	0

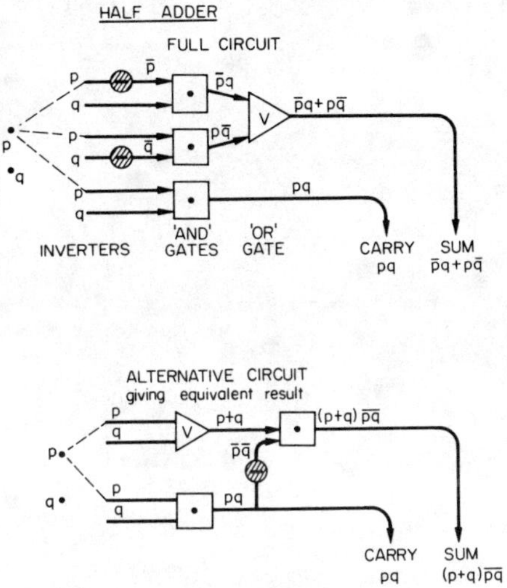

III.2. Logic and Computers II.

ADDITION

p	q	B/F$_{wd}$	CARRY	SUM
1	1	1	1	1
1	1	0	1	0
1	0	1	1	0
1	0	0	0	1
0	1	1	1	0
0	1	0	0	1
0	0	1	0	1
0	0	0	0	0

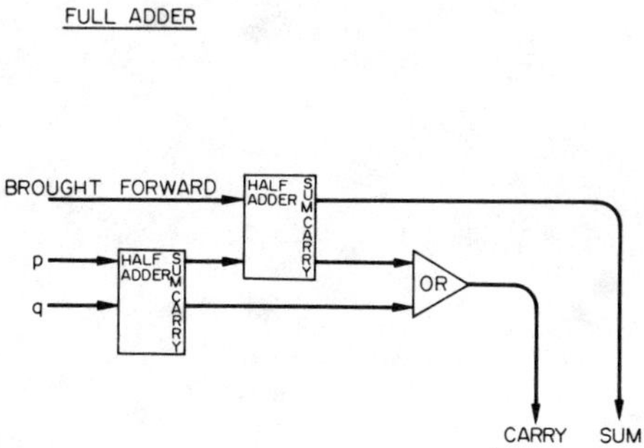

up a "full adder" which is necessary when adding three binary digits. This occurs when there is a carry forward from the previous column.

$$\begin{array}{r} 1\ 1\ 0\ 1 \\ 1\ 1\ 1\ 0 \\ \hline 1\ 1\ 0\ 1\ 1 \end{array}$$

APPENDIX IV

Background to Systems Thinking

Systematic thinking has been with us at least since the time of Aristotle. *Systems* thinking, *systemic* thinking, has sprung into prominence over the last two or three decades.

There is a connection between the two approaches though they are distinctly different modes of thought.

Systematic thinking implies the preparation of a logical framework so that the parts making up a particular branch of knowledge may be examined in logical order and possibly in increasing detail. It implies a static framework into which any particular item may be slotted, gradually building up an interlocking whole. As mentioned in Chapter 4, such frameworks can be regarded as "dynamic" systems having only one state.

Frameworks are important and advances in any branch of knowledge are not likely to occur unless the available data has first been organized in a framework, although after using a particular framework over a period of time for the organization of understanding and method it may become apparent that other frameworks are available and might equally be valid had they been used. However, once thought and knowledge have been developed in a particular way, it is the work of decades to break down the boundaries and to reassemble it in different ways.

Interest next shifts to the dynamic aspects of the interrelationships of the parts making up a whole. No longer pinned down within a single static framework, the parts that make up a whole are seen to be rich in their variety of interrelationships, constantly changing in their contacts with each other and mutually interacting rather than existing within a single chain of cause and effect. Time becomes important as the pattern of interrelationships is dynamic and changes over time.

Origins of thought leading finally to the development of the systems model can be traced back at least as far as Aristotle for the strands of empiricism, unification of science, evolution, and holism, and to Parmenides and Judaism for the concept of monism (oneness). The first two of these strands can be traced through Locke, the empiricists and the encyclopaedists to Comte the positivist, and on towards the logical positivists and Popper. Holism and Monism develop through Spinoza to the dialectic of Hegel and the Scientific Materialism of Marx. Darwin and later Whitehead take up the concepts of evolution and process.

Coming nearer to the present time, the holistic views of von Bertalanffy and Laszlo can be seen to be in similar vein to the *gestalt* of the German psychologists and the political views of Smuts. M'Pherson[1] brings in the views of de Chardin as process theology strongly linked to evolution of the system. De Chardin being a Jesuit does not limit his concept of system evolution entirely to the material plane and further interesting concepts on system evolution have been developed by Joel de Rosney, while at the Sorbonne and M.I.T. Rosney's concepts link the material and the non-material, an area that systems thinking with its important concept of hierarchy will eventually have to face.

Early system thinking was in scientific fields. Some important papers were published in the 1930s, J. Cannon (1932) contrasting the thermodynamic equilibria of machine states with the homeostatic steady state of the organism which "rests" in a state of tension and not a state of entropy. W. Koehler (1938) drew the distinction between open and closed systems, contrasting the laws of thermodynamics developed to explain machine systems considered in isolation as closed systems, with the laws needed to explain organic open systems which traded with their environment importing energy and giving back their output, yet dependent on their environment, "dying" when it dies.

Von Bertalanffy's work, based in physics and biology, was being carried out at the same time, but his rigorous explanation of open systems was not published until 1950. His paper "General systems theory; a new approach to the unity of Science" had great impact. From his work stemmed the Society for General Systems Research, a society devoted to the

[1] "A perspective on systems science and systems philosophy", *Futures* (June 1974).

advancement of systems theory in all fields, with a view to discovering overall principles and developing a common theory to cover all systems. In the scientific field attention was paid to problems of complexity by Ashby (1952), a doctor and director of a neurological institute, Gordon Pask (1958, 1961) was developing adaptive machines that learnt from experience and modified their own programmes, Grey Walter during this same period was building goal-seeking machines.

The social sciences were not slow in taking an interest in this new methodology. K. Boulding, an economist, published an important paper in 1956, "General Systems Theory; the skeleton of science". Katz and Kahn's *The Social Psychology of Organizations* (1966) built on a systems model a theory of organization. Writers on management theory were also using this model in the 1960s. Rensis Likert (1961) was writing on interaction processes and Cyert and March (1963) on the problem of determining goals. The ideas were put into practice through systems engineering, the technique of deliberately designing socio-technical systems.

Acceptance of this new direction of thought has not been too readily absorbed into everyday life, perhaps because of its complexity but also because of the difficulty there is in controlling dynamic situations that are given the opportunity to interact. To those in power control is important. The more fluid systems thinking could not be admitted to thought and allowed to exist side by side with the earlier static systematic thinking until tools not only to explain but also to control the dynamic situation exist. Much reliance is now placed on the newer mathematical techniques and the availability of the computer to process information for decision-making within the extrinsic feedback loops of process systems.

The systems viewpoint can be seen as a contrast to the reductionist methods in which knowledge is obtained by examining ever smaller areas at greater depth. The reductionist method is essentially analytic.

The systems viewpoint places emphasis on the synthetic process, the examination of parts in their relationhsip with one another. This approach is not always possible until the boundaries created by the framework in which knowledge has been organized for the past 300 years of more are partially broken down, and the partial breaking down of a long-standing framework may produce antagonism.

The systems concept is epitomized by emphasis on

Holism (viewing the system as an entity of a different order to the parts making it up).

Monism (having regard to the overall single purpose of the system).

Interrelatedness of parts (with emphasis on the richness of information flow between them).

In the important area of constructed systems, the emphasis is placed on:

The goal or purpose of the system.

Hierarchy, the organization of the sub-systems.

Information flow.

Control examination of the information flow (and subsequent action) better to achieve the stated goals.

Argument of the Systems Holistic Viewpoint

In the developing dialogue with scientific method, systems thinkers would claim that to continue down the reductionist route examining ever smaller parts loses some information, knowledge of the rich variety of interaction between the parts and that equally important to a knowledge of the parts themselves is a knowledge of how they link and behave as a whole unit; that the whole is more than the sum of the parts and of a different order that can be understood only by its examination as a whole; that analytic thinking (examination of parts) must needs be followed by synthetic thinking (when the parts are subsequently reassembled into their "whole" and examination made at the level of the "whole"). The claim is not that the systems viewpoint is the only one to be followed, but rather that both reductionist and systems approaches are necessary to understanding.

A similar problem may arise when only proximate cause and effect ($A \rightarrow B$) between two systems is admitted to a model. The systems thinker admits the rich variety of feedback loops that exist between systems of the 1st, 2nd, 3rd, 4th, . . . , *n*th order and explains this through the concept of mutual causality or mutual dependency ($A \leftrightarrow B$).

Value Assumptions Inherent in the Systems Model

A distinction must be made between

(i) the treatment of "values" within the model,

(ii) the value assumptions inherent in the model itself,

(a) the overall model,

(b) that part of the model that concerns "created" systems.

It is the second part that is of importance to this section.

Value Assumptions of the Model Itself

Systems theory rests on three basic principles accepted in all branches of science:

1. *Order* That there is order in the world and that it is not a completely random world.
2. *Value* That we are able to create measurement.
3. *Evolution* That systems differentiate and become more complex.

To which the systems modeller adds his own specific contribution of

4. *Holism* That the whole consists of more than the sum of the separate parts.
5. *Hierarchy* That one system exists within another in an ever-ascending scale.

In the specific area of *constructed* systems, further value assumptions are built into the general model:

1. That goals are capable of being stated (normally in writing).
2. That certain persons or groups have a right to state goals.
3. That hierarchy cannot be unlimited and that certain levels can be designated as autonomous (for practical control purposes).
4. That attention must be given to information flow and the organization of that information flow into decision and control areas.

Using a New Model

Altering the methodology is a "meta" concept. There is a change in the concept of how we look at the flux of phenomena and how we classify and categorize it:

Use model A to examine data and come to decisions —— that has resulted.

Use model B to examine data and come to decisions —— this has resulted.

Which of these ways of thinking has produced the "better" results and by what criteria can judgement be made between the two?

Why do we choose model B rather than model A?

APPENDIX V

System Process I: Positive and Negative Feedback

In a study of system dynamics it is useful to cover some of the "standard" modes of working of a system. Real-life systems will operate in an irregular manner but often their working can be analysed by relating the output states they show to known theoretical models. A knowledge of such standard modes of working can also help when an attempt is being made to predict future states of a real-life system. The present "tone" and some prediction of future states of a socio-technical system can be judged by examining the systems' working over time and, probably on a model, its reaction to disturbances and changes of input. Where we have a model we may then be able to relate its pattern of output states over time to the basic reaction patterns of some of the basic system structures and, seeing the way that the output of a specific system is moving as time elapses, it may then be possible to say "that looks like a —— system, let's check it for fit".

Growth Model: Positive Feedback

Growth can be linear
Fig. V.1 shows a step increase, which is often associated with sudden increase in *input*, akin to a disturbance of the system. It is not typical of *output* working. As a step increase works through the system it is more likely to be smoothed by interaction with other input parameters and the delays and interactions within the system itself into an output more typical of Fig. V.2.
Figure V.3 shows a linear increase from one level to another: the type of

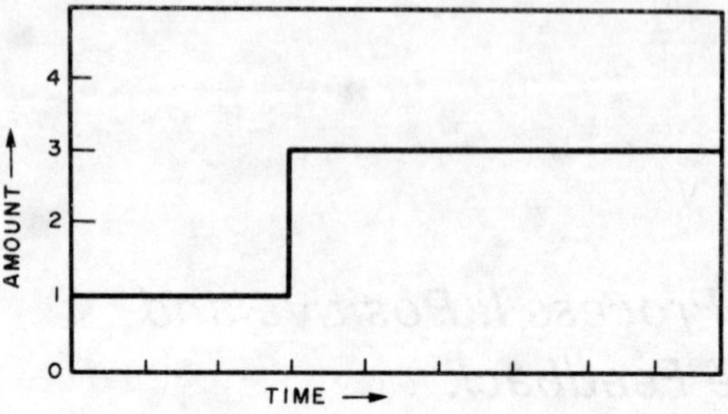

Fig. V.1. Step increase.

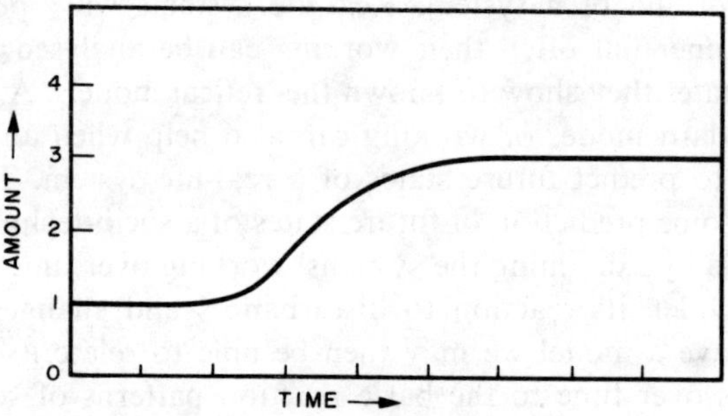

Fig. V.2. Smoothed output.

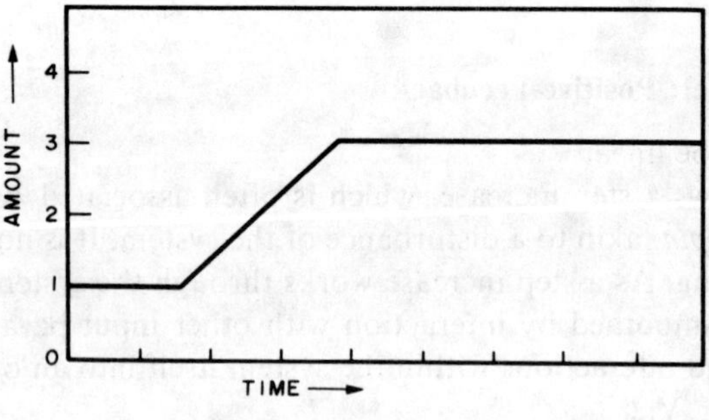

Fig. V.3. Ramp increase.

movement that any administrator might well be expecting to be able to arrange to accommodate new work. Relative to the amount of work being handled at the beginning of any time period the increase per time period is largest at the start of the slope and tapers off considerably towards the end. The increases are of fixed amount per time period and therefore of decreasing amount when related to the cumulated level at the beginning of each time period.

Exponential growth is a word frequently used in current literature. Exponential growth means a doubling in amount per fixed time period, although the phrase is used to cover any increasing growth situation that builds on the previous time period, be the increase more than double, exactly double or less than double per time period.

Figure V.4a shows an exponential curve that is doubling per time period. Figure V.4b a curve that is increasing by only half as much again per time period. Figure V.4c a curve that is more than doubling per

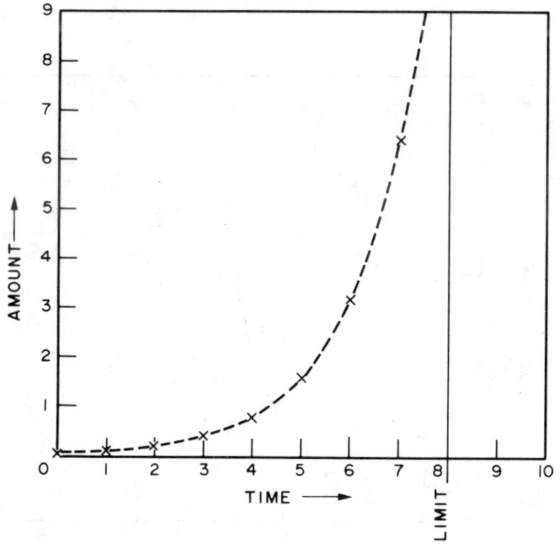

Fig. V.4 (a). Exponential growth curve approaching a limit (increase 100% per time period).

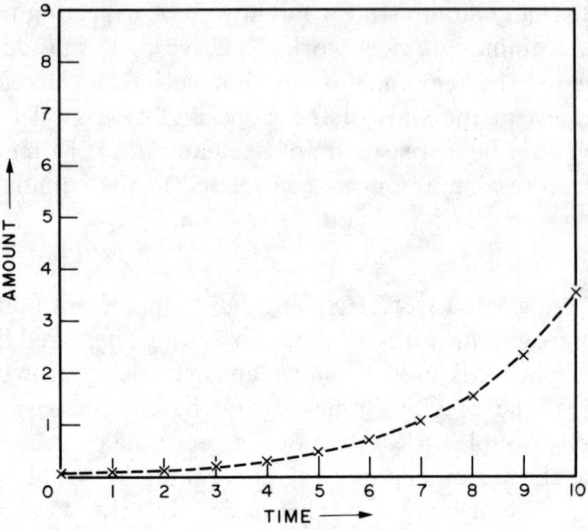

Fig. V.4. (b). Growth curve (increase 50% per time period).

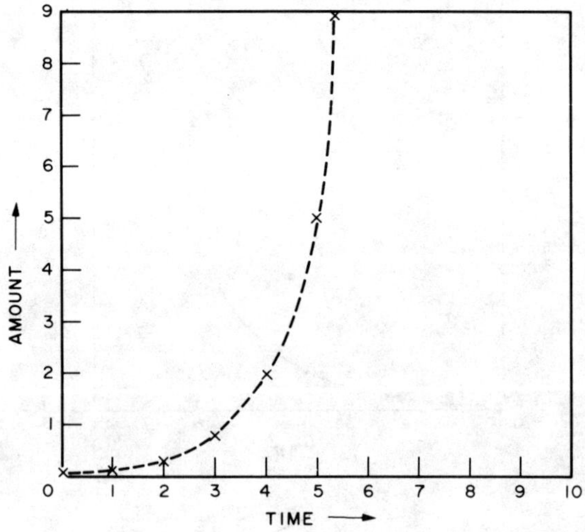

Fig. V.4. (c) Explosive growth curve (increase 150% per time period).

fixed time period or as it can also be put, doubling on a decreasing time period. This type of growth is often referred to as explosive.

Figure V.5 shows all these three curves on the same graph. The patterns are similar. The point at issue is the different speeds with which each curve approaches and leaves the top of the graph.

An example of an exponential curve might be that of a farmer and his wife with a large but fixed size of farm. He has two sons and two

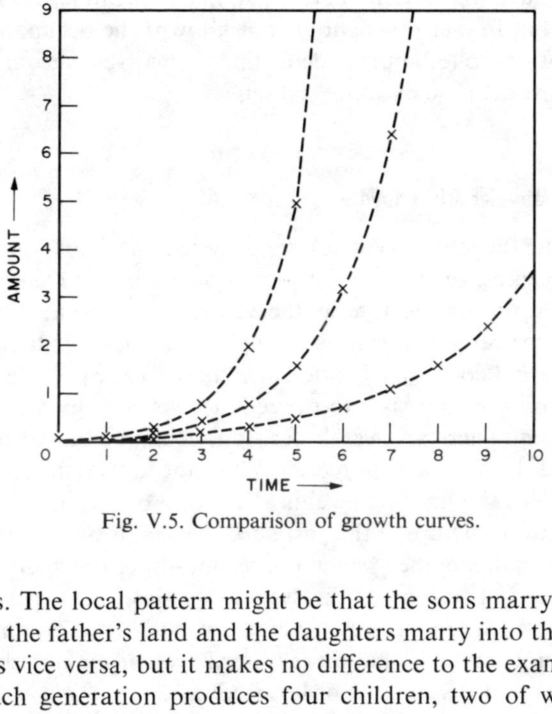

Fig. V.5. Comparison of growth curves.

daughters. The local pattern might be that the sons marry outside but take over the father's land and the daughters marry into the next farm. Often it is vice versa, but it makes no difference to the example. If each family each generation produces four children, two of whom marry outsiders and stay on the land, the pattern goes.

Families supported 1, 2, 4, 8, 16, 32, 64, 128, 256, 512, 1024,
by fixed farm land 2048, 4096, 8192, 16,384

In other words, the curve goes "off the graph" by about time 6. Obviously this great increase does not happen. Some sons join the army and do not come back. Some marry but do not have four children. Some go into industry, some die of starvation. Some look for other lands or worlds. Pressures and constraints mount as the system-carrying capacity of that particular environment is reached, the amount of people the farm can feed. The carrying limit may alter due to technical advances but it will remain as a limiting constraint at some point.

One problem with exponential growth is that the situation moves in so short a time period from well within the system-carrying capacity to well above. If the carrying capacity in this example is 52 families with a given technology (but in fact this figure is not known) the occupants appear well placed at time 5 (32) but suddenly find themselves in trouble at time 6 (64) and past the time of taking action.

Negative Feedback: First Order

The first-order negative feedback loop system has one variable that rises in succeeding time periods towards a limiting value, quickly at first then at a decreasing rate as the variable approaches its limiting value. This type of system can be exemplified by a water tank filled by a pipe with a ballcock that is gradually turned off by the level of the water in the cistern as it rises to the required level or by a single stock ordering system where an overall decision technique has to be applied to bring stock back to a required level but not to overshoot. The time taken to achieve the limiting level is a function of the size of the components and the structure of the particular system. Response time could be altered by changing the system to a second-order one by introducing more variables but as long as the system remains a first-order system, the response time can only be altered by altering the components; making the pipe larger so that more water flows, or making the periods at which stock is ordered more or less frequent.

Each point plotted is

$$\text{“Position in previous time period} + \frac{1}{N} \times \text{(The difference between the required level and the level measured)”}$$

where N is the fraction of the difference "absorbed" in each time period. As an example, starting with a variable value of 100 and building towards a limiting value of 800 with increases of 50% or one-half of the measured difference in each time period we obtain the values shown in Table 21.

TABLE 21

Time period	Position of variable	Measured difference required (800—actual)	Correction toward required position one-half of difference	New position variable
0	100	700	350	450
1	450	350	175	625
2	625	175	87	712
3	712	88	44	756
4	756	44	22	778
5	778	22	11	789
6	789	11	5	794
7	794	6	3	797
8	797	3	2	799

These figures are plotted as curve A on Fig. V.6.

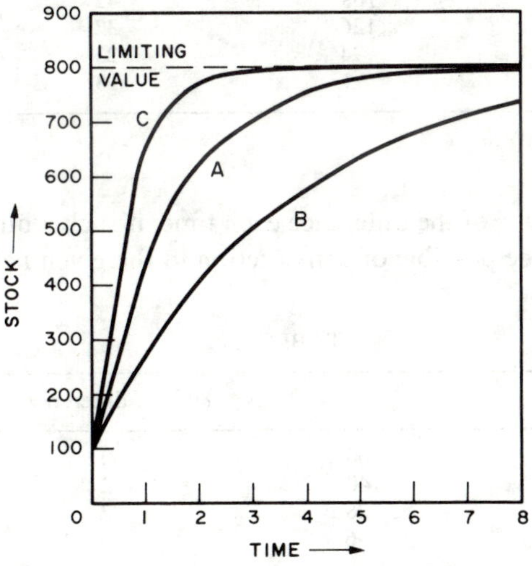

Fig. V.6. Negative feedback: first-order approach to a limiting value.

Theoretically the limiting variable is never reached, but in all practical situations it is reached as soon as the difference (required—actual) becomes less than the unit in which the system is capable of dealing, e.g. the smallest acceptable order may be 10 units in which case the limit is reached at time 6. If a component size is altered, but the structure remains the same, the speed with which the desired level is reached is altered, but the shape of the curve remains the same.

25% or one-quarter of the difference absorbed each time period would give us that shown in Table 22.

TABLE 22

Time period	Position of variable	Measured difference required (800-actual)	Correction towards required position one-quarter of difference	New position of variable
0	100	700	175	275
1	275	525	131	406
2	406	395	99	505
3	505	295	72	577
4	577	223	55	632
5	632	168	42	674
6	674	126	32	706
7	706	94	23	729
8	729	71	18	747

Curve B on Fig. V.6.

On taking up 80% of the difference each time, if such a quickly reacting system were to be possible of construction in the given field (Table 23).

TABLE 23

			80% of difference	
0	100	700	560	660
1	660	140	112	772
2	772	28	22	794
3	794	6	5	799

Curve C on Fig. V.6.

The obvious question is: why not construct a system that could absorb the whole of the difference in one time period? The answers are possible difficulties of construction, cost and side effects. If a water cistern's inlet is so large that it could be filled in one second the water would come out in such a swoosh that it would be unlikely to stay in the tank. Ordering goods from a wholesaler who could deliver immediately might involve large delivery costs and high stock-carrying costs.

Negative Feedback: Second order

First-order negative feedback systems are met only in the simplest of circumstances. The second-order negative-feedback system has two level variables. Often this situation may be occasioned by the introduction of a delay in the information channel. Typically the second-order negative-feedback system approaches its limiting value at too steep an angle, overshoots and then dies down to a dampened oscillation that

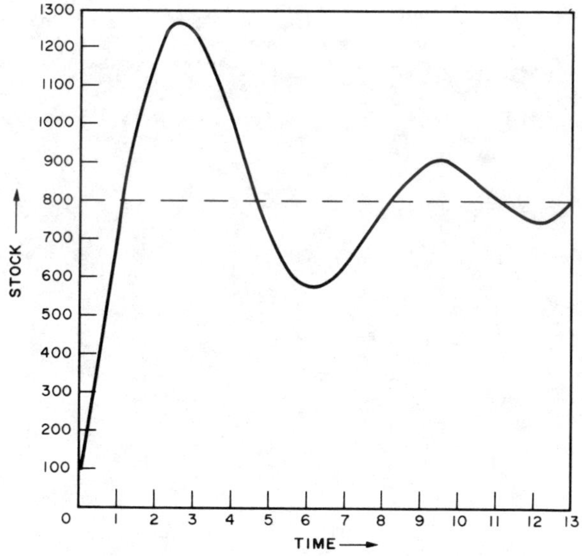

Fig. V.7. Negative feedback: second-order approach to a limiting value.

finally approaches the limiting value, or possibly continues to oscillate around that value, Fig. V.7.

The pattern of all higher-order feedback approximates that of second order but with less pronounced swing. Second-order feedback patterns are important as they are relatively easy to calculate and are a useful approximation of all higher-order feedback systems models.

If the various level variables and rates of flow of the second-order negative-feedback system are plotted on the same graph, they can be seen to peak at different points in time. An analysis of system working can be made from the pattern they show. In using such patterns to analyse the working of socio-technical systems, the equations taken to generate the flows are more usually not analytic algebraic equations from which any point in a curve can be calculated immediately, but simulation technique equations that, from a given starting-point, calculate the interaction and the values of the variables sequentially, each set of values being calculated from those existing in the preceding period of time.

APPENDIX VI

System Process II: System-carrying Capacity

Diagnosis of System Performance

Diagnosis of system performance has two main aspects:

1. To examine the inputs to a system and from these inputs to attempt to *predict* likely future states of the system under review (considered in this appendix).
2. To examine a system as it is currently operating and, being a constructed system, to attempt to *improve* the efficiency of working by examining and where thought necessary altering the structure of the system by altering some of its parts or the way they interact (considered in Appendix VII).

As example of (1) we will take a system where the output is beginning to behave exponentially. The model can be used to explore and diagnose many of the problem areas likely to be encountered by managers and if not to provide solutions, at least to show where the decision points are. As presented here the model is visual (graphic) and incorporates a timescale so that short-term and long-term positions can be seen together.

The Exponential System

Decision 1. The location of the system-carrying capacity.
In a socio-technological system, where the system output is approaching the saturation point of its environment it may be important to make

a time estimate of how soon the limit will be reached and if, in that time, technological breakthrough will enable the capacity limit to be raised, e.g. will advertising produce a bigger market or technical know-how to enable one to allow more cars on the road? If the point 1 on Fig. VI.1 is already reached and point 2 will be reached in 3 years, a technical breakthrough that raises the system-carrying capacity, say, 20% from A to B may only allow a further 2-year period of growth. A large-scale

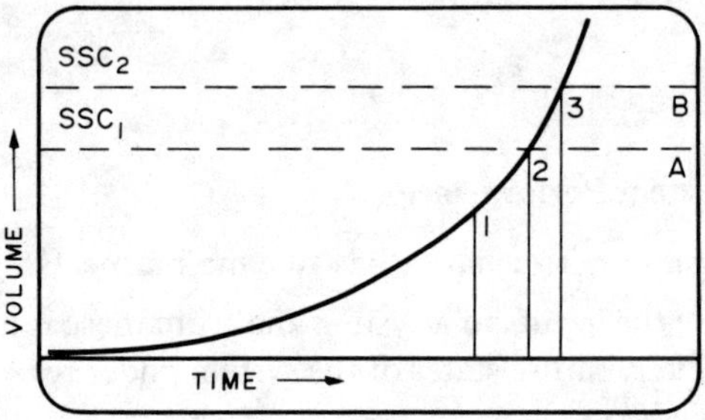

Fig. VI.1. Location of the environment's system-carrying capacity (SCC).

technical breakthrough of, say, 10 times or 1000% may produce the situation in Fig. VI.2 where in effect the system-carrying capacity has ceased to be a constraint that requires consideration for some years ahead. System-carrying capacity is an environmental constraint as far as a single organization is concerned, but the level will be determined by overall technical know-how and the speed with which that alters.

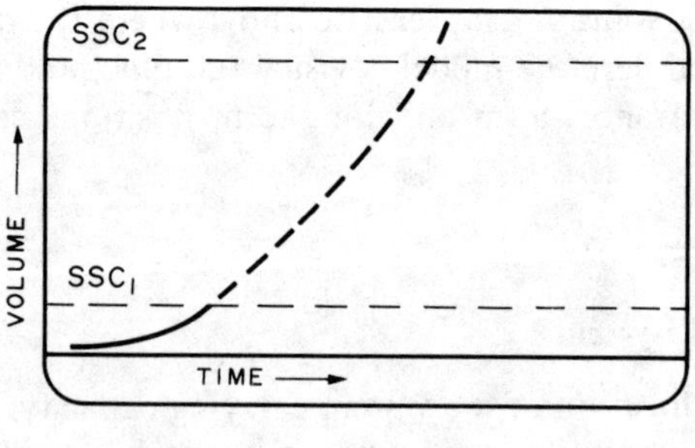

Fig. VI.2. Large-scale technological breakthrough alters location of the system-carrying capacity (SCC).

Beyond the technical constraint there is likely to be an absolute system-carrying-capacity level that is a function of quantity. The line itself is not necessarily straight and may fluctuate over time as it interacts with other systems. The manager requires to know what his constraints are, how likely they are to be altered in the few years ahead, and at what scale the change in level is likely to take place. An estimate of the system-carrying capacity level is necessary before further decisions can be undertaken using this model.

Decision 2. Relates to the curve on the graph. This is a single curve that embodies both output and marketing. Basically it relates to output, but of course output does not continue for long if the output is not bought or absorbed usefully.

The system-carrying capacity (SCC) is fixed, the curve is seen to be approaching the limit within a short time period (Fig. VI.3). Should some types of avoiding decision be taken at point A, or should the output be allowed to overshoot to point B to see what happens?

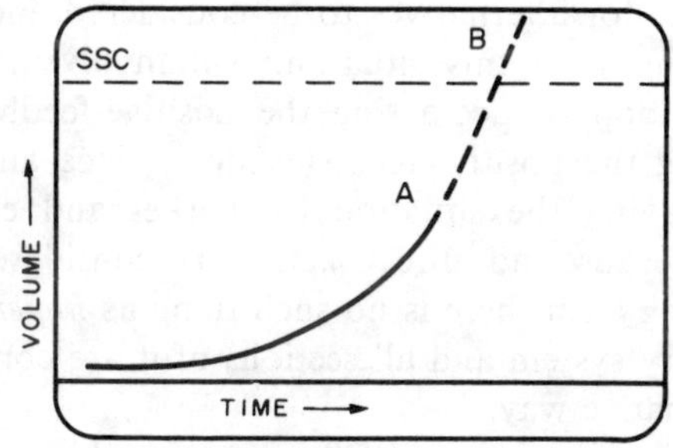

Fig. VI.3. Decision points.

Decision 3. If it is felt that some action is called for at point A (Fig. VI.4), such action will depend on viewpoints. Is a definite plan necessary to bring the level of output within the fixed SCC level (line A_1), or can it be left entirely for impersonal market forces to gradually make the situation unpleasant (overcrowding, a drop in selling price, a sharp rise in cost of provision of services) and so smooth off the curve in the same way? (Line A_2).

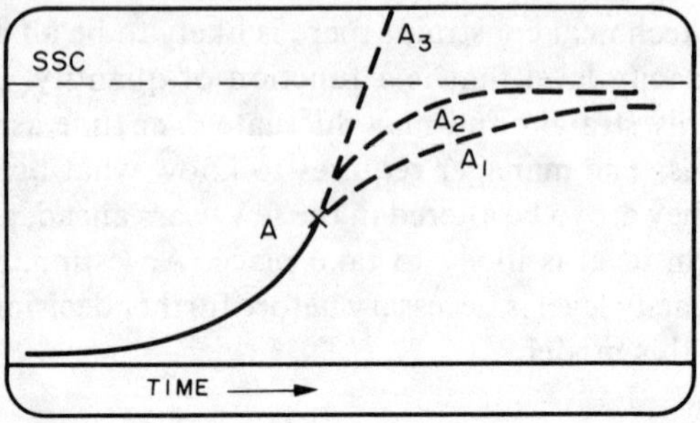

Fig. VI.4. Decision to alter or leave to market forces.

This decision to do or not to do is a crucial one. If intervention is to be carried out successfully it must take place at a point A because the timescale between point A and the time at which the output passes the SCC level is the minimum in which there is time for planning to take effect. At a later point in time only crash programmes could be introduced. The decision is between (i) planning and (ii) market forces. Planning takes time for alternatives to be considered and plans to be implemented. Planning in this situation will involve increasing the negative-feedback loop or decreasing the positive-feedback loop: in some way reducing the positive-feedback dominance and so slowing down growth. Leaving the situation to market and environmental forces is easier because no direct action is considered necessary, although in the long term there is no such thing as *impersonal* market forces, the monetary system and all sections of it are constantly being adjusted in a normative way.

World rubber production in the 1930s met with this problem. Plans were made to curtail output of natural rubber as all the output could not be absorbed. The plans were not implemented successfully and production continued at too high a level, the market was saturated and the price fell disastrously from the seller's point of view.

Decision 4. No decision to plan is taken at point A and the market forces do not in fact operate, so the output arrives at point B. It may possibly be found that a wrong estimate of the SCC has been made and that the system still functions in a tolerable manner at point B (Fig. VI.5). The

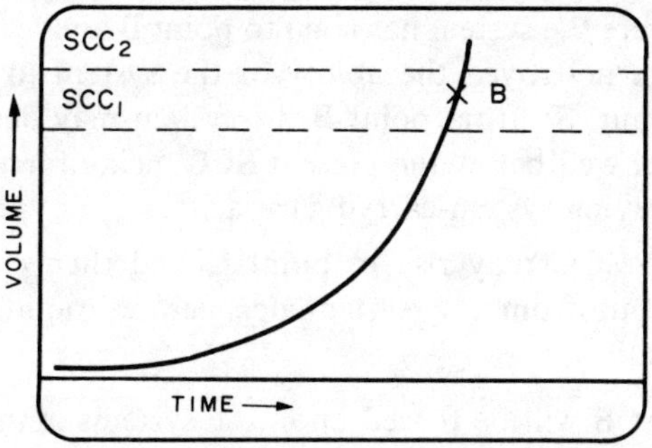

Fig. VI.5. Further estimation of the system-carrying capacity (SCC) level.

SCC has in effect been advanced to a higher level. Unless, however, there has been real technological breakthrough, the output is likely to pass the SCC at some point in the fairly near future. Many possibilities can occur from point B; these can be epitomized in four examples (Fig. VI.6):

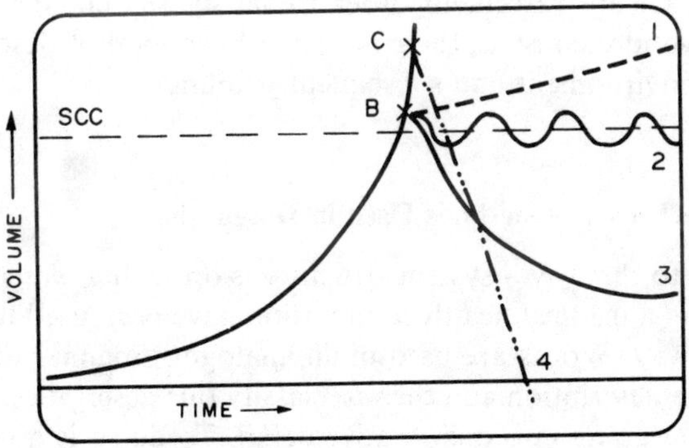

Fig. VI.6. Possibilities after passing the actual system-carrying capacity (SCC) level.

Line 1. A continued but steady small growth pressing against an SCC increasing slightly due to some technical advancement.

Line 2. An oscillation above and below the SCC, moving from crisis to crisis.

Line 3. Where the system has risen to point B above the SCC it may have destroyed the ability of the system to cope with the output. So from point B the system may decay to a stable level well below the present SCC, being forced there by the decaying system-carrying capacity.

or Line 4. The SCC may rise to point C and then collapse. So the output from the system degenerates rapidly to the zero position.

The situation at B will be forced upon the systems manager and from past experience it is very difficult to predict which of these events is likely to occur. The manager will then have little time to plan, though he may still be able to influence which possibility occurs. This example of exponential operation of a system exemplifies one of the ways in which a manager may examine his data and diagnose likely future outcomes. The model may be used to examine small-scale decisions, for example the decision whether or not to open a shop in a particular area. It may also show that when smaller companies that have a moderate market (SCC) are forced, in order to satisfy shareholder returns, to expand beyond their SCC, there is a great likelihood of destroying their own local environment and subsequently failing.

Descriptive Terms Sometimes Used in Diagnosis

In relation to the way a system structure is operating, *descriptive terms* often having a medical health connotation have been used for diagnosis in general way. Words are used in an analogous manner to build up a system state description and then to classify this description as a stereotype without going into quantitative detail. To do so is not a very safe procedure, yet perhaps because of emotional and motivational factors it is an approach frequently used, particularly in speeches, and because of this an explanation of the terms is included here.

Working Under Capacity

The system has some resources in all spheres that are not being used, and increased output could take place.

Normal Working (a little in reserve)

Excess capacity has been pared down and a balance between system parts obtained. Some reserves are being kept for expected problem situations.

Full Stretch

All reserves are being fully utilized. Any problem situations that arise, including expected problems, may involve a cutback.

Overstrained

The stress may be internal or external. The system can continue working for some time depending on its robustness, but parts are likely to suffer permanent damage in some degree and may not return to normal when the stress is removed.

Pathological functioning

The system continues to exist and to function not in the desired manner but in a manner which from a given standpoint, often that of the observer, can best be described as unhealthy or abnormal.

Neurotic

Again the system continues to exist and function but in an obsessive manner; paying greater attention to specific aspects of its functioning than is useful for the functioning of the whole system.

Crisis

The normal functioning of the system is interrupted by a situation for which it is not prepared and which it may not have the resources to overcome. If the system has the necessary resources available the effects of the crisis may be overcome. If not crisis will lead on to breakdown.

Breakdown

Some cessation of functioning is observed. This may be overcome by treating the part that breaks down as a sub-system and removing it from the main system. Alternatively the broken-down system may be absorbed by a larger system and further resources provided.

From the point of view of the system broken down, there will be disintegration and cessation to exist as a system. Provision of further resources may come at too late a time to prevent disintegration.

APPENDIX VII

Correction of Working in a Constructed System and System Checklist

The analytical approach to improving effectiveness may well not be useful for natural systems that evolve slowly as functioning wholes, and which may have taken millions of years to achieve their present state of balance.

But the strategies here described are concerned with man-created systems, technical and socio-technical systems, such as process and information systems which have been created out of their parts; systems which may have a lifespan of 5, 10, 20 years. Systems of this class may well function the better if aspects of their functioning are regularly inspected and where possible improved, without going to the extent of designing a completely new system. The system is already in operation. It is being examined for rectification and for improvement rather than replacement. The approaches are suitable for application to any man-created system. Such man-created systems are classed as *normative* systems. Compared with a biological system, for example a human being, they are of short evolution. The balance of their parts has not come about by interaction over thousands of years. Because of this lack of long evolutionary development we may well be able to improve performance by analysing and improving the operation *parts* of such systems, all the time remembering that it is the effectiveness of the *overall* functioning that is important.

As a general statement under normal working a system may tend towards a differentiation of its parts. Under stress a system is likely to

regress to a more "authoritarian" structure exemplified by a simplification of internal structure and a more direct control of each part.
Work may be carried out to locate and replace parts of the system that may have broken down, or alterations to detailed parts of the system may be carried out either to improve overall performance or to reduce cost while maintaining existing standards of performance.

Location of Faults

Malfunctioning may occur:

(i) In one or more *parts* of the system.

(ii) In the *interrelationship* of the parts or in the actual interfaces between the parts.

(iii) In the *operation* of the system, leading to a poor mode of working.

(iv) In the *use* to which the system is put and the goals it is attempting to achieve.

(v) In the *control* of the system, leading to sub-standard output.

Caused by:

faulty design of parts;

good design of parts but faulty interrelationship (incompatibility);

unreliability of parts;

poor maintenance;

poor operator training;

mismatch of goals and system used to achieve these goals;

poor monitoring of system working, allowing faults to develop to a point where they badly affect system output.

Certain types of system will be prone to particular types of malfunctioning. For example, there will be some difference between the types of fault likely to occur in a technology-dominated system where there is likely to be complete breakdown of parts and socio-technical systems that are more likely to be plagued by poor performance rather than the complete breakdown of parts.

Tracing of Malfunctioning in Technology-dominated Systems

Take our previous example of a car. It will not start. How can one approach the problem?

1. Collect information about symptoms.
2. Examine information and form hypothesis about likely cause of symptoms.
3. Inspect equipment and locate sub-system in which fault occurs.
4. Check the parts making up that sub-system.
5. Remove cause of trouble, repairing or replacing as necessary the cause and any subsequent damage that may have resulted from the cause.
6. Check for correct functioning.

As regards this problem, a car as a system can be said to have the sub-systems shown in Table 24.

Using an adaption of the principle of dichotomy the sub-systems not likely to be causing the trouble can be eliminated, lubrication, water

TABLE 24

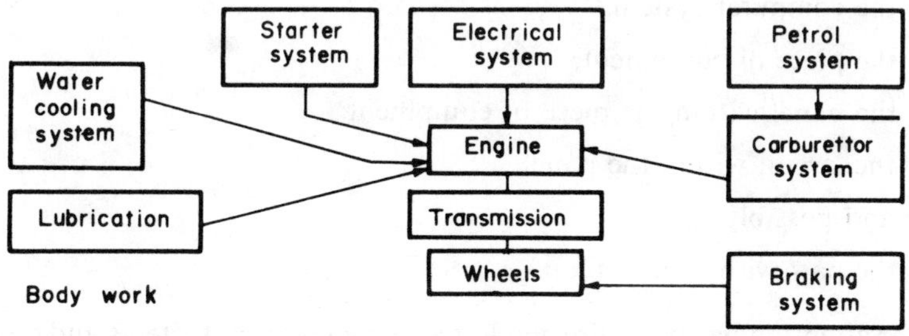

cooling. The starter motor turns, so we can concentrate on the petrol/carburettor and electrical systems. Petrol is checked to see that it is flowing, so concentration can take place on the electrical system which is the most likely cause. However, as work progresses it is seen that the whole engine is soaking wet and the cause is located as a split in the radiator, the water having been blown back over the engine whilst the car was moving.

It is the electrical system that does not function as the plugs are wet. These are dried out and after a lot of trouble the engine starts. However, the problem is not yet solved, for the water-cooling system must be filled with water and unless the cause of the trouble, the split in the radiator, is located and removed by plugging in some way, then symptoms in the electrical system will recur within a very short time.

To take another example within the same diagnostic framework. It might be found that the starter motor had jammed. This is freed and all parts of the starter motor system examined for correct functioning. It is found to be correct. However, the trouble recurs shortly. The fault is finally traced to faulty operator usage. The engine does not fire at the first attempt so the starter control is pulled several times in quick succession without sufficient pause being allowed between each attempt, resulting in the jamming. The fault lies not in the hardware system but in the liveware system itself. If the driver got so annoyed and pulled the starter so hard it finally came away in his hand, the fault could be said to lie in the liveware/hardware interface.

Locating techniques moving from large to small are used in finding faulty parts in computers, zeroing in on the faulty component from the overall position:

the computer system,

the piece of equipment,

the panel within the piece of equipment,

the circuit within the panel,

and possibly,

the part within the circuit.

So far attention has been directed to technical repair of systems and cost has not entered in. In the tracing and subsequent repair of faults in technological systems, the cost may not be considered the first few times the fault occurs, but very shortly cost will become a prime consideration. Cost of repair time and system downtime is kept to a minimum by replacing a unit rather than trying to repair it on the spot. The faulty unit can then be inspected in the factory and decisions made to repair or scrap. The system of which it is a part has been repaired and is working whilst these repair or scrap decisions are being taken. For any technological system the reliability of parts, availability of spares and the cost of maintenance and repairs are of vital importance. The situation contrasts strongly with social systems where these aspects are seldom considered in such detail.

Industrial Diagnosis

Moving to larger-scale socio-technical systems, the problem is more often one of poor operation rather than breakdown. Poor operation can make itself evident in two ways:

1. Poor technological operation, which reflects into costs, but which may be masked by the overall buoyancy of an expanding environment so that it is not noticed for a time.

2. Poor supporting decisions. The technical equipment may be in excellent working order, but managerial decisions may decide on the wrong product mix and marketing may be poor, so that the operation of the overall organization produces a very low return.

Investigation into low performance of complex socio-technical systems begins with a consideration of goals. Is the system designed to achieve the goals it is at present expected to achieve? For example, a steel mill may be highly integrated and automated ready to run continuously with high output. It is not likely to run efficiently from either a technical or cost point of view if only a few short-run orders can be obtained. Diagnosis of poor operation efficiency would cover:

1. Consideration of goals, and relationship between system as

designed and the present conditions under which it is expected to run.

2. Design of individual sub-systems and the degree of integration between sub-systems.

3. Technical efficiency with which sub-systems operate, including reliability and number of breakdowns.

4. Lack of control over the environment/system and system/environment interfaces leading to loss of "tension" in the open system at these points rather than through the ineffective working of the parts of the system itself.

If time is available it may be useful at this point to model the present situation and carry out a dynamic study to discover the relative effects of costs of improvements and benefits obtained. *Sensitivity analysis* will show which of the technical improvements will reflect most strongly into costs and available resources can be concentrated at these points. Subsystems working in highly integrated systems will be affected by the operation of previous stages. Improvements at certain key points in a highly integrated complex system may set off chain reactions of the type discussed in "mutual causality" and produce dramatic improvement. Location of these pressure points and concentration of available resources is a key technique in industrial diagnosis. But it is not easy and if a wrong analysis is made and resources are devoted to allaying symptoms rather than curing a cause, the total effect may merely be the expenditure of expensive and "one-off" resources for very little result and eventual collapse.

Although many optimizing techniques are available to ensure optimal working of the various parts of a system, it is the overall improvement in working of the whole complex system that is sought. It is unlikely that *analytical* optimizing techniques are powerful enough to cover the whole of a complex system and for this reason dynamic *simulation* techniques covering operation of the whole system are recommended in order to synthesize the first-stage analytic models and discover an improved but not necessarily optimal mode of operation.

Systems Checklist

The checklist[1] following has been built up from the description of a system given in earlier chapters. Using this model we may ask questions about all aspects of the systems functioning with a view to improving certain parts and hence improving the overall functioning of the whole.
Section A is concerned with elucidating the stance that a particular observer takes up in relationship to any given system; his style of observation.
Section B is concerned with a description of the system under review and with isolating the given system from the rest of the environment.
The way a checklist is set out normally gives the impression that it is to be filled in sequentially, starting at question 1. To some extent only is this true of this form. There can usefully be iteration between at least section A and parts S1–10 of section B. As parts of section B are filled in it may be deemed necessary to go back and modify the approach first set out in section A.
Section C examines in some detail the control aspects of the system isolated. In most cases the meaning of questions asked will be evident from a previous reading of the text.

Measurement

Key aspects of each part of the system are questioned. Each of these questions requires an answer in word description, unit if any suitable one is available, and the resultant effect on cost. Where it is possible to devise quantitative units and later to correlate such units with monetary values, three answers to each of the questions posed in the questionnaire can be given:

Present situation and cost	Possible improvements Estimated cost	Expected benefit to overall system if changed, expressed in monetary terms

The specific task envisaged is to locate poor functioning of parts of the normative system under review and to improve such aspects, always

[1] An earlier version of this checklist first appeared in the *Journal of Systems Engineering*, University of Lancaster, Vol. 3, No. 1, 1972, Donald.

with a view to improving *overall* performance. To obtain perfect functioning is nearly always prohibitively expensive but in the middle range of functioning some improvements can often be achieved without too much expense, though any correlation between improved performance as measured in some unit and the £'s cost of such improvement is probably non-linear.

Although accuracy in measurement of the improvement may not be possible because a satisfactory unit has not been developed it should still be possible to show an *approximate* cost or benefit from such an improvement.

Measurement at the Margin

Again *total* costs (reasonably easy to calculate) and *total* benefits (not so easy to calculate or predict) of any system may not be so easy to obtain as all experiment within an undertaking starts from an on-going situation. However, it is submitted that this method of appraisal is quite suitable at the margin—to give *incremental* costs of proposed alterations and *incremental* expected benefits to be obtained from such changes, discounting the cash flow over a somewhat short time horizon. If marginal costs and benefits are then built up over several successive changes to a system, the amount of costs and benefits measured may soon aggregate a substantial coverage of the totals involved.

The analysis proposed has therefore two separate objectives:

(a) To improve an existing normative system of any type by examining *aspects* of its working and suggesting improvements in its control and operation.

(b) To calculate *incremental* costs and benefits (rather than *total* costs and benefits) of the proposed changes as a method of approach to the problem of the cost effectiveness of systems.

The Model

By definition a normative system comprises what its author or examiner decides *is* the system and, having such power, he needs to make sure that his definition of the boundaries of the system to be reviewed is a useful one. His own experience of past occasions and an understanding of what others have found to be effective systems to isolate for study are his only guide here.

Questionnaire for Examination of a System in Operation

Section I

A. GENERAL FRAMEWORK OF THE EXAMINATION

Type of system (S) *under review*
- (i) Reality system
- (ii) Model of a reality system
- (iii) Conceptualized system
- (iv) Abstract system

Observer (O)

O.1 Standpoint of observer (prospect taken)

What aspects is observer interested in?

(e.g. if a socio-technical system is it technology, information flow, values, economic and markets, social aspects?)

Does the observer place himself within or outside the system?

If outside { Distance from the system; Depth (altitude) of analysis (observation) undertaken }

If within His position within the system

O.2 *Attitude of observation* Descriptive
Classificatory
Analytic
Synthetic

O.3 *Mode of observation* Static
Dynamic

O.4 *Concerned with*
- (i) Representational aspects of the system
  Control (steering) aspects of the system
  Predictive possibilities of the system
  Planning and growth processes of the system
- (ii) External relationships system/environment
  Systems internal working parts and interfaces
- (iii) Development of the system (i.e. structural change that may take place within the system or within the environment)

The observer then either (1) constructs his system model or (2) isolates his physical system for study or constructs overtly his abstract system.

B. DESCRIPTION OF THE SYSTEM and ITS OVERALL PROPERTIES

S.1 Name of system under review
Position in system hierarchy
(i) Larger system of which part
(ii) Sub-systems
(iii) Any system with which the system is known (or expected) to be in a relationship of mutual causality

S.2 BOUNDARIES of system
Define
Permeability or impermeability
Security
System model. Open
Information-tight
Closed

S.3 TOTAL COST of operation (process system and control system) if available.

S.4 Analysis to be taken to the depth which will allow the system to be classified as.

Deterministic ☐

Probabilistic ☐

Self-organizing ☐

S.5 Is the system Reactive? (stimulus-responsive)
Proactive? (planned-response)
Impactive? (self-starter)

S.6 GOAL of the system if it is goal-seeking and how and by whom these goals have been defined
OR
Description of the on-going DRIVE that causes optimization of the system
Are the defined goals long term, short term or both?
Who has authority to state goals?

S.7 Overall criteria
Who "censors" goals?
Hierarchy structure

S.8 CRITERION used for measuring the achievement of the goal. Ranking of the criteria if there are several

S.9 A short description of the VALUE JUDGEMENTS used as justification for employing the above criteria as measure of effectiveness of the system

S.10 ENVIRONMENT (necessary where the system model has been classified as an open system or information-tight, but not if it is closed)
Environment$_1$ (i) Present state
Interactions with system
Possible future states
(ii) Boundary E_1/E_2

Environment$_2$

S.11 INPUTS

1. Materials
2. Energy (human and material)
3. Information (input system)

S.12 OUTPUTS

In general terms (see C.1 for detailed description)

OVERALL STATE OF SYSTEM

S.13 Is output tied to static level or fluctuating, randomly or seasonally?

S.14 Output response to change in input by controller—Time delay in input–output response, active/sluggish

S.15 Oscillation/attenuation achieved by present control

S.16 Noise. Extraneous/built-in/random

S.17 Redundancy, and liability to breakdown in functioning (i.e. need for redundancy)

C. INTERNAL ASPECTS OF THE SYSTEM

Structure	consisting of interrelated sub-systems (STR)
STR 1	Perception sub-systems
2	Decision-making sub-systems
3	Implementation sub-systems (action)
4	Goal formulation sub-systems (positive feedback) + advisory sub-systems
5	Control sub-systems (negative feedback)
6	Advisory sub-systems
7	Information sub-systems

Properties	of the structure (PR)
PR 1	Parts involved—number of sub-systems of each kind
2	Coupling—pattern in which sub-systems joined
3	Interfaces between parts. Opaqueness. Gaps
4	Compatibility of parts
5	Mutual dependency of parts

Action process	of system (ACPR)
ACPR 1	Normal *process* within the system
2	Mechanisms of *change* in structure
	(i) Self-regulatory: homeostasis programmed growth/decay
	(ii) Change in variety and complexity of structure variety and complexity of response
	(iii) Change in durability and transience

Limits of acceptable change and crisis (breakdown) points.

SECTION II

CONTROL ASPECTS	PRESENT SITUATION			POSSIBLE IMPROVEMENTS			
	Description in words	Unit if any	Cost £'s (if available)	Description in words	Unit if any	Cost £'s (single cost or per period)	Expected benefit to total system
C.1 Output measured							
1.1 Is output continuous or discrete?							
1.2 Is measurement continuous, intermittent or random?							
1.3 If intermittent, what intervals?							
1.4 What is measured? How many characteristics of the output? Unit used? (£'s, Statistical quantity, Ranking, Descriptive)							
1.5 Important aspects as yet unmeasured? Reason? (No unit, Too expensive, No time, Other). Information screened out							
1.6 Delay in measurement?							
C.2 The Sensor							
2.1 Physical type? (Process/Human, Self-recording/other)							
2.2 Efficiency in measurement?							
2.3 How many sensors? (redundancy?)							
2.4 "Noise" (i.e. wrong information) introduced? (Accidentally, By design, Too much data, Useless data)							

C.3 Control loop							
3.1 Is it discernible? If so is it (a) internal? (b) external? (a) intrinsic? (b) extrinsic? Does it contain (a) Physical content of same type as main process? (b) information only? Timing of loop Response time of system 3.2 FEEDFORWARD of part process of information interaction in time 3.3 FEEDBACK 3.3.1 Positive/Negative? 3.3.2 Amplitude? 3.3.3 Length of time of total feedback (delay) and its effect on system? 3.3.4 "Noise" in feedback link? 3.3.5 Tendency to produce oscillation/attenuation of fluctuations in the the system under control? 3.3.6 Redundancy: Ability of feedback channel to carry sufficient information? Performance under expected partial breakdown?							

CONTROL ASPECTS	PRESENT SITUATION			POSSIBLE IMPROVEMENTS			
	Description in words	Unit if any	Cost £'s (if available)	Description in words	Unit if any	Cost £'s (single cost or per period)	Expected benefit to total system
C.4 Standard							
4.1 In what unit(s) is the standard expressed? 4.2 Is the standard fixed/variable? If variable, between what limits? 4.3 At what intervals is standard revised? On whose authority? 4.4 Are present data being fed in to keep it up to date?							
C.5 The Comparator							
5.1 Is each measurement characteristic compared with standard separately? 5.2 Is an interpretive unit used to interrelate data before comparison with standard?							
C.6 The Decision-maker							
6.1 Automatic or Human? 6.2 If automatic, is the control system monitored? (see control of control) 6.3 If human, individual or group? Degree of rational thinking/ emotion entering into decision?							

6.4 Choice allowed: "go–no go" multiple choice (are all choices included)/open-ended? 6.5 Absence from station? 6.6 Effectiveness of interfaces? (a) with control system (i) to D/maker (ii) from D/maker (b) with lower level decision-makers							
C.7. Controller							
7.1 Is position separate from decision-maker? 7.2 Criteria used for control? 7.3 Limits: single/double (high/low) trends? 7.4 Nearness of the two limits? (on–off and possible oscillation) 7.5 If more than one controller, their relationship in series/parallel, etc.? 7.6 Effectiveness of interface? (a) with control system (i) to controller (ii) from controller (b) with higher-level decision-makers							
C.8 Effector							
8.1 Human or automatic? 8.2 Intrinsic/extrinsic?							

CONTROL ASPECTS	PRESENT SITUATION			POSSIBLE IMPROVEMENTS			
	Description in words	Unit if any	Cost £'s (if available)	Description in words	Unit if any	Cost £'s (single cost or per period)	Expected benefit to total system
8.3 Continuous/intermittent? at what intervals? 8.4 Method of converting information current to action current? 8.5 Loss of efficiency in effector, % 8.6 Delay/lead in the effector 8.7 Input: controlled aspects-characteristics unit, used? Uncontrolled aspects-reasons for not controlling							
C.9 Control on the control system (monitoring)							
9.1 Intervals at which the control system is monitored? 9.2 Can control lapse? Intrinsic/extrinsic control? 9.3 If control is not working will system fail safe?							
C.10. Net costs and benefits							
10.1 Total costs and benefits for items where change is envisaged 10.2 Resultant net cost of envisaged change							

Cost Aspects

The net cost and benefit for the improvements proposed are then calculated,

	Capital	Running cost per annum
Total cost of improvements	£	£
Less any existing items no longer required	£	£
Net cost of improvements	£	£
Estimated marginal benefit per annum to be gained from making such changes		£

Capital cost would require to be discounted over a reasonably short (to allow for changes in technology) period to see if the proposed changes were likely to produce a net present benefit when total annual costs were taken into account.

In more complex situations, rather than calculate one single figure, it may be more informative to work out the cost and benefit for a range of improvements and later select between high and low points.

Conclusion

The checklist probes into all aspects of the purpose and operational effectiveness of any "on-going" system. Its most important aspect is to promote the asking of relevant questions within a systems context.

Further Reading

As most writings tend to cover specialist fields or to be written from a particular viewpoint, a short introduction is given to each work.

Systems

Those interested in the *development of systems theory* could start with collections of readings:

F. E. Emery (Ed.), *Systems Thinking*, Penguin, 1969.
S. L. Optner (Ed.), *Systems Analysis*, Penguin, 1973.
J. Beishon and G. Peters, *Systems Behaviour*, Harper & Row (Open University), 1972.

Many of these readings are taken from articles not books, and so much time will be saved by not having to trace past issues of journals. But notice in the introduction the criteria by which these readings have been chosen. There are many other historical articles that are important.

In the line of *general system theory*, the historical development is traced in

L. von Bertalanffy, *General System Theory*, Penguin, 1973,

a book which contains a large number of references for continued reading, and

G. J. Klir (Ed.), *Trends in General Systems Theory*, Wiley, 1972.

The series of annual yearbooks published by the Society for General Systems Research from 1958 onwards,

General Systems Yearbooks, Society for General Systems Research, contain much historical evidence as well as a multitude of specialist articles on the most varied topics. Some of these make quite difficult reading.

Problems of *variety and complexity* are tackled by

W. Ross Ashby, *An Introduction to Cybernetics*, 2nd Edn., Methuen University Paperbacks, 1959.
N. Moray, *Cybernetics, Machines with Intelligence*, Burns & Oates, 1963.
D. A. Bell, *Intelligent Machines*, Sir Isaac Pitman, 1962.

The *control engineer's* approach is shown in

J. J. DiStefano III *et al.*, *Feedback and Control Systems*, Schaum's Outline Series, McGraw-Hill, 1967, and the *mathematical* basis in

Mesarovic and Takahara, *General Systems Theory: Mathematical Foundations*, Academic Press Inc., 1975.

System engineering aspects are covered by

Journal of Systems Engineering, published six monthly at the University of Lancaster,

a journal that has appeared twice yearly since 1969 covering a wide range of system concepts and practical applications. From issue Vol. 5, No. 1 it has been renamed the *Journal of Applied Systems Analysis*.

The *philosophical* concepts on which system theory is based are covered by:

N. Weiner, *The Human use of human beings*, Eyre and Spottiswoode, 1950.

C. West Churchman, *Challenge to Reason*, McGraw-Hill, 1968.

E. Laszlo, *Introduction to Systems Philosophy: Towards a New Paradigm of Contemporary Thought*, Gordon & Breach, 1972.

P. K. M'Pherson, "A perspective on Systems", *Futures* (June 1974), Science & Systems Philosophy (journal article).

Collections of papers appear at random intervals and cover all manner of points of interest:

M. D. Mesarovic (Ed.), *Views on General Systems Theory*, John Wiley, 1964.

J. H. Milsum (Ed.), *Positive Feedback*, Pergamon Press, 1968.

Transactions of The Society for General Systems Research: Conference on Cybernetics, Vienna, 1972, Transcripta Books, London, 1972.

Transactions of the Institute of Electrical and Electronic Engineers on Systems, Man and Cybernetics, 1977 SMC-7(5).

A useful *student's book* is

P. Kilgannon, *The Student's Systems Analysis*, Ed. Arnold, 1972, and *Business Data Processing and Systems Analysis*, Ed. Arnold, 1978.

Information

Information systems have produced much literature, the following are concerned with information aspects of *general systems*:

J. L. Jolley, *Data Study*, Weidenfeld & Nicholson, 1968;

F. Keay, *The Numerate Manager*, Geo. Allen & Unwin, 1969;

A. M. McDonough, *Information Economics and Management Systems*, McGraw-Hill, 1963;

R. Mace, *Management Information and the Computer*, Accountancy Age, 1974;

J. R. M. Simmons, *Management of Change: The Role of Information*, Gee & Co., 1970;

and specifically of *Management information systems*:

Institute of Cost & Management Accountants, *Management Information Systems and the Computer:*

Part I: "Design of a Management Information System",
Part II (1): "Computer Applications",
Part II (2): "Computer Applications".

D. H. Li, *Design and Management of Information Systems*, Science Research Associates, 1972.

F. H. George, *Anatomy of Business: Introduction to Business Cybernetics and Executive Information Systems*, Assoc. Business Programmes, 1974.

D. A. Yewdall, *Management Information*, Pan, 1969.

A. Wilkinson, *Information for Managers*, Pitman, 1971.

Management from the Systems Viewpoint

Work in the *sociology and social psychology* field including *business organization* is epitomized by

A. K. Rice, *The Enterprise and its Environment, a System Theory of Management Organisation*, Tavistock Publications, 1963;

D. Katz and R. L. Kahn, *The Social Psychology of Organizations*, John Wiley, 1966;

E. J. Miller and A. K. Rice, *Systems of Organization. The Control of Task and Sentient Boundaries*, 1967,

and in *psychology* by

R. M. Gagne and others, *Psychological Principles in System Development*, Holt, Rinehart Winston, 1963.

Systems thinking is brought across from its origins in science to a *management* context in

S. Beer, *Decision and Control*, John Wiley, 1966.

S. Beer. *Brain of the Firm*, Allen Lane, 1972.

de Hanika, *New Thinking in Management*, 1968; Heinemann, 2nd edn., 1972.

J. C. Emery, *Organisational Planning and Control Systems*, London, 1969.

R. A. Johnson, F. E. Kast and J. E. Rosenzweig, *The Theory and Management of Systems*, 2nd edn., McGraw-Hill, 1967.

F. E. Kast and J. E. Rosenzweig, *Organisation and Management: A systems Approach*, McGraw-Hill, 1974.

E. R. McLean and J. V. Soden, *Strategic Planning for MIS*, John Wiley, 1977.

E. Mumford, *The Computer and the Clerk*, Routledge & Kegan Paul, 1967.

A. L. Patz and A. J. Rowe, *Management Control and Decision Systems*, John Wiley, 1977.

The work of Professor Forrester at the Massachusetts Institute of Technology on the dynamics of systems has produced many books on *time-based simulation*:

J. W. Forrester, *Principles of Systems*, Wright-Allen Press Inc., Cambridge, Mass., 1968;
J. W. Forrester, *Industrial Dynamics*, M.I.T. Press, Cambridge, Mass., 1961;
J. W. Forrester, *Urban Dynamics*, M.I.T. Press, Cambridge, Mass., 1969;
J. W. Forrester, *World Dynamics*, Wright-Allen Press Inc., Cambridge, Mass. 1971;

further specialist work in this line being contributed by

Dennis L. Meadows, *Dynamics of Commodity Production Cycles*, Wright-Allen Press, Cambridge, Mass., 1970;
Donnella Meadows, *et al.*, *Limits to Growth*, Universe Books, New York, 1972;

This latter title being a very readable non-specialist work.

The International Institute of Applied Systems Analysis

In 1972 IIASA, the International Institute of Applied Systems Analysis, was set up at Laxenburg, Austria. Over 15 countries are now members including Austria, Bulgaria, Canada, Czechoslovakia, Federal Republic of Germany, German Democratic Republic, France, Hungary, Italy, Japan, Poland, Sweden, the U.K., the U.S.A. and the U.S.S.R.

IIASA's charter includes "to increase understanding through the development of uniform standards and terminology (of applied systems analysis)". Amongst other things IIASA will be publishing a handbook and monographs on the "state-of-the art".

Index